11/13

JOY of KOSHER

JOY *of* KOSHER

Fast, Fresh Family Recipes

DRESS THEM UP FOR ENTERTAINING • **DRESS THEM DOWN** FOR EVERYDAY

Jamie Geller

WM

WILLIAM MORROW

An Imprint of HarperCollinsPublishers

ALSO BY JAMIE GELLER

Quick & Kosher: Recipes from the Bride Who Knew Nothing

Quick & Kosher: Meals in Minutes

● ● ●

HarperCollins books may be purchased for educational, business, or sales promotional use. For information please write: Special Markets Department, HarperCollins Publishers, 10 East 53rd Street, New York, NY 10022.

FIRST EDITION

Designed by Paula Russell Szafranski

Food photography by Andrew Purcell, with food styling by Carrie Purcell and prop styling by Paige Hicks
Lifestyle photography by Zoe Berkovic, with food and prop styling by Jessica Leiser, makeup by Olga Postoachi, and wardrobe styling by Naila Ruechel
Recipe editing and testing by Sheilah Kaufman and Paula Jacobson
Recipe testing by Terry H. Tretter
Wine pairings by Gary Landsman

Library of Congress Cataloging-in-Publication Data

Geller, Jamie.
  Joy of kosher : fast, fresh family recipes / Jamie Geller.
    pages   cm
Includes bibliographical references and index.
  ISBN 978-0-06-220782-1 (hardback)
  1. Jewish cooking.   2. Kosher food.   I. Title.
TX724.G446 2013
641.5'676—dc23   2013013310

13 14 15 16 17 ID/RRD 10 9 8 7 6 5 4 3 2 1

**This book is dedicated to Henry Kauftheil,
a visionary, a mentor, an amazing person.**

As chairman of Kosher Media Network, Henry believes in the mission of bringing kosher food to the mass marketplace. He is devoted to his family, his friends, and the countless individuals who turn to him for aid, and most of his time—day and night—is dedicated to *chessed* and *tzedakah*, the Jewish formula for tending to the needs of others in a manner that respects the dignity of every individual and the nobility of all God's creations.

Everybody who knows him loves and respects him. It is impossible not to.

Fruit, Flower, and Mint Ice Cubes, page 65

Contents

Introduction

Confessions of the Bride Who Knew Nothing

I wrote most of this book on my iPhone at three in the morning. Yes, the touchscreen is very tiny and almost invisible in the dark. My thumbs hurt.

Much of the time, I also was balancing my baby on my lap or sitting beside her crib, breathing quietly and praying that she would sleep for an hour or two. I could teach juggling to Barnum & Bailey.

If you and I are already acquainted—maybe you've read my other books or my magazine, or we met on line at the supermarket, or online at my website—you already know all about me, and you can skip to the next section. But if my name is new to you, you'll get more out of this book if we get to know each other right now.

You may as well know that most people call me the Bride Who Knew Nothing. That title might bother some folks, but not me. Because it's true.

Embarrassing, but true.

So a few confessions are in order. I was raised on takeout, not home cooking. My wonderful mom shared many of life's secrets with me (mostly about how black makes you look two sizes smaller, and that no woman should be without a classic cashmere sweater), but she'd never be caught in a frilly apron standing in front of a stove, and neither would I. It was policy. Instead, she gave me the vaulting confidence to pursue a high-octane career as a TV producer. That was enough for both of us. That, and her certainty that I would one day become the first Jewish woman president of the United States.

And I wasn't always kosher. Jewish, yes. Kosher, no. Till I was in my midtwenties, those "old dietary restrictions" never meant much to me. Yet somewhere between covering the Oscars and practicing yoga, I gravitated to Jewish observance, a lifestyle that had been dropped by my family in recent generations. I wanted to marry someone from a traditional Jewish family. When Hubby and I met, we knew this was *it*! We were engaged in like five minutes, and we were married two months later, before you could say, "What just happened?"

I quickly discovered that being part of his family meant celebrating more than a hundred traditional festivals annually, complete with six-course dinners for the immediate family, the extended family, and a few people they thought were aunts and uncles—not sure. Hubby's family dinners were entirely homemade, preferably using recipes handed down from Bubby, his great-grandma. And they were kosher.

Let's say I didn't fit in. Let's say I was overwhelmed.

But ya gotta know me to understand my reaction. My kindergarten teacher dubbed me a hard worker. (What kind of work is there in kindergarten?) So the Great Kitchen Challenge only spurred me to confront my culinary clumsiness. Hubby was amused. He's from a family of caterers and had never seen anybody mess up peeling an onion. Well, I was gonna show him. I'd show 'em all.

And I did. Like a runner who didn't notice the finish line, I didn't just learn to cook; I sprinted into cookbooks, magazines, a website, and a TV show. Hubby is not laughing anymore except for, well, sometimes.

Now we're eight years into our beautiful marriage, we have five children, and my corporate image has boiled down simply to Mommy. Like an aspiring actress, I hunger for great reviews, especially when it comes to feeding my family. And the best review is "More please, Mommy." That's when I glow. I feel like I'm doing what every mother has done since the first cavewoman lit a fire and burned the woolly mammoth burgers.

But here's my next confession: I still don't like to cook.

I love to *eat*. I love to watch my children eat. And I adore the looks of delighted anticipation on the faces of dinner guests when I bring out a tantalizing dish. But I still want to get out of my kitchen as fast as I can.

Might as well totally 'fess up.

I am not a natural-born killer cook, and my grandfather would say I'm "no *balabusta*." That's a Yiddish word that, like all Yiddish terms, is dripping with unstated meanings. Simply, a balabusta is a homemaker. But a "real balabusta" is someone who serves a ten-course—all homemade, all perfect—meal to fifty people, and she made the place cards and re-covered all the dining room chairs. (She prepared all this last week while taking care of her six kids, making sure they wore matching outfits every day, and chairing the charity bazaar at their school.) And her kitchen is spotless after the party, even before her guests leave.

I'm not one of those. I'm the kind of homemaker who just stares at the dirty dishes in the sink, hoping they will do themselves. I'll leave the room and come back to check if they're still there. And then, once it's clear they ain't goin' nowhere on their own, I go to sleep and pray to God that by morning He will make a miracle (akin to the splitting of the sea) in my very own kitchen. And you already know that if this had happened, you would be holding a very different book.

I hope that you and I will become friends. Here's a little shortcut, a few things you should know about me:

I love olive oil, Hubby, avocados, and my kids, but not necessarily in that order.

Yes, I taste test every recipe. That's why I look this way.

Kitchenphobia is an inherited disorder. My mother designed her new house *without* a kitchen—really.

My career in television taught me that people will believe illusion. That's how I can keep a straight face when telling my toddler that a kiss will make it all better.

When I became kosher, I was shocked to discover that kosher food is really good, even the wine.

I love Middle Eastern music and food with inexplicable passion.

I'm more at home in a made-for-TV kitchen than in my own.

I'm so self-critical I think that even this confession isn't enough.

When people argue over whether Jewish mothers or Italian mothers stuff their kids more, I go out for a sandwich.

If you're a novice cook, I feel your pain. If you're not, can you send me a recipe?

•   •   •

And I want you to meet my immediate family, the main cast of characters in the sitcom of my life:

Hubby   He's my idea man, my other half, my soul mate. And a darned good cook.

Little Momma

This is my sweet seven-year-old, wise as a grandma, and my number one sous chef, now that she can read the ingredient list and do the math when we multiply a recipe by eight. Sensitive, caring, and so responsible, she makes me feel like I have a deputy mom on board.

Miss Bouncy

My six-year-old, who loves life, wakes up with a *jump,* gets dressed in a flash, and doesn't stop bouncing all day. It gets a little scary when she holds The Baby and bounces at the same time, but she hugs her so tight, with such love, that I don't have the heart to stop her. If you happen to be beside her, she'll reach up to hold your hand, whether it's to cross a street or to walk four paces into the next room.

Angel Face

At four *"and* a half," he knows that with his innocent mug, he can get away with anything. He'll get out of his bed ten times, just to give me one more kiss and hug. He loves "wabbits" and "woosters" and is learning to tie his "thoes." Irresistible.

Bruiser

Almost three, and already a bulldozer, the king of the jungle gym, and one heck of a chunky little linebacker. And he can look fierce despite his long eyelashes, curly blond hair, and coy smiles. Also a great hugger and kisser—must have learned that secret from Angel Face.

The Baby

She's the yummiest butterball on the block, and so happy to be at the party. She already loves food as much as the rest of us. When she coos and lays her head on your shoulder, you never want to put her down.

● ● ●

So you see this book is really about my life, unabashedly including my struggles in the kitchen and the triumph when I overcome the voice inside me that says, "I can't." And maybe I talk too much. Hubby asks why I have to tell you *everything*. I guess it's because I want you to understand my message: If I can put really good food on the table, anyone can.

And don't let the kosher thing throw you. Kosher is not tedious, not limited, and not complicated. My recipes are authentically kosher, but there's no slaving in the kitchen (slaving over a hot stove is so yesterday), plus no bubby or rabbi is required. My recipes are easy, scrumptious, nutritious (well, except for the ones that aren't), and fun.

If you don't believe me, try a few of the recipes in this book. They're foolproof, actually, because I'm the fool who worked them over and over, and they became go-to recipes for my family meals. I really try to feed my family well.

That's because food is an expression of love. And it doesn't matter if you've never eaten kosher, always eat kosher, or go "kosher casual." What's important is that food brings us together, and we all want to share our best, most delectable meals with the people we love. And when it's kosher, we're also pulling in thousands of years of love and tradition.

So join us at our family table. You'll discover, as I did: You don't have to be kosher to love kosher. Who knew?

JOY of KOSHER

Raw Root
Vegetable Salad,
page 108

How to Use This Book

We've all had the experience of trying some fancy new recipe to impress dinner guests; often the food looks fantabulous, but the taste is sort of blah. Know what I mean? Think about it. Wouldn't it be better to take the same recipes you use every day—your best stuff, the recipes everyone loves—and dress 'em up? I thought about how to take my super family meals—real food, simple food, great food; the recipes that come out right every time—and make them worthy of entertaining everyone from your next-door neighbor to the Queen of England. (Okay, to be honest, the Queen of England has never come over for dinner. But week after week, my home is visited by the Sabbath Queen, and that's even better.)

The more than 100 core recipes in this book include either a Dress It Up or Dress It Down complementary recipe. That's over 200 recipes total—dishes that do double duty for entertaining or everyday.

We all have our go-to recipes that are easy, foolproof crowd-pleasers. Now you'll have even more. The Dressed Down recipes are quick solutions for fast, fab family dinners. The Dressed Up recipes include simple presentation tweaks, special garnishes, or an extra ingredient or two to take them from everyday to holiday. I promise these recipes will become part of your tried-and-true recipe inventory. In the following pages you'll find all the tips, techniques, and abracadabra you need.

Along with each recipe, you'll also find a combination of some or all of the following:

Make It a Meal   Suggested pairings with another recipe or two in this book or alternative complementary dishes to create an entire, well-balanced family meal. I thought it through, because you've got more to do than figure out what goes with what.

Make It Pareve   Food that is neither meat nor dairy is called *pareve*. Sorta neutral, but not wishy-washy—more like congenially flexible. Water is pareve. Eggs are pareve. Bread (unless made with milk or other dairy) is pareve. Make It Pareve offers substitutions for the meat or dairy component in the recipe to allow more varied uses.

Pair It   Because dining is about the entire package, I give you a suggestion for the perfect wine to pair with the dish.

Variation(s)   After I finish giving you a recipe, I often think of another way to do it, or an alternative presentation. This is where I share those ideas.

Time-saver(s)   You know what those are: little tricks to help you zoom out of the kitchen and into the sunshine.

Quick Tip(s)   Things that make the whole job easier, better, faster. Stuff my mother would have taught me, if she had known.

Equipment and Ingredients List
You will need this equipment
(don't panic—nothing hard to get)

I'm gonna assume your kitchen is stocked with the basics including:

Cheesecloth or T-shirts   For your soup. Don't ask. (See page 24.)

Melon baller   I call for this in lots of my Dress It Up recipes, for hollowing out onions for stuffing, cucumbers for shooters, potatoes for nacho bites.

Sharp knives   Personally, I like using a large chef's knife for most things, but you should choose knives that make you feel comfortable. Just make sure they're sharp.

Slotted spoons and wooden spoons   I've got lots and lots of wooden spoons, could build a tree house for my kids with them.

Stainless-steel skimmer   Like tongs, I use this baby over and over again. Great for fishing things out, and of course for skimming the stuff that comes to the top of your soups, stews, and sauces.

Tongs   Like having a third hand!

Now here's an additional list of really handy, not-your-everyday kitchen gear. These tools are not so over the top that you have to search all over to find them. If you're an online shopper, JoyofKosher.com has links to purchase the equipment and foods listed below. Do whatever is quickest and easiest for you. The idea is to get you to the crazy good food fast.

Bundt pan and tube pan   Fancy-in-a-flash bakeware. Amazing what a difference they make in presentation. Watch the eyebrows go up.

Dutch oven   I love bright colors, and it can be quite a decorative piece. I once bought the 13¼-quart size. Needed a cart to haul it out of the store, Hubby to help me get it into the oven—and it almost snapped an oven rack. So go a little smaller.

Fine-mesh colander   Line it with cheesecloth (or a T-shirt) if you want your soup crystal clear.

Mandoline or julienne peeler   That's mandoline with an *e*, not the instrument. My third-grade teacher was right: spelling is everything.

Oversize oven-to-table sauté pan   Perfect for one-pan meals, cooking in large quantities, and entertaining.

Pastry bags and tips   Don't get all freaked, we're not decorating cakes! These are primarily used for piping things into things for Dress It Up recipes.

Plastic bowl, large (10-quart)   You'll need this baby to knead your challah dough. A friend told me she uses her laundry bin. Try to avoid that; nobody wants to find a sock in the challah.

Ring molds   Individual portions are a key Dress It Up element. Use ring molds to create beautiful single servings.

Springform pan   You'll need one for at least two of the dairy recipes in this book.

Stock pot (12-quart) If you want to make the entire batch of my crystal-clear chicken soup. Otherwise a 6-quart will do for halving the recipe.

Zester For grating and making decorative curls. Hubby calls this "the zest book" because it has more than a dozen recipes that call for the zest of a lime, lemon, or orange (make sure you've got a lot of those on hand, too). He seems to have some sensitivity to orange zest that can't quite be explained scientifically; his bloodhound nose sniffs it out even when no one else can tell it's there. So I usually write that orange zest is optional, in case you're sensitive to it, too.

Ingredients You'll Need on Hand

A Note About Herbs I often call for dried herbs. (That's because bugs aren't kosher, and checking every fresh herb for them is tedious work. Faster and easier to use the dried variety.) Dried herbs and fresh-frozen chopped herbs that come in a tray are great substitutes for fresh herbs. The general rule is that dried is more potent than fresh, so it's a 1:3 ratio, that is, 1 teaspoon dried = 1 tablespoon fresh. For frozen herbs, 1 cube = 1 teaspoon fresh.

I select frozen herbs over dried when the taste really relies on fresh, especially in things that are not cooked, so you don't get that papery taste.

If I call for fresh herbs and don't give a dried equivalent, it's because there's really no compromising on that recipe. Many kosher supermarkets (if you're lucky enough to live near one) carry fresh parsley, mint, and cilantro that have been checked for bugs—although they do cost. Time is money in this case.

Spices Assuming your cabinet is stocked with the basics, these are some additional ones I call for, some quite frequently.

- Ground sumac
- Za'atar
- Ground caraway
- Ground white pepper
- Dry mustard

- Ground cloves
- Ground nutmeg
- Ground and whole allspice
- Ground cardamom

And when I say salt . . .

There's regular table salt, and then there's the coarse-grained salt known as kosher salt (because it's used in the process of making meat kosher). I use Diamond Crystal kosher salt. Always. It's more forgiving than other kosher salts and not as salty, so you are less likely to oversalt. If you use Morton's, for instance, you have to adjust and use less than I call for. I even use kosher salt in baking (except when I call for sea salt).

I call for coarse flake sea salt in certain recipes that benefit from the flavor or texture of large, coarse flakes. Gefen makes a very good coarse flake sea salt from the Dead Sea.

Granulated sugar

This is just regular white sugar, folks. I say granulated so you won't confuse it with the light brown or confectioners'—which I also specify where needed, because I'm just that kinda gal.

Margarine

I'm not a fan of margarine; it's really artificial. I use Earth Balance Buttery Sticks (which also comes in a nice round tub) in all my nondairy cooking and baking. It's plant-based, vegan, made without artificial ingredients or hydrogenated oils, and is free of gluten, lactose, and eggs. Now, I personally don't have anything against dairy, gluten, or eggs, but when I need a substitute for that rich, buttery taste, I prefer to go as natural as possible. Whenever I call for "margarine," I'm using Earth Balance.

Coconut milk

An incredibly creamy replacement for chemical-laden nondairy whipped topping or nondairy creamer. (It's super for making homemade pareve whipped cream, page 256.) I use the full-fat variety.

Soy milk

I like Zen Soy, the creamiest of soy milks on the market. You will also notice that it is completely nondairy, while some other soy milks are made on dairy equipment (indicated by the initials "DE" or "D" next to the kosher certification), and so are considered virtually dairy and cannot be mixed into a meat recipe.

Broth

My favorite packaged broth is the Manischewitz line of all-natural broths. Chicken, low-sodium chicken, vegetable, and beef—I love them all because they're building-block ingredients that make a dish sing. (Try cooking rice in broth in place of water, and you'll see what I mean.) I always keep a case of chicken broth on hand, and a few boxes of the veg and beef as well.

Cooking spray

Almost every recipe starts with it, so stock up.

Oils

I keep only three or four in my kitchen:

Olive oil/extra virgin olive oil   I'd love to buy the absolute highest quality, but Hubby freaks if olive oil is more expensive than a trip to Italy. So I buy Bertolli extra virgin, in jugs the size of a two-year-old, from Costco, and I use it for everything. Extra virgin olive oil is meant to be used in uncooked preparations, such as salad dressings, or for finishing a dish. For high-temperature cooking, use regular olive oil. I love the rich and fruity flavor of olive oil, so I never use light olive oil; it's not light in calories or more healthful for you (in fact, cold-pressed extra virgin is the most healthful), just lighter in flavor.

Toasted sesame oil   The aroma alone makes me want to dance. Fantastic for Asian cooking and fun for salad dressings, or for sniffing when you're feeling down.

Canola oil   Your best all-purpose oil. I use it for frying and for my challah.

Mustard, mustard, and more mustard

I use 'em all, but not together.

- Dijon
- Country Dijon/grainy mustard
- Honey Dijon
- Spicy mustard

Nuts

For fun things.

- Pistachios
- Hazelnuts/filberts
- Walnuts
- Almonds

Tomato paste

A major building block ingredient; always have a few cans on hand.

Pure vanilla extract

Not that synthetic imitation stuff.

Chocolate

Good quality, with a high percentage of cocoa—bittersweet (70% cacao or more) or semisweet (60 to 70%), depending on your taste buds. Keep extra for snacking.

Wine

"Cooking wine" is a no-no! Always have a decent dry red and dry white on hand for cooking (and sampling while cooking). No need to splurge, but always use something that you would actually drink.

I recommend these relatively inexpensive kosher wines for most uses. The bottle descriptions below (provided by experts with supersensitive palates) will give you some idea of what they're like.

On a budget:

Red by W   Lively and youthful in color, blackberry and pomegranate on the nose; clean and silky in the mouth, with flavors of grenadine and fresh berries, followed by a crisp finish.

White by W   Bright and refreshing, with lively aroma of grapefruit, elegant floral notes, and white peach flavors.

For a refreshing splurge:

Ramon Cardova Rioja   Dark berry, oak, and nutmeg aromas with delicious spicy and fruit flavor.

Baron Herzog Chenin Blanc   Focused and crisp, with intense passion fruit and citrus flavors; finishes with a touch of sweetness.

*Colorful Mustard
String Beans,
page 107*

About the Kosher Thing

Kosher refers to preparing foods according to Jewish law and avoiding certain foods altogether. It's ancient as the Bible, yet totally modern in its application, and millions of people have incorporated this way of thinking about food into their lives. You don't have to be kosher to enjoy kosher food, just as you don't need to be a card-carrying member of PETA to eat a vegan meal.

Sophisticated kosher restaurants that impress kosher and nonkosher patrons alike can be found in most major American cities: Japanese steakhouses, Spanish tapas bars, French bistros, and restaurants serving outstanding fare from India, North Africa, and the Middle East. Moreover, a steadily increasing number of kosher wines is winning awards in prestigious international competitions. For instance, Israel's Carmel Single Vineyard Kayoumi Shiraz won the top Rhône Varietal Wine of the Year award over every top winery in the world, and the 2009 Celler de Capçanes Montsant Peraj Ha'abib Flor de Primavera received a 95 rating from Robert Parker's *Wine Advocate*. Prized by world-class restaurants and home gourmands, the relatively new array of kosher wines makes kosher cooking a viable gourmet choice. The erroneous perception that only people who have a family rabbi want to eat kosher is rapidly evaporating.

Volumes have been written on the details of what makes food kosher, but in short, the rules are:

1. Milk and meat (and their products) are never cooked or eaten together. In a strictly kosher kitchen, in fact, separate pots, pans, cooking utensils, dinnerware, flatware, and even appliances in some cases are designated for meat or dairy.

2. Foods that are neither meat nor dairy (vegetables, fruit, and eggs, for example) are called "pareve" and can be included in either meat or dairy meals. In fact, people who are allergic or sensitive to dairy products know that kosher-certified "pareve" on a food label assures them that there is *not a trace* of dairy.

3. Pork and shellfish are off the menu.

4. A fish is kosher if it has fins and scales (removed before cooking, of course), which pushes seafood like shark and catfish right outta your kosher kitchen. Fish is intrinsically pareve, but it cannot be mixed or even plated with meat.

5. Meat must be slaughtered in accordance with Jewish law (which is the most humane method of slaughter) and "koshered" by soaking in water and salting to remove blood. Blood of any type is not kosher. In fact, eggs are examined for bloodspots and are discarded if they're found.

6. Processed foods require rabbinic certification. This means that a rabbi or rabbinic agency expert in these laws has monitored the processing of the foods and guarantees that no nonkosher ingredients are in them. A rabbi does not bless the food. His job is to keep a sharp eye on the process.

Fortunately, the kosher food industry has exploded, making available thousands of ingredients and products previously unheard of by kosher cooks. My recipes will take you beyond the traditional and expected foods and flavors, and they can be made with ingredients that are now readily available.

In short, this book presents darn good food that happens to comply with kosher dietary laws for the convenience of traditionally observant Jews. But this is not an exclusive club. Everyone can enjoy these scrumptious, hearty, elegant, and authentically kosher—not "kosher-style"—recipes.

Think about it. The term "kosher home" evokes the image of a place where family values are paramount, where guests are welcomed any time of the day or night, and the aroma of delectable food is always in the air.

It's all about family—whether it's immediate family, extended family, your neighbor's extended family, or the cousins from abroad whom you've never met but you just know you'll love the instant they arrive at the airport. It's about thinking of your entire community as your family, too.

Family values are not unique to Jewish homes; they are emphasized in many cultures. If you grew up with these values—or wish you had—you will find this book familiar and uplifting. The connection between family and food is deep and meaningful. And a kosher meal brings it all together.

Soups AND Starters

MEAT

Crystal Clear Chicken Soup with Julienned Vegetables and Angel Hair   25
DRESS IT DOWN *Chicken Noodle Alphabet Soup*

Cocktail Meatballs with Sweet 'n' Sour Sauce   28
DRESS IT UP *Deconstructed Meatball Bruschetta*

Ktzitzot (Israeli Mini Burgers)   33
DRESS IT UP *Hummus-Topped Ktzitzot*

Anita's Lachmagine (Miniature Ground Beef Pies)   38
DRESS IT UP *Pine Nut Lachmagine with Parsley Tahini*

PAREVE

Eggplant Caviar   40
DRESS IT UP *Eggplant Caviar Crostini*

Lemon Lover's Hummus   42
DRESS IT UP *Tricolor Hummus Trifles*

Falafel Poppers with Lemon Sesame Schug   46
DRESS IT DOWN *Falafel Sandwiches*

Cilantro Corn Cakes   49
DRESS IT UP *Cilantro Corn Cakes with Avocado Aioli*

Tropical Fruit Guacamole   51
DRESS IT UP *Deconstructed Tropical Guacamole*

Uputzi's Vegetarian Chopped "Liver" Pâté   53
DRESS IT UP *Vegetarian Chopped "Liver" Pâté Bread Cups*

Baked Herbed Gefilte Fish   58
DRESS IT UP *Baked Carrot-Stuffed Gefilte Fish*

Fancy Crudités with Garlic Ranch Dip   61
DRESS IT DOWN *Quick Crudités*

Chilled Coconut Berry Soup   63
DRESS IT UP *Fruit, Flower, and Mint Ice Cubes*

Baked Sweet Potato Chips   66
DRESS IT UP *Purple, Orange, and White Chips (Dairy)*

DAIRY

Cool Cucumber and Avocado Cream Soup   68
DRESS IT UP *Cool Cucumber and Avocado Cream Shooters*

Smashed Red Potato Nachoes   70
DRESS IT UP *Nacho Potato Bites*

Poppy's Sour Cream Potato Soup   72
DRESS IT UP *Poppy's Potato Soup Cups*

Friday: 2:00 p.m.

First thing you gotta know . . .

Chicken soups are like snowflakes: no two are alike. A good chicken soup conveys your love and emotions more than any other classic dish. Maybe it has something to do with tradition . . . or kosher salt. Don't ask me how. I'm not a mystic.

Chicken soup is a luscious example of the way people like my grandparents consistently cooked up perfection without a recipe or measuring spoon. Nowadays, folks are obsessed with precision. Was that ⅛ teaspoon turmeric or ¼? What, *exactly*, is a pinch of salt? Back in the day, my grandmother (we called her Ma) used measurements like "a mouthful," "a handful," "*a bissel* [a little]" and "a bissel more." She must be really laughing it up in heaven, watching us squint at our fancy measuring devices. The handful method was good enough for her.

I blush to confess that I pull out the measuring cups and spoons just like everybody else. Since my grandparents never taught me to cook, I try to re-create their dishes from the taste memory archives in my head. There are no recipes, just my palate. Besides, I don't know if my hand is the same size as Ma's.

My first soup as a new bride was an immeasurable lesson in humility.

I was preparing for the first Shabbos after my wedding. (*Shabbos* is generally translated as "Sabbath," but I prefer the Hebrew term. It's cozier, and it links me to millions of women who devised special Shabbos delicacies over the past 3,000 years or so.) The whole Shabbos thing was fairly new to me, as was kosher cooking, but I was determined to serve Hubby an authentic Old Country soup he'd never forget. And when I say "Old

Country," I don't mean the Ozarks or Nashville. I'm talking about shtetls with tongue-twisting names like Pshischa and Sighisoara. That's where they made real chicken soup.

The broth I presented to Hubby that evening resembled machine oil more than anything else, and there were 4-inch carrots standing straight out of the bowl like tree trunks. Hubby bravely dug in. He never even asked for a chainsaw. Now that's love.

I was right about one thing. He never forgot it. And he never let me forget it.

After the Great Chicken Soup Disaster, I worked like a fiend to find out how to get chicken soup rich, but clear. My mother (who never ever cooked) told me to spill out the water after boiling up the chicken—you know, to get rid of all that stuff that comes to the top. So I'd boil the water, toss it out, and start over with clean cold water. Did that three or four times till I realized I should never trust my mother on these things. I loaded up the water with powdered chicken soup mix to give it a flavor. Who needs a chicken?

Since then, I've learned some great tricks. I've discovered cheesecloth. But in my opinion, nothing strains the soup as clear as a T-shirt. No kidding. And the secret to perfect broth is lots of chicken, the real stuff, and tons of fresh herbs and veggies. I use a method I call "sacrificial vegetables." Don't worry, it's not a cult thing. I cook down every little bit of these veggies, zap the life out of them for all their nutrients and color, then infuse that into my best-ever broth. I feel like I've really worked those veggies. After I've boiled and simmered them beyond recognition, I toss them (much to Hubby's dismay) with peace of mind, knowing they have given over all they had to my savory soup.

And yes, scientifically, chicken soup does have healing powers.

Crystal Clear Chicken Soup with Julienned Vegetables and Angel Hair

Kosher Status: Meat • Prep: 15 minutes • Cook: 4 hours •
Chill: Overnight • Total: About 12 hours •
Yield: 6 quarts, 24 servings at 1 cup per serving

Note: For optimum flavor and results, this soup has to be started the night before.

My grandparents Ma and Uputzi (which means "daddy" in Hungarian) made a phenomenally flavorful, golden, clear chicken soup. (My other grandparents, Grandma and Poppy, favored a dark, rich, earthy soup, with lots of chicken feet. Those scaly feet! They'll never enter my kitchen.) For about eight years, I struggled, slightly crazed, to re-create that soup. I remember Ma serving it piping hot, along with paper-thin slices of raw daikon sprinkled with salt. We would dip them in our soup and purr. This wasn't just a bowl of soup; it was an experience. But the actual soup recipe remained a mystery.

Then one fine morning, as I was driving down I-95, talking to my sister on the phone (hands free!), she mentioned that Aunt Debbie actually had the recipe. Nearly drove off the road. Well, thank God for Aunt Debs, because I never would have gotten this right. There's a green pepper and cauliflower in this chicken soup! Who knew?

STOCK BASE

1 chicken, cut into 8 pieces (about 3½ pounds)

2 bone-in chicken breasts (about 1½ pounds)

4 or 5 beef marrow bones (about 2 pounds)

5 medium carrots, quartered

2 large parsnips, quartered

2 small turnips, quartered

2 medium parsley roots, quartered, or sub in a combo of more parsnips and turnips

1 large green bell pepper, halved, ribs and seeds removed

1 large onion

3 tablespoons kosher salt

20 parsley sprigs

½ head cauliflower, broken into florets

7 garlic cloves

20 black or white peppercorns

4 whole allspice

SOUP

1 large zucchini, cut into ⅛-inch julienne

1 large carrot, peeled, cut into ⅛-inch
   julienne

1 large daikon, peeled, cut into ⅛-inch
   julienne

1 pound angel hair pasta, cooked and
   drained, at room temperature

1. Place the chicken, marrow bones, carrots, parsnips, turnips, parsley roots, green pepper, onion, and 1 tablespoon of the salt in a 12-quart stockpot. Cover with 6 quarts cold
water and bring to a boil over high heat. Skim and discard the foam that forms at the
top when it comes to a boil.

2. Add the remaining 2 tablespoons salt, the parsley, cauliflower, garlic, peppercorns, and
allspice and return to a boil. Simmer, covered, over low heat for 1 hour. Remove the
4 chicken breasts and allow them to cool slightly. Remove the meat from the bones.
Shred or chop the meat and store it in the fridge to serve in the soup or for another use.
Return the bones to the pot. Continue simmering, covered, over low heat, for at least
2 hours more.

3. Strain the entire contents of the pot through a colander lined with cheesecloth or a
clean old T-shirt. Discard all the solids or save them for another use. Chill the broth
overnight.

4. To serve the soup, remove the surface fat and pour the broth into a large pot. Bring to a
simmer over low heat and cook until warm, 10 to 15 minutes. Add the zucchini, carrot,
daikon, and the reserved chicken, if desired. Simmer 5 minutes to cook the vegetables
and heat the chicken. Be careful to keep the soup over low heat; bringing the soup to a
boil can make it cloudy. Season to taste with salt.

5. Place ¼ cup angel hair in each soup bowl and ladle the hot soup over the pasta. Serve
immediately.

6. This soup can be frozen after the surface fat is removed. You can freeze the breast meat
separately if you want to use it for other dishes.

You will need a 12-quart pot for this recipe. Only have a 6-quart? Simply halve the recipe. If you like marrow bones, don't toss them. Knock the marrow out onto a plate (that's what real experts do, but it's not cheating to use a knife or tiny spoon) and spread it on your bread like butter. That's how Ma and Uputzi used to serve it to us. There are, of course, those who suck the marrow directly from the bones, but I don't want to be seen publicly endorsing such an act.

TIME-SAVER

When I first discovered the creative things you can do with a mandoline, I got into using it for everything—until Hubby sliced a finger along with the French fries and our dinner guests arrived just after the ambulance. Warning: Cutting those beautiful julienned veggies can be dangerous. I love using my handheld julienne peeler for jobs like these—it's easier than pulling out the entire contraption. But if you're lazy, short on time, or have no mandoline or julienne peeler to speak of, buy the packages of pretty shredded carrots to get the elegant look of beautiful julienned veggies. Then just chop some scallions (carefully) for taste and color, and toss 'em in.

DRESS IT DOWN

• Chicken Noodle Alphabet Soup •

ABC noodles were a treat, and growing up we all fought over the carrots. This spells my childhood—as well as Friday nights at my grandparents' house—in a bowl.

Replace the julienne veg with ¼-inch diced carrots and the angel hair with a box of alphabet noodles, cooked and drained.

PAIR IT DRAPPIER CARTE D'OR CHAMPAGNE

The texture of soup makes "bubbly" a great choice for a little contrast. Since chicken soup is classic, stick with the classic bubbly: Champagne!

Cocktail Meatballs with Sweet 'n' Sour Sauce

Kosher Status: Meat • Prep: 15 minutes • Cook: 18 minutes • Total: 33 minutes • Yield: 25 meatballs

It's not a party until you bring out the cocktail meatballs with little toothpicks in them. Treats on toothpicks talk to me. They say, "Eat me, now!" And I do.

MEATBALLS

Cooking spray

1 pound ground beef

1 large egg, beaten

¼ cup plain dry bread crumbs

2 tablespoons ketchup

2 teaspoons honey mustard

2 teaspoons Worcestershire sauce

2 teaspoons kosher salt

1 garlic clove, minced, or 1 cube frozen
   minced garlic

1 teaspoon dried oregano

1 to 2 tablespoons canola oil

SAUCE

1 cup ketchup

¼ cup packed light brown sugar

¼ cup honey mustard

3 tablespoons red wine vinegar

1 teaspoon kosher salt

1. Spray a baking sheet with cooking spray.

2. Prepare the meatballs: Combine the beef, egg, bread crumbs, ketchup, mustard, Worcestershire, salt, garlic, and oregano in a medium bowl; mix well. Roll about 1 tablespoon of the beef mixture into a ball with the palms of your hands. Transfer the ball to the prepared baking sheet. Repeat with the remaining mixture to make 25 meatballs.

3. Heat the canola oil in an extra-large sauté pan over medium heat and add the meatballs. Cook, turning often, until the meatballs are brown on all sides, 5 to 7 minutes. Carefully add 3 tablespoons water to the pan. Cover and cook 4 minutes more.

4. Prepare the sauce: While the meatballs are cooking, combine the ketchup, brown sugar, mustard, vinegar, and salt in a small saucepan. Heat over medium-low heat until warm.

5. Serve the meatballs on toothpicks with the warm sauce for dipping.

QUICK TIP

If you don't have an extra-large sauté pan, work in batches: Transfer the browned meatballs to a plate, brown the second batch, then return them all to the pan to simmer.

DRESS IT UP

• Deconstructed Meatball Bruschetta •

Bruschetta is an elegant and easy appetizer that becomes hearty and delicious with the addition of mini meatballs.

Plate six servings of four cocktail meatballs per person. Make the bruschetta topping: Seed and finely chop 3 tomatoes (preferably the on-the-vine variety), and combine them with 1 tablespoon minced red onion, 6 thinly sliced basil leaves, 1 tablespoon extra virgin olive oil, and salt and pepper to taste. Make the garlic toast: Cut a baguette into ¼-inch slices, toast them, and rub the hot bread with a garlic clove. Spoon the topping on the meatballs and serve with two slices of garlic toast.

MAKE IT A MEAL

For four entrée portions, serve about six meatballs per person. The Deconstructed Meatball Bruschetta just needs a simple salad to complete the meal. The Cocktail Meatballs with Sweet 'n' Sour Sauce would be perfect over a bed of couscous tossed with pine nuts and chopped scallions.

PAIR IT BARON HERZOG JEUNESSE CABERNET SAUVIGNON

It's party time! Let's go with a crowd-pleasing semidry red wine.

Sunday: 3:00 p.m.

In a past life, I must have been a raven-haired Arabian princess . . .

Even though all of my known ancestors hailed from Eastern Europe, something about Middle Eastern stuff—the music, the aromas, the desert, the food—really stirs my blood. Middle Eastern, Iberian, and North African Jews, known as Sephardim, absorbed the tastes and rhythms of their surroundings. So at the very least, I somehow must have inherited some Sephardic genes. *Ktzitzot* speak to my soul.

Ktzitzot are itsy-bitsy beef patties popular in Israel. It would be a shame to call 'em sliders. That just makes them sound trendy, when in fact, they've been around forever. My sister-in-law, Chanie, makes them in her sleep. She learned from her mom and her Iraqi grandmom. When Hubby's brother, Greg, married Chanie, ktzitzot became part of the family repertoire.

One day, Hubby asked me to make them. Super unfair. Never met a ktzitzah in my life. What's more, Chanie and Greg have since moved to Israel and I'm stuck with an e-mail "recipe" written in grandma-style. No measurements.

So there I am, up to my wrists in a bowl of chopped meat, and Hubby is trying to recall the look, feel, shape, and weight of the ktzitzot he had learned to love. He's going, "No, more like this; no, maybe more like that. Here, let me try. . . . This is it!" he shouts. "This is what it's supposed to look like!"

It's somewhere between a hockey puck and a squashed tennis ball. Aha!

The next time I formed my mini patties, Hubby still stood over me like a backseat driver. *What? I got this!* I thought, but I let him direct anyway. He better love me for this.

Dress It Up! Hummus-Topped Ktzitzot, page 34

Ktzitzot (Israeli Mini Burgers)

Kosher Status: Meat • Prep: 15 minutes • Cook: 18 minutes • Total: 33 minutes • Yield: 10 ktzitzot

Ktzitzot are perfect when fresh, but get a little rubbery if reheated. Chanie says that to be really authentic you're supposed to pan-fry them with a touch of oil. But she always baked them, and that's what Hubby wants. So that's what Hubby gets. I much prefer frying them, with the authentic inclusion of sumac, cinnamon, and cumin. My Sephardic soul knows the difference.

Cooking spray

1 pound ground beef

1 large egg, beaten

1 small onion, minced

2 garlic cloves, minced

½ cup plain dry bread crumbs

¼ cup chopped fresh parsley or

   1½ tablespoons dried

2 teaspoons kosher salt

½ teaspoon ground sumac or paprika

½ teaspoon ground cumin (optional)

½ teaspoon ground cinnamon (optional)

Canola oil, for pan-frying (optional)

1. Preheat the oven to 425°F. Spray a baking sheet with cooking spray.

2. Combine the beef, egg, onion, garlic, bread crumbs, parsley, salt, sumac, and the cumin and cinnamon, if using, in a medium bowl; mix well.

3. Divide the beef mixture into 10 equal portions. Roll a portion between the palms of your hands to make a compact ball. Flatten the ball into a patty about ½ inch thick and transfer it to the prepared baking sheet. Repeat with the remaining portions. Bake the patties, flipping them halfway through, until done in the centers and browned on the tops, 15 to 16 minutes for medium or 18 minutes for well-done, then serve.

4. Alternatively, pan-fry: Briefly sear both sides in 3 tablespoons hot canola oil over medium heat. Reduce the heat to medium-low and continue cooking for 4 minutes per side for medium, 5 minutes per side for medium-well, or 6 minutes per side for well-done.

Purplish-red sumac is a traditional spice in Middle Eastern cooking. It has a lovely tangy lemony flavor that's great in meat, on salads, and sprinkled on hummus. It's usually available in Middle Eastern markets or spice shops. If you can't find it, you can sub in paprika—it doesn't taste the same, but it has a similar look. Chanie uses paprika in place of sumac all the time, so I guess that makes it okay. I do happen to have a jar of genuine sumac, and I love it!

DRESS IT UP

• Hummus-Topped Ktzitzot •

Place ktzitzot on a pretty platter. Top each patty with a dollop of Lemon Lover's Hummus (page 42), a sprinkle of sumac, and a drizzle of olive oil. Scatter some fresh parsley leaves around the platter.

MAKE IT A MEAL

Ktzitzot Pita Sandwiches

Instead of making small patties from the meat mixture, make four large burgers and pop them into pitas or onto buns stuffed with lettuce and slathered with Lemon Lover's Hummus (page 42) or Parsley Tahini (page 39) or both.

PAIR IT ELVI MATÍ RIOJA

Ktzitzot explode with flavor, so pair them with a spunky wine! This spicy but light red Rioja from the rich Ebro Valley in Spain will complement this dish with true Sephardic flair.

Monday: 7:15 p.m.

Let me tell you about my neighbor Anita . . .

She's the kind of woman who cooks, cleans, grills, takes out the garbage, and drives while her husband rides shotgun. She does it all with a certain flair that's hard to describe and impossible to duplicate. I admire her. I want to be like her.

But only sometimes, because Anita is fearless. Just listen.

At the time we lived in the suburbs, thirty miles north of Manhattan. People from New York City call it "the country," but that's because to them any place out of the five boroughs might as well be the Amazon jungle. So here I was in the wild country, roughing it with no sidewalks, few street lights, and spotty cell phone service. We wore reflectors in the street at night. No, we were not on camp time. Every snap of a branch could bring you face-to-face with a representative of nature you'd rather not meet. Promise not to tell my mother: There were even bear sightings.

So once upon a time, there were three bears that just happened to show up in our neighborhood. They were not cute and cuddly. They were not out for a stroll, letting their porridge cool. They were real bears, for goodness' sake! I locked my kids indoors, closed the curtains, grabbed a kitchen knife, and listened for news reports.

Meanwhile, Anita took it all with true pioneering spirit. Good soul that she is, she volunteered to walk a friend home after calmly arming herself with a broom and a cleaver. Oh, and nobody ever saw those bears again. Maybe they saw Anita.

Okay, she's one of my craziest friends, but I think she's super cool. And she's one of the best cooks on the planet. I call her for everything.

Anita's Lachmagine
(Miniature Ground Beef Pies)

Kosher Status: Meat • Prep: 10 minutes • Cook: 30 minutes • Total: 40 minutes • Yield: 48 lachmagine

The common spelling of this dish is lachmagine, *but you may see it spelled* lahm b'ajeen. *Transliteration from Arabic is tricky business, so we won't get all uppity about this. Lachmagine are sweet miniature minced meat pies that are popular in Israel, Syria, Lebanon, and Turkey. I always thought these mini pies were traditional fare, but the author of* Aromas from Aleppo, *the queen of Syrian cuisine Poopa Dweck (now there's an exotic name!), says that mini pies are "an American thing." 'Scuse me? Lachmagine American? Next thing, they'll be telling us that shish kebab was invented in Hoboken. Anyway, she insists that in Syria these pies were originally the size of a wrap. But Anita makes minis, and so do I. I like using them as a starter or as a side, and they're unbeatable party food. Traditional lachmagine calls for* temerhindi, *tamarind concentrate, so go stock up at your local souk. I'll wait. Anita is too practical to mess with temerhindi. She makes a sweet paste of more readily available ingredients: prune butter and tomato paste. And you don't have to make your own pie dough on a flat rock in your backyard. Anita says prepared pizza rounds are fine, and that's good enough for me.*

Cooking spray

2 medium onions

½ pound ground beef

1 cup prune butter

¾ cup tomato paste

Juice of 1 lemon

¾ teaspoon kosher salt

48 frozen 3-inch pizza rounds, not thawed

1. Preheat the oven to 350°F. Spray 4 baking sheets with cooking spray.

2. Finely grate the onions or puree them in a food processor. Combine the onions with the beef, prune butter, tomato paste, lemon juice, and salt in a large bowl. Mix until very well combined and completely smooth.

3. Place the pizza rounds on the prepared baking sheets and top each round with about 1 tablespoon of the meat sauce. With the back of a spoon, spread the sauce all the way to the edges.

4. Bake until the meat mixture is cooked through, about 30 minutes. Serve warm.

Resist the urge to add more meat. You are going for a saucy meat paste here, spread out to the edges. More meat results in a less flavorful lachmagine, and it will look like a dry, shrunken burger on a round of dough as opposed to a glistening mini meat pie.

DRESS IT UP

• Pine Nut Lachmagine with Parsley Tahini •

Top the pies with pine nuts and serve with a sesame sauce.

Decorate each round of meat paste with pine nuts before baking. Just before serving, garnish with chopped fresh parsley and serve with parsley tahini on the side.

To make **Parsley Tahini**: Combine ½ cup sesame paste, ¼ cup fresh lemon juice, ½ cup coarsely chopped fresh parsley, and ½ to ¾ teaspoon kosher salt in a food processor; pulse to chop. With processor running, slowly add water until a pourable consistency is reached.

MAKE IT A MEAL

Make a 7-inch round personal pie for each person. Serve with a simple Persian Cucumber Salad: Thinly slice Persian cucumbers, toss with sliced red onions, and drizzle Parsley Tahini over the top. Serve additional tahini on the side for dipping or drizzling on the pie.

PAIR IT BARTENURA OVADIA ESTATES ROSSO DI MONTEPULCIANO

This is a great party wine that goes down smooth 'n' easy.

Eggplant Caviar

Kosher Status: Pareve • Prep: 10 minutes • Cook: 12 minutes • Total: 22 minutes • Yield: 1½ cups caviar

Here's another recipe from my sister-in-law, Chanie. Last time I visited Greg and Chanie, she served some fab new salads. New to me, anyway. My favorite was the eggplant dip, and I couldn't figure out what made it so different. I cornered Chanie in the kitchen and demanded, "Tell me now what you did here." She explained that only the eggplant was sautéed. The red pepper and red onion were diced and tossed raw with the warm eggplant, so they soften slightly but still retain their shape and crunch. No measurements, of course. I've learned to expect that from Chanie.

When I came home, I did my best to re-create that dip. Wasn't sure if I got it just right until my friend Tzippy (the first guest to taste it) cornered me in my kitchen and pleaded, "Tell me now what you did here."

¼ cup olive oil

2 small Italian eggplants, diced (about 4 cups)

2 garlic cloves, minced

Kosher salt

¼ cup diced red bell pepper (about ¼ small pepper)

¼ cup diced red onion (about ½ small onion)

1 teaspoon chopped fresh parsley

1 teaspoon balsamic vinegar

Pita chips, for serving

Heat the olive oil in a large sauté pan over medium heat. Add the eggplant and sauté 2 minutes, stirring well to coat the eggplant with the oil. Add the garlic and ½ teaspoon salt. Cover and cook until the eggplant is lightly golden and softened, about 10 minutes. Remove from the heat. Mix in the pepper, onion, parsley, and vinegar; season with salt. Transfer the caviar to a bowl and serve warm with pita chips.

VARIATION

You can throw the caviar in a food processor and purée it for a creamy dip. It's almost like baba ghanoush. Not as pretty as the caviar, but definitely delish.

• Eggplant Caviar Crostini •

I love serving individual toast points or small slices of bread topped with Eggplant Caviar. It's divine.

Toast twenty ¼-inch-thick baguette slices to make crostini. Top the crispy crostini with 1 tablespoon of the Eggplant Caviar and small leaves of fresh herbs like basil, parsley, or chervil. To save time, you could sub water crackers for the baguette slices.

MAKE IT A MEAL

Create a Middle Eastern tasting plate with Eggplant Caviar and your choice of the following: Ktzitzot (page 33), Lachmagine (page 38), Falafel Poppers (page 46), and/or Lemon Lover's Hummus (page 42), along with warm pita and an Israeli chopped salad (made with a base of chopped cucumbers and tomatoes dressed in fresh lemon juice and salt; some people add chopped bell peppers or red onions and olive oil and freshly ground black pepper).

PAIR IT BARTENURA OVADIA ESTATES ROSSO TOSCANO

At under $10 a bottle, you can stock up on this light, fruity Italian wine.

Lemon Lover's Hummus

Kosher Status: Pareve • Prep: 5 minutes • Cook: 0 minutes • Total: 5 minutes • Yield: 2 cups hummus

If you live in an uberfriendly small town like ours, everyone is on the welcome bandwagon when a new neighbor moves in. The multicolored dressed-up version of this recipe looks great in little mason jars, delivered with your pita crisps (see Make It a Meal). Who says it has to be cookies or a pie? Believe me, they'll appreciate some good hummus after all those pies.

I've created many a hummus recipe, and every member of my family has a favorite. Angel Face will even clean up all his toys to get Lemon Lover's Hummus, and I have to agree with his taste: It has the deepest, most authentic flavors and is by far my best and creamiest rendition of this dip. You should have some of this stuff ready at all times, just in case you get new neighbors. Listen, if nobody moves in, you can always eat it yourself.

One 15½-ounce can chickpeas, rinsed well and drained

1 tablespoon tahini paste

1 garlic clove

Grated zest and juice of 2 medium lemons

¾ teaspoon kosher salt

¼ teaspoon ground cumin

½ cup extra virgin olive oil

Combine the chickpeas, tahini, garlic, lemon zest and juice, salt, and cumin in a food processor. Pulse to coarsely chop. With the processor running, slowly add the olive oil, stopping once to scrape down the sides of the bowl. The mixture will be smooth and creamy. The hummus can be stored in an airtight container in the refrigerator for up to 1 week.

QUICK TIP

For a more subtle lemon taste, use the zest and juice of only one lemon. This will be closer to the classic flavor of hummus.

• **Tricolor Hummus Trifles** •

Make a double batch of Lemon Lover's Hummus to create colorful layered trifles.

To make the layers: For the red pepper layer, place 1 cup hummus, ½ cup coarsely chopped roasted red bell peppers, and ¼ teaspoon salt in a food processor; blend until smooth and set aside. For the spinach layer, place 1 cup hummus, ½ cup frozen chopped spinach (thawed and drained well), ¼ cup extra virgin olive oil, and ¼ teaspoon salt in a food processor; blend until smooth. Do not add anything to the third cup of hummus.

Transfer the three types of hummus to separate pastry bags fitted with large tips. Pipe the hummus in three layers in small trifle dishes or mason jars.

MAKE IT A MEAL

Serve a scoop of hummus on a bed of lettuce tossed with chopped tomatoes and cucumbers. Drizzle with extra virgin olive oil and sesame seeds, and serve with homemade Pita Crisps.

To make **Pita Crisps**: Split pitas in half, cut the two disks into quarters, and place them in a single layer on a baking sheet. Sprinkle the pitas with sumac, za'atar, or a spice of your choice. Spray with cooking spray and bake at 350°F until golden brown and crisp, 8 to 10 minutes.

PAIR IT GOOSE BAY SAUVIGNON BLANC

Hummus needs a refreshing wine to cleanse the palate between bites. The citrus flavors in this dish will match beautifully with a crisp sauvignon blanc.

Tuesday: 10:00 a.m.

Music is blasting in the kitchen . . .

You know that Middle Eastern desert sound, with some guy hitting a drum at 300 slaps a minute, somebody plucking furiously at a tight-stringed oud, and another guy yelling like he's herding sheep. Anyway, I'm chopping hot peppers and smashing garlic to the beat; my baby is sitting near me, laughing and pounding her chubby little fists on the counter.

And then—Hubby walks in. All blond-haired and blue-eyed. He lets me know I might want to go outside because "your camel got loose and is running down the driveway."

Big deal. I was only channeling my Arabian ancestors while trying to create a truly great Yemenite *schug*, a spicy paste consumed for centuries by people with iron guts. I was gonna introduce it to the Western world and take my bows, waving graciously to the paparazzi. Then my friend Judy tells me that a recipe for schug had already debuted in the April 2011 special sandwich issue of *Saveur*. It was called "a fantastic condiment for pita and falafel sandwiches." So much for secret recipes. Ah well, nothin' new under the sun, as the wise man said.

Falafel Poppers with Lemon Sesame Schug

Kosher Status: Pareve • Prep: 15 minutes • Chill: 30 minutes • Cook: 8 minutes •
Total: 53 minutes • Yield: 20 poppers

Let me define schug for you. This stuff is no timid little dip; we're talking **Hot! Hot!
Hot!** *In my recipe, I temper it to mildly scalding by seeding the jalapeños, mixing in a
bell pepper, and then combining equal parts schug with 100 percent sesame seed paste,
lemon juice, and salt. You want authentic schug? Don't seed your jalapeños, and lose
the bell pepper in favor of three more medium jalapeños. Oh, and traditionally, schug is
eaten straight. I double-dare you. But first you have to get the guy with the sheep and the
drums. So don't blame me if your schug experience is too civilized. I did my best.*

FALAFEL POPPERS

One 15½-ounce can chickpeas, drained
and patted dry

¼ cup coarsely chopped fresh cilantro or
1½ tablespoons dried

3 scallions (white part plus 3 inches of the
green), coarsely chopped

4 garlic cloves, smashed

1 tablespoon dried parsley

1 tablespoon ground cumin

1 teaspoon ground coriander

1 teaspoon kosher salt

½ teaspoon ground white pepper

1 teaspoon baking powder

2 tablespoons all-purpose flour

1 large egg, beaten

Cooking spray

Canola oil, for frying

LEMON SESAME SCHUG

½ green bell pepper, ribs and seeds
removed

6 to 8 medium green jalapeño chiles
(8 ounces)

6 garlic cloves

5 tablespoons extra virgin olive oil

Kosher salt

¼ cup tahini paste

2 tablespoons fresh lemon juice

ASSEMBLY

20 grape tomatoes

20 Persian cucumber rounds

EQUIPMENT

Twenty 6-inch skewers or long cocktail toothpicks

1. Prepare the falafel batter: Combine the chickpeas, cilantro, scallions, garlic, parsley, cumin, coriander, salt, and pepper in a food processor and puree until almost smooth. Sprinkle in the baking powder. Add the flour and egg and pulse until the batter comes together. Transfer the batter to a bowl, cover, and refrigerate for 30 minutes.

2. Meanwhile, prepare the schug: Place the pepper, chiles, garlic, olive oil, and ½ teaspoon salt in a food processor. Pulse until a coarse thick paste is formed.

3. In a small bowl, stir together ¼ cup of the schug with the tahini, lemon juice, and ½ teaspoon salt. Store the remaining schug in an airtight container in the fridge for up to 1 week.

4. Lightly spray a baking sheet with cooking spray. Line a plate with two layers of paper towels.

5. Heat 2 inches of canola oil in a large, deep, heavy-bottomed skillet over medium-high heat to 350°F. Remove the chickpea batter from the fridge, and with damp hands, roll it into 20 balls. Place the balls on the prepared baking sheet. Using a slotted spoon, carefully lower the falafel balls into the hot oil. Fry the balls until brown and crispy, about 7 to 8 minutes, turning them while frying to cook evenly. Transfer the balls with the slotted spoon to the prepared plate to drain.

6. Skewer each falafel ball with a grape tomato and a cucumber round. Serve the poppers with Lemon Sesame Schug for dipping.

You can serve poppers with store-bought tahini if you don't have time to make the Lemon Sesame Schug.

Using 6 to 8 jalapeños will give you a super spicy, almost scalding, schug. For a simply spicy, more tolerable version, use 3 or 4 jalapeños.

DRESS IT DOWN/MAKE IT A MEAL
• Falafel Sandwiches •

Falafel is the ultimate Israeli street food. In several Jewish neighborhoods here in the States, any pizza place worth its weight in kosher salt serves up falafel. Falafel Poppers with Lemon Sesame Schug is an elegant presentation of this fast-food classic.

Enjoy authentic and hearty falafel by layering the falafel balls in pita pockets with salads of your choice—think red cabbage salad, Israeli chopped salad, even classic coleslaw or sauerkraut. Smear in my fab Lemon Sesame Schug; add pickles, fries, hummus, and plenty of tahini, and you're good to go.

PAIR IT CARMEL KAYOUMI WHITE RIESLING

Too much schug and you'll need a fire hydrant to cool your palate. A chilled riesling will do the trick.

Cilantro Corn Cakes

Kosher Status: Pareve • Prep: 15 minutes • Cook: 16 minutes • Total: 31 minutes • Yield: 16 cakes

Corn fritters by one of my favorite chefs, David Kolotkin, inspired this recipe. How I got from that to my subtly sweet Cilantro Corn Cakes, I can't exactly say. That's just how my mind works. Hubby says probing my mind is asking for trouble. He just doesn't go there.

Cooking spray

1 cup yellow cornmeal

½ cup all-purpose flour

2½ tablespoons granulated sugar

1 teaspoon kosher salt

1 teaspoon baking soda

½ teaspoon ground cumin

2 cups frozen corn kernels, thawed, or canned corn, drained

2 large eggs, beaten

¼ cup finely chopped fresh cilantro or 1½ tablespoons dried

Juice of 1 lime

1 tablespoon hot sauce (optional)

Canola oil

Salsa, for serving (optional)

1. Spray a baking sheet with cooking spray.

2. Combine the cornmeal, flour, sugar, salt, baking soda, and cumin in a medium bowl. Add the corn, eggs, cilantro, lime juice, and hot sauce, if using, and stir until well moistened. Using slightly wet hands, form about 2 tablespoons of the dough into a ball. Flatten it into a ¼-inch-thick patty and place it on the prepared baking sheet. Repeat with the remaining mixture to make 16 cakes.

3. Heat 2 tablespoons canola oil in a large skillet over medium heat. Working in batches, pan-fry the cakes until golden brown and cooked through, 3 to 4 minutes per side. Keep the first batch warm on a plate tented with foil while you're cooking the second batch, adding another 2 tablespoons oil if necessary. Serve immediately with salsa, if desired.

Microwave hard limes for 20 to 30 seconds. Let them cool before halving and juicing so the hot juice doesn't burn you. It's painful. And embarrassing. What are you gonna tell people? "I got in a fight with a lime!"

PREP AHEAD

Best served fresh, these corn cakes do not keep well and will dry out and lose their lightness. If you want to prep ahead, form the cakes and keep them refrigerated on a plate, tightly covered with plastic wrap, for up to 3 days. Bring to room temperature and pan-fry.

VARIATION

Instead of serving your corn cakes with salsa, try drizzling maple syrup on them as they do in the South.

DRESS IT UP

• Cilantro Corn Cakes with Avocado Aioli •

Add avocado aioli and some citrus for a delightful taste and color complement.

In a food processor, purée 2 pitted and peeled avocados with ¼ to ½ cup mayonnaise and ¼ teaspoon salt. Dollop the aioli on the corn cakes, and top with a grapefruit segment or mango slice and a sprinkle of chopped chives.

MAKE IT A MEAL

Enjoy morning or night. These versatile corn cakes go great with Argentinean Brisket (page 200) for dinner. For breakfast, drizzle the cakes with maple syrup and serve them alongside beef or chicken sausage links.

PAIR IT BARON HERZOG PINOT GRIGIO

Grab this easy white wine with a slightly herbal twist to pair with these pan-fried patties.

Tropical Fruit Guacamole

Kosher Status: Pareve • Prep: 15 minutes • Cook: 0 minutes • Total: 15 minutes • Yield: 2½ cups guac.

I don't care if you've heard me say this before—I'll say it a hundred times over: Avocados are one of God's great gifts to this world (along with sunsets, calla lilies, and Hubby). I put avocados on most everything. Eat 'em plain, too—all they need is a sprinkle of kosher salt. When I'm feeling really wild, they get a drizzle of olive oil.

Guacamole is a common way to enjoy this fruit. (It's a fruit, not a vegetable. Trust me.) So I'm combining it with more fruit. Here goes.

3 ripe avocados, pitted, peeled, and diced (about 2 cups)

3 tablespoons fresh lime juice (about 1½ limes)

½ teaspoon kosher salt

¼ cup diced mango

¼ cup diced pineapple

2 tablespoons finely chopped red onion

2 tablespoons coarsely chopped fresh cilantro

Tortilla chips, for serving

Place the avocados, lime juice, and salt in a medium bowl. Using a fork or potato masher, mash the avocados until fairly smooth. Gently stir in the mango, pineapple, onion, and cilantro. Serve immediately with tortilla chips.

• **Deconstructed Tropical Guacamole** •

Layer it up for a pretty, upscale look.

Layer ¼- to ½-inch slices of avocado, mango, pineapple, and red onion (even add watermelon for a splash of color) on a salad plate or platter. Drizzle extra virgin olive oil on top, add a sprinkle of salt, and serve with lime wedges and fresh cilantro for garnish.

PAIR IT ELVI INVITA

Go for this unusual, but quite delicious, white wine blend to complement this unique guac.

Uputzi's Vegetarian Chopped "Liver" Pâté

Kosher Status: Pareve • Prep: 10 minutes • Cook: 16 minutes • Chill: 3 hours •
Total: 3 hours, 26 minutes • Yield: 4 cups pâté

To Europeans, lunch is dinner—the main meal. My mother always told us how, back in the Old Country, Uputzi (my granddad) would come home from work smack in the middle of the day for a full hot lunch spread. In America, our family kept that custom. On weekends, no one wanted to miss lunch (really "dinner," which is lunch, you understand), especially at Uputzi's house. One of my yummiest memories is his faux liver pâté. Spread it on fresh bread and eat it with a light salad dressed simply in oil with a dash of salt, and you're in pâté heaven. It was the kind of food that comes out of only the finest kitchens in the world, and Uputzi's was one of them.

1 cup walnut halves

3 tablespoons olive oil

1 large onion, chopped

1 pound mixed mushrooms (such as
    button, shiitake, and cremini), chopped

4 large hard-cooked eggs, quartered
    (see Quick Tips)

1 garlic clove

1 teaspoon dried thyme

1 teaspoon kosher salt

1 teaspoon red wine vinegar

Freshly ground black pepper

2 to 3 tablespoons mayonnaise

Crackers or crostini, for serving

1. Preheat the oven to 350°F.

2. Spread the walnuts in a single layer on a baking sheet and toast in the oven until fragrant, about 6 minutes. Set aside to cool.

3. Heat 1 tablespoon of the olive oil in a large sauté pan over medium heat. Add the onion and sauté until slightly softened, about 4 minutes. Add the mushrooms and the remaining 2 tablespoons of oil. Sauté until the mushrooms are softened and most of the liquid has evaporated, 10 to 12 minutes. Transfer to a food processor. Add the walnuts, eggs, garlic, thyme, salt, vinegar, and pepper to taste. Process until almost smooth, 2 to 3 minutes. Add the mayonnaise and continue processing until creamy.

4. Transfer the pâté to a bowl and cover with plastic wrap. Chill at least 3 hours or overnight. Serve with crackers or crostini.

QUICK TIPS

For perfect hard-cooked eggs, start with large eggs at room temp. Place the eggs in a pot large enough to hold them in a single layer without crowding. Add cold water to cover the eggs by 1 inch. Bring just to a boil over high heat. Remove the pot from the heat and cover with a tight-fitting lid. Let stand for 12 minutes. Pour off the water, then shake the pot gently so the eggs bump into one another and the sides of the pot and the shells crack all over. Run cold water over the eggs to stop the cooking. Peel the eggs under cold running water.

Be sure to remove and discard the tough, woody stems from the shiitake mushrooms.

• Vegetarian Chopped "Liver" Pâté Bread Cups •

We're going to put this pâté into a creative container: the bread! Makes it both impressive to look at and easy to eat. Fab for parties and holidays. Exquisite taste presented in festive finery.

Transfer the chilled pâté to a pastry bag fitted with a large tip. Cut a baguette on the diagonal into 2-inch slices and hollow out the bread in the center, leaving ¼ inch on the bottom to make a little "bowl." Pipe the pâté into the baguette, garnish with sliced scallions, and serve immediately so the cups don't become soggy.

This presentation idea is also great for crudités and dip. Pipe or pour your dip into the little bread cups and stand up a few pieces of veggies in it to garnish.

MAKE IT A MEAL

Serve scoops of pâté and egg salad on a bed of chopped romaine. Top with finely diced red bell pepper and drizzle on ranch dressing, or thin the Garlic Ranch Dip (page 61) with water and drizzle it on top.

PAIR IT GOOSE BAY RESERVE PINOT NOIR

The liver may be faux, but we can still take advantage of the genuine richness of "meaty" mushrooms. A light red wine will work beautifully here.

Thursday: 10:00 a.m.

When I was expecting baby #5 . . .

Everywhere I waddled, I evoked concerned comments and homespun advice. Around here, that's not an invasion of privacy; it's more like the whole community rooting you on. We do it for everybody.

Finally, thank the Lord, the day comes. And the minute you come home from the hospital with that neat little bundle wrapped in blankets, your family wants dinner.

That's when all your wonderful neighbors cook dinner for you and your brood—for two weeks. And friends like Anita bring over double portions, so you can freeze the extras for when the meals stop coming. That's real *cheesed.* (The usual translation of that Hebrew word is benevolence, but whoa, what an understatement. We're talking about neighbors coming in to wash your laundry, do homework with your kids, tend your garden, and feed your goldfish. It's all about over-the-top caring, and in my world, it happens every day.)

So anyway, when I came home with my daughter, my neighbor Miriam delivered this fish. Now gefilte fish and I have sort of a love-hate relationship. I know a frozen fish loaf doesn't have eyes, but the minute I open the package, I feel like it's looking at me and saying, "*Nu,* vat you gonna do vit me?" Yes, it has a bit of a Yiddish accent.

Gefilte fish is an acquired taste, like tuna tartare, but way over on the other side of the palate. But Miriam's version was a stunning surprise. As I savored the last bite, I thought, *I must remember this for my next book.*

Baked Herbed Gefilte Fish

Kosher Status: Pareve • Prep: 5 minutes • Cook: 2 hours • Chill: Overnight •
Total: About 10 hours • Yield: 8 servings

*I much prefer baking my gefilte fish as opposed to the traditional method of boiling. I just
don't like how the words "boiled fish" sound, but that of course is neither here nor there.
Boiled gefilte fish (blech, again!) can get really soggy and waterlogged, depending on how
long you leave it in the pot and the level of your heat. I find baking always produces a
firmer-textured, tastier gefilte.*

¼ cup olive oil, plus more for drizzling

2 teaspoons paprika

2 teaspoons dried parsley

2 pinches ground allspice

½ teaspoon kosher salt

½ teaspoon freshly ground black pepper

One 22-ounce loaf frozen gefilte fish,
  paper removed, not thawed

1 large onion, sliced in rounds

2 garlic cloves, minced

1. Preheat the oven to 350°F.

2. Pour the olive oil into the bottom of a 9 x 5-inch loaf pan. Add the paprika, parsley, 1
   pinch of the allspice, the salt, and pepper. Roll the frozen loaf in the oil and spices to
   coat. Remove the loaf from the pan, arrange the onion on the bottom of the pan, and
   place the loaf on top of the onion. Sprinkle with the garlic and the remaining 1 pinch
   allspice. Finish with a drizzle of olive oil. Bake, covered, for 2 hours.

3. Cool the gefilte fish completely, then place it in a resealable container and refrigerate it
   for at least 4 hours or overnight. Serve cold, sliced and topped with the onions.

PAIR IT BARON HERZOG CENTRAL COAST MERLOT

Gefilte fish is not flaky and certainly not a pushover. It can stand up to *chrein* (horseradish) and a
good medium-bodied red wine.

• **Baked Carrot-Stuffed Gefilte Fish** •

A slice of gefilte with a carrot round cooked smack in the center is a thing of beauty and wonderment. Surprise—with this little trick, it's not at all hard!

Thaw the fish in the paper, at room temperature, for 1 hour and 45 minutes. Stand the fish upright with one end flat on the counter; open the paper at the top. Position the long handle of a wooden spoon at the center of the top of the fish and gently push the handle down the length of the fish to create a hole. Trim the ends of a long, thin carrot so that the carrot is the same length as the loaf, and then push the carrot through the hole. Important: Be sure that your carrot is thin, otherwise it will not cook through in the 2 hours.

Rewrap the paper at the top, and twist both ends to secure. If needed, place the fish in a large resealable bag to roll it back into shape. Refreeze for 2 hours.

Follow the instructions, omitting the parsley. After rolling the fish in the oil and spices and placing it over the bed of onions, top with the torn leaves of 1 small bunch of fresh parsley. Continue as above with the garlic, allspice, and drizzle of olive oil. Bake as instructed.

Soups and Starters

59

Fancy Crudités with Garlic Ranch Dip

Kosher Status: Pareve • Prep: 15 minutes • Cook: 0 minutes • Chill: 1 hour •
Total: 1 hour, 15 minutes • Yield: 2 cups dip, 8 cups crudités

I love this elegant presentation for crudités, and you're going to love this dip. You can triple it, bottle it, use it as perfume, and store it in your fridge for at least two weeks. It's also great thinned out and used as a salad dressing. If you're going fancy-schmancy with your entertaining, you could opt for a dichromatic green-and-white veg look in elegant vintage silver cups. But I happen to love clear glass (or plastic!), so my guests can see that their crudités already have been dipped for them. The vibrant mix-and-match colors are so bright and cheery that the veggies are irresistible.

6 garlic cloves

2 cups canola oil

1 cup plain soy milk

Regular or light mayonnaise or soy sour cream

4 scallions (white and light green parts), coarsely chopped

Juice of 1 lemon (about ¼ cup)

2 tablespoons coarsely chopped fresh dill

2 teaspoons kosher salt

Freshly ground black pepper

8 cups cut assorted fresh vegetables, for dipping

1. Place the garlic in a small pot or sauté pan and cover with 1 cup of the canola oil. Bring to a boil over medium-high heat and reduce to a simmer. Cook until the garlic is browned and soft, about 10 minutes. Remove the garlic from the oil. Discard the oil. Let the garlic cool slightly.

2. Combine the remaining 1 cup canola oil, the soy milk, ½ cup mayonnaise (or soy sour cream), scallions, lemon juice, dill, salt, pepper to taste, and cooled garlic in a food processor. Puree until the mixture comes together to form a smooth, thick dip. Thicken with mayonnaise or thin with water to reach the desired consistency. Transfer to a container, cover, and refrigerate for 1 hour or up to 3 days.

3. To serve, spread crushed ice on a rimmed serving tray. Nestle eight small glass cups into the ice. Pour ¼ cup of the dip into each glass. Fill the glasses with the vegetables and serve immediately.

I love using an array of pretty, bold-colored veggies: crisp green beans, crunchy Persian cucumbers, ruby-red radicchio, and those cute miniature carrots with the greens on top. Something as simple as using miniatures or cutting your veggies on the diagonal makes this just a touch more elegant.

TIME-SAVER

To cut down on your cutting time, choose vegetables such as snap peas, green beans, radishes, and baby carrots.

DRESS IT DOWN
• Quick Crudités •

For everyday meals, make it simple. Serve the dip in a bowl in the center of a platter surrounded by baby carrots.

MAKE IT A MEAL

This dip is great on your favorite pasta or potato salad. Toss in cubed meat or cheese to make this a hearty one-bowl meal. I also love to add a handful of greens to my pasta and potato salads; they add a pop of color and fresh bright flavor to a heavy carb.

PAIR IT FLAM BLANC

After all that garlic, freshen your breath and enjoy a fab white! This sauvignon blanc and chardonnay blend is both fruity and floral, and that's a mouthful!

Chilled Coconut Berry Soup

Kosher Status: Pareve • Prep: 15 minutes • Cook: 0 minutes •
Total: 15 minutes • Yield: 4 to 6 servings

I am a huge fan of coconut milk. It's rich, creamy, and, well, coconutty. This is not your typical fruit soup—it's dreamy and decadent. Make a batch of the dressed-up ice cubes and keep them on hand. You can use them to turn your everyday punch, lemonade, iced tea, or water pitcher into an eye-popping showstopper.

1½ cups frozen blueberries, not thawed

1½ cups frozen strawberries, not thawed

Two 14-ounce cans coconut milk

¼ cup honey

Grated zest and juice of 1 medium lemon

1 pinch of kosher salt

1. Purée the blueberries, strawberries, coconut milk, honey, lemon zest and juice, and salt in a blender until smooth.

2. Strain the soup to remove the seeds and skin by pressing it through a fine-mesh sieve with a wooden spoon over a large bowl.

3. Serve immediately, or transfer the soup to a container, cover, and refrigerate for up to 2 days. If there is any separation, just give the soup a good stir before serving chilled.

VARIATIONS

You can, of course, sub in regular, soy, rice, or almond milk for the coconut milk; but keep in mind that they vary in thickness, so that will affect the creaminess of your soup.

Throw in some booze for the grownups. Walders Vodka & Vanilla would make a *great* addition to this soup.

Make it a dessert: Freeze the soup. Remove it from the freezer, put it in a food processor, and pulse it until smooth. Return to the freezer until ready to serve. Scoop into individual bowls topped with dollops of whipped cream and a few fresh blueberries.

• Fruit, Flower, and Mint Ice Cubes •

Garnish the soup with large ice cubes filled with fresh berries, mint leaves, or edible flowers such as purple orchids.

To make the cubes: Place a blueberry, a strawberry slice, a mint leaf, or an orchid in each section of an ice cube tray that makes large cubes; they take longer to melt. Cover with water and freeze overnight. Note: Use only edible flowers that have not been processed with chemicals; you can find them in grocery stores.

PAIR IT BARTENURA PROSECCO BRUT

When pairing soup, always look for something fun and bubbly. The texture of bubbles provides a contrast to the soup.

Baked Sweet Potato Chips

Kosher Status: Pareve • Prep: 15 minutes • Cook: 25 minutes •
Total: 40 minutes • Yield: 4 servings

Baked, not fried, these guys are sweet and crispy around the edges. And they have beta carotene, so they're good for you. The kids love 'em, and I love 'em, so that's reason enough for them to go into this book. They're simple to make, too. I like to add a little salt, making them sweet and salty.

2 medium sweet potatoes, scrubbed and
   cut into ⅛-inch slices
¼ cup olive oil

½ teaspoon kosher salt
Honey mustard, for dipping (optional)

1. Preheat the oven to 400°F.

2. Divide the sweet potatoes between 2 rimmed baking sheets and drizzle the olive oil on top. Toss the potatoes with the oil so they are well coated. Spread the potatoes in a single layer. Bake until golden brown and crispy, 20 to 25 minutes, flipping once halfway through. Sprinkle with the salt and serve immediately with honey mustard for dipping.

DRESS IT UP

• Purple, Orange, and White Chips (Dairy) •

Multicolored chips topped with a dollop of sour cream look gourmet but are super simple.

Along with sweet potatoes, also use purple and Yukon gold potatoes. To serve, top each chip with ½ teaspoon sour cream and a small sprig of fresh dill or chives.

PAIR IT WEINSTOCK RED BY W

Sweet potato chips are easy to eat, so go for an easy-sippin' red.

Cool Cucumber and Avocado Cream Soup

Kosher Status: Dairy • Prep: 10 minutes • Cook: 0 minutes • Chill: 2 hours •
Total: 2 hours, 10 minutes • Yield: 4½ cups soup

My friend Victoria came up with a pasta dish with avocado cream sauce. Just listen to that sound—avocado cream, avocado cream. So smooth. So indulgent. While Victoria was telling me all about her creation, I tuned her out entirely, lost in an avocado cream fantasy.

Forget the pasta, I just wanted that sauce! So I ditched the noodles and went straight for the gold: a cool, creamy dreamy smooth soup.

1 large cucumber, peeled, seeded, and
    cut into chunks
3 ripe medium avocados, pitted and
    peeled
½ cup plain Greek yogurt

1 garlic clove
Juice of 1 small lime
1½ teaspoons kosher salt
Fresh dill or cilantro, for garnish
    (optional)

Puree the cucumber, avocados, yogurt, garlic, lime juice, salt, and 1½ cups water in a food processor until smooth. Transfer the soup to an airtight container and refrigerate until very cold, about 2 hours. Before serving, the soup can be thinned with a little water, if necessary, to reach the desired consistency. Garnish with fresh dill or cilantro.

VARIATIONS

You can sub in regular yogurt for this soup. It will be a little less rich and creamy, but still good; just be sure to pour off any liquid that may have collected at the top of the container.

Make your own Greek yogurt. Line a fine-mesh sieve with a clean T-shirt or cheesecloth. Place the strainer in a bowl large enough that the excess liquid can drip down and collect at the bottom of the bowl. Spoon the yogurt into the strainer and place in the fridge, covered with plastic wrap, overnight. This will leave you with Greek-style yogurt that is rich and creamy.

Best served as soon as it's fully chilled, the soup can last in the fridge for 1 to 2 days, but the top layer will darken as the avocados oxidize. Remove this layer with a spoon before serving. If you place plastic wrap directly on the soup, keeping out all air, it will help delay the formation of that dark layer.

• Cool Cucumber and Avocado Cream Shooters •

Serve the soup as a shooter in cucumber cups.

Take one large, straight English cucumber and cut off both ends. Peel the cucumber vertically, leaving strips to create stripes. Cut the cucumber into 2-inch-long cylinders and scoop out the insides, leaving ¼ to ½ inch on the bottom to form cups. Just before serving, fill them with the soup and garnish with a small dollop of Greek yogurt, some chives, and a light dusting of paprika. You can make about 4 to 5 shooters per large cucumber, and each shooter holds about 1 tablespoon of soup.

MAKE IT A MEAL

Serve the soup with crusty sourdough bread and a simple tomato-garlic salad.

PAIR IT BARTENURA SPARKLING MOSCATO

The subtle sweetness of this popular wine is a real crowd-pleaser!

WHAT IS GREEK YOGURT?

This recipe calls for Greek yogurt, so let's talk about what makes this yogurt different from all other yogurts. The rich texture of Greek yogurt is achieved by straining it through a cloth, a paper bag, or a filter to remove the whey. Because the whey is removed, even nonfat varieties are rich and creamy. The consistency achieved is between yogurt and cheese, and the distinctive tangy taste is preserved.

Smashed Red Potato Nachos

Kosher Status: Dairy • Prep: 15 minutes • Cook: 25 minutes • Total: 40 minutes • Yield: 4 to 6 servings

Ian Knauer lives on a farm in rural Pennsylvania, grows his own potatoes and herbs, keeps chickens, and hunts for his din din. When I first saw him dig up a few potatoes and make this recipe on his American Seed *cooking show, it struck me as the most amazing thing ever! Could practically taste it right through the screen. And the whole time I'm wondering,* Why didn't I think of that?

Ian deep-fried his smashed potatoes before topping them with cheese and broiling them in the oven. I skipped that step because of the extra calories—okay, really because of the extra time. But if you can spare the minutes, frying makes them taste beyond words.

Cooking spray

2 pounds small red-skin potatoes
(about 24), scrubbed

2 tablespoons olive oil

½ teaspoon kosher salt

1 cup shredded cheddar cheese or
Mexican blend

½ cup sour cream

½ cup salsa

½ cup guacamole

2 scallions (green part only), chopped

1. Spray a baking sheet with cooking spray.

2. Place the potatoes in a medium pot and cover them with cold water. Bring to a boil, covered, over medium-high heat. Cook the potatoes until fork tender, 12 to 15 minutes. Drain and set aside until cool enough to handle.

3. Preheat the broiler on high heat.

4. Place a potato on a cutting board. Using the palm of your hand or the bottom of a plate or measuring cup larger than the potato, smash down until the potato is about ¼ inch thick. Using a spatula, transfer the smashed potato to the prepared baking sheet. Repeat with the remaining potatoes. Drizzle the olive oil over the potatoes and sprinkle with the salt.

5. Broil the potatoes until golden brown, 5 to 8 minutes. Sprinkle the cheese on top and broil until the cheese is melted and bubbly, 1 to 2 minutes. Remove the pan from the oven. Using a spatula, carefully transfer the potatoes to a platter. Top with dollops of the sour cream, salsa, and guacamole and sprinkle with the scallions. Serve immediately.

PAIR IT SEGAL'S SPECIAL RESERVE CHARDONNAY

A rich chardonnay is a true soul mate to this creamy dish.

DRESS IT UP

• **Nacho Potato Bites** •

Choose the largest small red-skin potatoes you can find, and boil them as directed on page 70.

Once drained and cool enough to handle, slice off the tops and bottoms so the potatoes can stand without falling over. Using a melon baller or small paring knife, carefully scoop out the insides of the potatoes while keeping the outsides intact. Mix the scooped-out potato flesh with 1½ cups shredded cheese and ½ cup salsa in a medium bowl. Evenly distribute the filling among the potatoes. Place the potato bites on a greased baking sheet or oven-to-table platter and broil until the cheese is melted and bubbly, about 1 to 2 minutes. Top with sour cream or guacamole and a few scallions. Bake any excess filling as a small casserole and brown the top with extra cheese. No need to waste yummy goodness.

Poppy's Sour Cream Potato Soup

Kosher Status: Dairy • Prep: 8 minutes • Cook: 30 minutes • Total: 38 minutes • Yield: 10 cups soup

Uputzi wasn't the only cook in our family; my other grandfather, Poppy, was nicknamed Chefu, Romanian for chef. A butcher by trade, he was amazing in the kitchen. He and my grandmother each had their specialties. Anytime we stopped by their house off Philly's Northeast Avenue, there was always something tasty and fresh for us to eat. I loved sitting at their tiny kitchen table enjoying this sour cream potato soup.

Poppy's original rendition of this soup consisted simply of potatoes, water, salt, pepper, sour cream, and small square luckshen. *(It may sound like Chinese, but it's Yiddish for noodles.) I've beefed up his recipe by replacing the water with veg broth and subbing small red-skin potatoes (eye appeal) for his peeled, diced russets. Can't be sure exactly how much sour cream he used, so I just put in the whole darn container. This rich soup immediately transports me back to his kitchen table with my legs dangling above the floor.*

3 tablespoons butter

1 large onion, finely diced

1 quart vegetable broth, such as Manischewitz All Natural Vegetable Broth

1 pound very small red-skin potatoes, quartered

One 16-ounce container sour cream

Kosher salt

Ground white pepper

2½ cups cooked small pasta (such as square noodles, ditalini, or orzo)

1. Heat the butter in a large pot over medium heat. Add the onion and cook, stirring continually until translucent, about 10 minutes. Do not let the onion brown.

2. Add the broth and potatoes and bring to a boil. Reduce the heat and simmer until the potatoes are fork tender, 10 to 15 minutes.

3. Temper the sour cream by placing it in a large bowl and slowly, so that it doesn't curdle, whisking in 1 cup of the soup. Pour the tempered sour cream into the soup. Mix well and heat through. Season with salt and pepper.

4. Place ¼ cup noodles in each of eight bowls and ladle the soup over the top. Serve warm.

Small square noodles by Manischewitz can be found in your local supermarket under the name Egg Noodles Flakes.

This recipe keeps the cooked noodles separate from the soup so they don't get mushy. Portion the noodles into bowls and top with hot soup just before serving.

VARIATION

Serve as a chilled soup. Omit the noodles and puree with a dash of nutmeg until thick and creamy. Top with chopped chives.

DRESS IT UP

• Poppy's Potato Soup Cups •

Make a spice rub to rim mugs for a fun presentation.

Combine 2 tablespoons each paprika and celery salt in a small bowl. Dip the edges of ten 8-ounce mugs in water and then in the spice rub. Fill the mugs with soup and garnish with a dollop of sour cream.

MAKE IT A MEAL

This soup is perfect with fresh buttered pumpernickel rolls.

PAIR IT SHILOH LEGEND

A medium-bodied red here would be a surprising, out-of-the-box pairing. This blend includes shiraz and merlot with great fruit flavors and a fabulous finish.

Sides AND
Salads

MEAT

Triple Deli Pasta Salad with Creamy Italian Dressing   77
DRESS IT UP *Deconstructed Chef's Salad*

Cranberry Chestnut Challah Stuffing   79
DRESS IT UP *Stuffed Baked Onions*

Hearty Mushrooms with Herbs and Wine   84
DRESS IT UP *Mushroom Phyllo Cups*

Pastrami-Fry Salad with Creamy Chili Dressing   86
DRESS IT UP *Pastrami-Fry Tomato Cups*

PAREVE

Daddy's Deep-Dish Potato Kigel/ Kugel   91
DRESS IT UP *Pastrami Potato Kugel (Meat)*

Spiced Apple Challah Kugel   94
DRESS IT UP *Apple Challah Kugel Towers*

Winter Citrus Salad   96
DRESS IT UP *Winter Citrus Brûlée*

Red Hasselback Potatoes   98
DRESS IT DOWN *Roasted Red Potatoes*

Easy Cranberry and Pine Nut Couscous   100
DRESS IT UP *Cranberry Couscous Squash Bowls*
DRESS IT UP *Cranberry Couscous Eggplant Boats*

Rice Salad with Toasted Nuts, Apples, and Onion Dressing   102
DRESS IT UP *Apple and Nut Rice Ring*

Mustard Green Beans   106
DRESS IT UP *Colorful Mustard String Beans*

Raw Root Vegetable Salad   108
DRESS IT DOWN *Asian Roasted Root Vegetables*

Sweet Potato Casserole   110
DRESS IT UP *Marshmallow-Topped Sweet Potato Casserole*

Easy Scallion Cornbread   112
DRESS IT UP *Pretty Cornbread*

Avocado Salad with Butter Lettuce and Lemon Dressing   116
DRESS IT UP *Mock Crab Salad in Avocados*

Yerushalmi Kugel   118
DRESS IT UP *Yerushalmi Raisin Kugel*

Zucchini and Red Bell Pepper Sauté   121
DRESS IT DOWN *Zucchini Coins*

Roasted Brussels Sprouts with Herb "Butter"   122
DRESS IT DOWN *Garlic and Thyme Brussels Sprouts*

Wilted Spinach with Crispy Garlic Chips   124
DRESS IT DOWN *Garlic Wilted Spinach*

Triple Deli Pasta Salad
with Creamy Italian Dressing

Kosher Status: Meat • Prep: 15 minutes • Cook: 8 minutes • Total: 23 minutes • Yield: 4 servings

Hubby and I agree on the big things: nuclear disarmament, the lousy economy, what color to paint the house. But when it comes to food, it's totally Venus versus Mars. So I'm a sucker for Waldorf Salad—soft butter lettuce, nuts, apples, yogurt dressing (page 132)—while way over there, light years away, is Hubby and his chef's salad (with iceberg lettuce yet). It's gotta have lots of chopped deli meat and store-bought pareve creamy Italian dressing! And I've been serving it to him just that way for years—really. Even though I'm a hotsy-totsy cookbook author. Even though I run all over the world preaching home cooking.

But deep in my heart, I knew I could do better. So I came up with this semi-homemade Creamy Italian. And it's good. I mean really good. I'm so proud of myself. And now we can eat salad together and live happily ever after. (Well, I did sub in romaine for the iceberg, but either Hubby didn't notice or he didn't want to blow the truce.)

2 tablespoons mayonnaise

1 tablespoon extra virgin olive oil

1 tablespoon red wine vinegar

1 tablespoon fresh lemon juice

¼ teaspoon kosher salt

¼ teaspoon dried oregano

¼ teaspoon dried basil

¼ teaspoon red pepper flakes (optional)

1 cup cooked elbow macaroni or other short pasta

1 cup shredded romaine or iceberg lettuce

½ cup cubed smoked turkey (about 3 ounces)

½ cup cubed salami (about 3 ounces)

½ cup cubed roast beef (about 3 ounces)

15 grape tomatoes, halved

1 Persian cucumber, unpeeled, diced

2 cremini or button mushrooms, diced

1. Prepare the dressing: Combine the mayonnaise, olive oil, vinegar, lemon juice, salt, oregano, basil, and red pepper flakes, if using, in a small bowl. Mix well and set aside.

2. Toss together the pasta, lettuce, turkey, salami, roast beef, tomatoes, cucumber, and mushrooms in a large bowl. Add the dressing and toss to coat well.

Tailor this recipe to your liking using corned beef or pastrami, bell peppers, red onions, green beans, or celery. The idea is a crunchy, colorful salad where all the veggies and meat are diced to the same size as the pasta.

DRESS IT UP
• Deconstructed Chef's Salad •

Serve a wedge of iceberg lettuce or ½ romaine heart with little piles of the deli meat and vegetables on a chilled plate. Double the amount of dressing and serve on the side in individual glasses.

MAKE IT A MEAL

This hearty salad is already a meal. The above quantity will serve two as an entrée.

PAIR IT HARKHAM WINERY CHARDONNAY

This tasty chardonnay has a touch of creaminess to it, yet its tartness makes it a perfect contrast to this salad.

Cranberry Chestnut Challah Stuffing

Kosher Status: Meat • Prep: 10 minutes • Cook: 50 minutes • Total: 1 hour • Yield: 8 to 10 servings

In the dead of winter, my folks would drive us up to New York City from Philly. We'd catch a few Broadway shows and shop like crazy. We snacked on little bags of hot roasted chestnuts bought from a street vendor wearing fingerless gloves. The aroma of fresh roasted chestnuts in winter is my New York.

So when I noticed bagged roasted and shelled chestnuts in a store recently—wham! I instantly saw Times Square . . . snow . . . funny gloves. There was no snow and no hot aroma when I opened the bag, but once baked in the oven with my stuffing, they were divine.

2 tablespoons olive oil

1 large onion, coarsely chopped

4 celery stalks, coarsely chopped

1 cup roasted and peeled chestnuts, quartered

1 cup dried cranberries

¼ cup finely chopped fresh sage or 1 tablespoon dried

2 tablespoons finely chopped fresh parsley or 2 teaspoons dried

8 cups ½-inch cubes white or whole wheat challah

2 cups chicken broth, such as Manischewitz All Natural Chicken Broth

1 teaspoon kosher salt

1 teaspoon freshly ground black pepper

1. Preheat the oven to 400°F.

2. Heat the olive oil in a large Dutch oven or ovenproof sauté pan over medium-high heat. Sauté the onion and celery until softened and the onion is translucent, 8 to 10 minutes. Add the chestnuts, cranberries, sage, and parsley and cook 2 minutes more. Stir in the challah, chicken broth, salt, and pepper. Remove from the heat. Cover and bake for 30 minutes. Uncover and bake until lightly browned, 10 minutes more.

QUICK TIPS

You can find bags of roasted and peeled chestnuts in the snack aisle at the supermarket. This recipe doesn't require day-old or stale bread, although it's a great use for any leftovers on hand. Challah, hot dog and hamburger buns, even sandwich bread—use it all, mix 'n' match it, cube it, and make stuffing or Spiced Apple Challah Kugel (page 94).

MAKE IT PAREVE

Use vegetable broth in place of chicken broth.

MAKE IT A MEAL

Serve with Sour Mash Whiskey–Glazed Whole Roasted Turkey (page 168).

PAIR IT WEINSTOCK RED BY W

A robust red wine would overwhelm this dish, so go for the soft fruity flavors in Red by W to complement the red berry flavors of the stuffing.

• Stuffed Baked Onions •

Serve the stuffing in baked onions.

Peel 5 medium red onions and 5 medium yellow onions and trim the bottoms so the onions can stand upright. Trim about ½ inch from the top and scoop out all but 2 or 3 layers from the inside using a melon baller or small paring knife. Bake the onions at 440°F, covered, in a baking dish with ½ inch water for 30 minutes. While the onions are baking, prepare the stuffing as on page 80. When the onions are done, pour out the water from the pan, then lightly spray it with cooking spray. Fill each onion with about 3 heaping tablespoons of stuffing, mounding it on top a bit. Reduce the oven temperature to 350°F and bake, uncovered, until heated through and golden brown, 40 to 50 minutes. While the onions are baking, spoon the remaining stuffing into a greased casserole dish. Cover and bake until lightly browned, about 30 minutes. After the stuffing has been cooked and cooled, you can freeze it in a tightly sealed container. To serve, thaw and bring to room temperature before warming in a 350°F oven for about 20 minutes. If you want to prepare only enough stuffing for the 10 onions, quarter the main stuffing recipe.

Wednesday: 5:30 p.m.

I want it.

The Mother of the Year award.

Today Angel Face came home from kindergarten with a shiny badge pinned to his shirt. He got it for knowing his colors. I can't remember the last time anybody gave me an award. Or the last time I was jealous of a four-year-old.

Maybe I'm not good enough. Observe, people: Here's where old-fashioned Jewish guilt rises to the surface. Jewish moms dish it out liberally with the brisket, but not only to anyone standing nearby. We throw it at ourselves, too. It's tough to be both disher and dishee. We tell ourselves we're not joyous enough with our kids; we're not attentive enough to our husbands; we don't call our mothers often enough. We should cook more, play more, smile more.

So I'm not perfect, but that's no reason not to get the Supermom Award. Way back when, in my TV producer life, I was there when glamorous stars picked up Emmys and Oscars. Did they deserve them? Did they call their mothers enough?

9:00 p.m.   Listen, never mind Mother of the Year. I'll settle for Mom of the Day. And if I can't earn one of those shiny badges, just tell me where I can buy one and I'll pin it on myself. I'm not proud.

Hearty Mushrooms with Herbs and Wine

Kosher Status: Meat • Prep: 8 minutes • Cook: 24 minutes • Total: 32 minutes • Yield: 4 to 6 servings

Among the many ventures in my life, I went through a vegetarian stage. I loved nothing more than rich, earthy beefy mushrooms as a satisfying sub for meat. Beef broth (you can use veg if you want to keep it pareve) and red wine make this a really sumptuous side.

½ cup beef broth, such as Manischewitz
    All Natural Beef Broth

1 tablespoon Dijon mustard

1 tablespoon tomato paste

½ teaspoon kosher salt

½ teaspoon freshly ground black pepper

3 tablespoons olive oil

1 small onion, diced

2 garlic cloves, minced

1½ pounds button or cremini mushrooms,
    quartered

⅔ cup dry red wine

1 tablespoon chopped fresh thyme or
    1 teaspoon dried

1 tablespoon chopped fresh parsley or
    1 teaspoon dried

1. Whisk the broth, Dijon, tomato paste, salt, and pepper in a small bowl until smooth; set aside.

2. Heat the olive oil in a large sauté pan over medium-high heat. Add the onion and cook until slightly softened, about 5 minutes. Add the garlic and sauté 2 minutes more. Add the mushrooms and sauté until golden brown, 5 minutes. Raise the heat to high and add the wine. Cook, stirring and scraping the browned bits from the bottom of the pan with a wooden spoon, until the wine evaporates, about 5 minutes. Add the broth mixture, reduce the heat to a simmer, and cook until slightly thickened, 2 to 3 minutes. Add the thyme and parsley and stir to combine. Serve warm.

VARIATION

Makes a great dairy appetizer cooked with white wine and vegetable broth and topped with a little goat cheese or feta.

• Mushroom Phyllo Cups •

Serve in individual phyllo cups.

You will need 12 sheets (12 x 16½ inches) frozen phyllo dough, thawed. Stack 4 layers at a time, spraying each layer with cooking spray. Cut the phyllo stacks into six 5½ x 6-inch pieces and press them into muffin cups. Fill each cup with 2 tablespoons cooled mushrooms. Bake at 375°F until golden brown, 10 to 12 minutes. Garnish with a sprinkling of chopped fresh parsley before serving. Makes 18.

MAKE IT A MEAL

Top your favorite steak with these mushrooms. Or make the mushrooms with white wine and chicken broth and pair them with Crispy Salt and Pepper Chicken with Caramelized Fennel and Shallots (page 179).

MAKE IT PAREVE

Sub in vegetable broth for the beef broth and white wine for the red. The red wine doesn't make this dish "meat," of course, but once you switch from beef to vegetable broth the white wine is a better match.

PAIR IT SHILOH WINERY SECRET RESERVE SHIRAZ

The earthy rich flavors of this recipe will pair perfectly with an aged shiraz. This robust Israeli shiraz was made for this dish.

Pastrami-Fry Salad with Creamy Chili Dressing

Kosher Status: Meat • Prep: 12 minutes • Cook: 18 minutes • Total: 30 minutes • Yield: 6 servings

I got the idea for this salad from the kosher restaurant Prime Grill in New York City. Greens + fried crispy bits of beef = sinfully gooood.

½ cup extra virgin olive oil

¼ cup soy sour cream

¼ cup seasoned rice vinegar

1 teaspoon kosher salt

1 teaspoon ground cumin

1 teaspoon chili powder

1 teaspoon garlic powder

½ teaspoon freshly ground black pepper

¼ teaspoon cayenne pepper (optional)

1 pound thinly sliced pastrami

1 head Boston lettuce, washed and torn
    into 1-inch pieces (about 6 cups)

One 1-ounce bunch basil, torn into 1-inch
    pieces (about 1 cup loosely packed)

3 ripe tomatoes, sliced

1. Prepare the dressing: Whisk together ¼ cup of the olive oil, the sour cream, vinegar, salt, cumin, chili powder, garlic powder, black pepper, and cayenne, if using, in a small bowl.

2. Line a baking sheet with paper towels.

3. Heat the remaining ¼ cup of oil in a large sauté pan over medium-high heat. Using tongs and working in batches, fry the pastrami in a single layer until crisp and deep, dark red, almost blackened, 7 to 9 minutes. Drain on the prepared baking sheet and let cool slightly.

4. Toss the lettuce and basil with half the dressing in a large salad bowl. Top with sliced tomatoes. Crumble the pastrami into bits by hand or chop with a knife. Top the salad with the pastrami-fry. Drizzle with the remaining dressing and serve immediately.

DRESS IT UP

• Pastrami-Fry Tomato Cups •

Serve the salad in individual tomatoes.

Divide the recipe above in half, omitting the tomatoes. Instead, cut ⅛ inch off the tops of 8 beefsteak tomatoes. Use a melon baller or grapefruit spoon to scoop out the insides. Leave about ¼ inch of flesh and skin around the whole tomato so it holds its shape. Toss the greens and pastrami-fry with dressing and fill each tomato with salad.

MAKE IT PAREVE

Use tempeh "bacon" in place of pastrami.

MAKE IT A MEAL

Serve with a cup of soup. Something thick and hearty like mushroom, potato, or tomato.

PAIR IT PSAGOT CABERNET FRANC

Salty pastrami needs a red wine with a slightly higher acidity than a cab or merlot. This cab franc will do it justice, and the green notes in this wine pair well with the salad, too!

Friday: 9:00 a.m.

Ironically, I've always been surrounded by incredible cooks . . .

There was Poppy, aka Chefu (Dad's dad), and Uputzi (Mom's dad), not to mention Hubby's dad—a professional caterer, no less. Of course, there's Hubby himself, the ultimate chef who taught this bride who knew nothing everything she now knows.

And then there's my dad. If we wanted something good to eat in our house, Daddy made it. He was the sole inheritor of a special recipe from Chefu for a deep-dish potato pudding. Hard and crunchy outside, soft and sticky inside. Total perfection, for a baked potato pudding.

But Chefu didn't call it potato pudding. He called it *kigel.* Now, not everyone is aware of the Jewish version of "You say tomato, I say tomahto . . ." but it's very much with us, even today. How you pronounce certain Yiddish words marks which part of Europe you—or more likely your grandma or great-grandma—came from. Some people say *kigel* (keegle), others say *kugel* (kuhgel). Real experts can place you within twenty miles of your great-great-grandpa's birthplace the instant you say anything. So if you're dining with such a person and say, "Please pass the kigel," don't be surprised if someone says, "Aha! A *lantsman* from Hotzenplotz!" (What's a lantsman? Someone from the same place, of course.)

Anyway, I clearly remember how Mom would cajole Daddy to make Chefu's kigel, and then my sister and I would come running. We'd watch wide-eyed as he'd hand-grate the potatoes and keep our vigil at the oven window as it baked. He would have to hold us back while it cooled so we wouldn't burn ourselves. The instant he declared it ready, we'd all fight over the corner pieces.

I got it into my head that I just had to have that recipe. So I asked Dad. You have to understand that he's uber Old World manly, yet domesticated at the same time. Kinda like a football player who can pull off doing ballet. (Or like Bruiser, my two-year-old son, who can wear his sister's tutu and her glittery headband in his long hair, but no one would mistake that macho tyke for a girl.) Dad gave me the recipe over the phone: "one egg per potato, use a little bit of oil, not olive because I don't like the taste, a little bit of salt, a little pepper, and that's it."

"No onions?" I asked.

"No onions," he said, "we didn't put in onions."

"I can't believe there are no onions."

"Listen, you want the real recipe or not? Go ahead, put in onions! But it won't be Chefu's kigel."

Until now, I was considered the potato kugel queen of my 'hood. But somehow I couldn't master Chefu's exact recipe. Tried it over and over. Nothing worked. And Hubby was away for a few days. What's a girl to do?

Call Daddy! "Please, *puhleeease* come and show me how to do this!" And he did. He drove from Jersey to my house to make this simple four-ingredient kigel with me. It's a three-hour drive, and he arrived before 8:00 a.m.

To watch a natural in the kitchen is like watching a perfectly trained acrobat. Daddy moved with total confidence, with his big bushy salt-and-pepper mustache (which lots of Europeans his age seem to have). He grated those potatoes and talked me through the whole process. I couldn't wait to try the kigel. The instant it was ready, I pulled it out and took a bite—burned my mouth as usual, but it was well worth it. This was the glistening, crunchy, sticky kigel I remembered.

Superb.

It's a true family heirloom: And now that recipe has passed from father to father, to daughter, to you, and all is well with the world.

Daddy's Deep-Dish Potato Kigel/Kugel

Kosher Status: Pareve • Prep: 15 minutes • Cook: 1 hour, 30 minutes to 1 hour, 40 minutes • Total: 1 hour, 55 minutes • Yield: 6 to 8 servings

My friend Judy was helping me sort recipes for this book and saw the dressed-up version of Chefu's recipe. "Um, shouldn't this go in the 'Mains' section, not the 'Sides'?" she asked innocently. Kugel? A main? I never laughed so hard! Judy, love ya, but in a Jewish home, this is a side. If I served potato kugel, even one stuffed with pastrami, my family would just sit there all night, waiting for the main.

1 tablespoon plus 1 teaspoon canola oil	7 large eggs
3¾ pounds russet potatoes (about 7 large)	1½ teaspoons kosher salt
	½ teaspoon freshly ground black pepper

1. Preheat the oven to 400°F.

2. Brush an 8-inch square glass baking dish with the 1 teaspoon canola oil. Wipe the oil all over the bottom of the dish and up the sides using a paper towel. Set aside.

3. Peel the potatoes and rinse them in cold water. Grate the potatoes into a large bowl on the smallest side of a box grater. Pour off all the water. Add the eggs, the remaining 1 tablespoon oil, the salt, and pepper. Mix really well by hand, breaking up the yolks, until everything is thoroughly combined and the batter is smooth. Pour into the prepared dish and bake until the top is crispy and deep golden brown and a toothpick comes out clean, 1 hour, 30 minutes to 1 hour, 40 minutes.

4. Check your kugel at the 45-minute, 1-hour, and 1-hour-and-15-minute marks. If your kugel has risen in the center, use a fork to poke holes in it, then use the back of the fork to pat down and flatten it. You want a perfectly flat top. If your kugel doesn't rise, don't worry; this is a good thing.

5. Remove the kugel from the oven. Using a knife, separate the kugel from the walls of the baking dish, being careful not to break the kugel and paying special attention to the corners. Place a square serving platter over the kugel and invert the kugel onto the platter. It is best to cut the kugel in squares at the table, to order, so it does not dry out.

The baking dish *must* be glass—really, the result will be nothing like what you see here if you use anything other than glass. The shiny brown finish is one of the best parts of this potato kugel. If you want to make a larger kugel, the ratio is 1:1; translation, one egg per potato. If you are not going to serve this kugel immediately and will be refrigerating and rewarming it, up the oil in the batter from 1 tablespoon to ¼ cup. Otherwise the kugel will dry out considerably when reheated.

VARIATION

Add 1 finely grated raw onion or 1 caramelized diced onion, cooled, to the potato mixture before baking.

DRESS IT UP/MAKE IT A MEAL

• **Pastrami Potato Kugel (Meat)** •

Just for Judy, I am pseudofiling this as a "meal."

Make it even heartier with meat. Pour half the potato mixture into the baking dish. Top with ½ pound sliced pastrami. Pour on the remaining potato mixture and bake as directed. Great served with mustard, it's almost like a knish.

PAIR IT BARON HERZOG CHARDONNAY (WHITE) OR MERLOT (RED)

Okay, in addition to the kigel/kugel thing, there's a bit of controversy over whether kugel is rich enough for a red wine, or if it should go with a white. Let your palate decide. These Baron Herzog wines are as classic as this dish.

Spiced Apple Challah Kugel

Kosher Status: Pareve • Prep: 15 minutes • Rest: 10 minutes • Cook: 45 minutes • Cool: 10 minutes •
Total: 1 hour, 20 minutes • Yield: 9 to 12 servings

Nobody in the family thought I could do it, but I did. I mastered Great-Grandma Martha Geller's Challah Kugel. Even she says it tastes just like hers.

So I put that recipe in my first book, never thinking I'd revisit it. Until I tasted Chef David Kolotkin's Apple Challah Bread Pudding for dessert at our Joy of Kosher *magazine shoot. There were six of us there, and I suddenly felt the desperate need to cling to every morsel of that pudding. No, I didn't want to share (no matter what Mrs. Eskin taught me in kindergarten). And no, I wouldn't give up my plate.*

I came home inspired. So here I blend the two recipes into something worthy of both side and dessert status. Officially, it's a side, though some people would call it a dessert. Jews do this kind of thing, you know. We serve desserts as sides—even a kugel that looks and tastes like an apple blueberry crumb pie. It's our way of getting double dessert. It's an ethnic thing. You got a problem with that?

Cooking spray

2 cups sweetened applesauce

¾ cup soy milk

3 large eggs, beaten

½ cup granulated sugar

1 teaspoon ground cinnamon

½ teaspoon ground nutmeg

¼ teaspoon ground allspice

¼ teaspoon kosher salt

One 1-pound challah, cut into ½-inch cubes (about 12 cups)

2 medium Granny Smith apples, peeled, cored, and cut into ½-inch dice (about 2 cups)

1. Preheat the oven to 350°F.

2. Spray a 9-inch square baking dish with cooking spray.

3. Stir together the applesauce, soy milk, eggs, sugar, cinnamon, nutmeg, allspice, and salt in a medium bowl. Combine the challah and apples in a large bowl. Pour the applesauce mixture over the challah and apples. Toss to coat, then let sit 10 minutes. Stir it once more to combine, then transfer to the prepared baking dish. Bake until golden brown and set, 40 to 45 minutes. Cool 10 minutes before slicing and serving.

If you're comfortable with the whole dessert/side dish thing, then serve it with your main, otherwise add a little sticky note right here in your book indicating that this should be filed as a bread pudding dessert. In which case, you can finish it off by making a glaze. Whisk together 1 cup confectioners' sugar with 2 tablespoons soy milk and ½ teaspoon vanilla extract. Drizzle the glaze on the pudding just before serving, warm or at room temp, as a sweet finish to any meal.

DRESS IT UP
• Apple Challah Kugel Towers •

Bake the kugel in individual ramekins or ring molds and serve with a drizzle of apricot honey.

Liberally grease twelve 2-ounce ramekins. Fill each with about 1 cup of the challah mixture and bake for 30 minutes. Whisk together ⅓ cup honey with 2 tablespoons apricot preserves in a small bowl. Carefully run a paring knife around the edges of the ramekins and invert the kugels onto serving plates. Drizzle the flavored honey over the warm kugels.

MAKE IT A MEAL

Serve this at brunch alongside eggs.

PAIR IT ELVI WINERY ADAR BRUT CAVA

Something this sweet calls for a nice bubbly. Try this one blended into a mimosa (sparkling wine and orange juice).

Winter Citrus Salad

Kosher Status: Pareve • Prep: 25 minutes • Cook: 0 minutes • Total: 25 minutes • Yield: 4 to 6 servings

When I was young, single, naïve, and much thinner, I used to go to my friend Miriam Shira's house for Shabbos. Without fail, she would start lunch with half a grapefruit. So the years have passed. She's had seven kids and she's still thinner than I am. I figure it's time to get back to grapefruit.

3 small grapefruits

3 small oranges

6 tangerines

1 head radicchio, shredded

2 tablespoons chopped fresh mint

2 tablespoons extra virgin olive oil

1 tablespoon white wine vinegar

Freshly ground black pepper

1. Cut off and discard the tops and bottoms of the citrus. Place a cut side of one fruit on a cutting board. With a curved motion, working from top to bottom, use your knife to slice away the peel and pith. Repeat all the way around the entire fruit until all the peel and pith is gone. Lay the peeled fruit on its side and slice it into ¼-inch rings. Repeat with the remaining fruit.

2. To assemble the salad, spread the radicchio on a serving platter. Layer the fruit in a decorative pattern on top of the radicchio and sprinkle with the mint. Drizzle the olive oil and vinegar over the top. Season lightly with the pepper.

QUICK TIP

If you happen to have those cute and colorful ceramic knives, they are great for cutting citrus.

DRESS IT UP
• Winter Citrus Brûlée •

Brûlée the citrus before serving.

Heat the broiler to high with the rack 6 inches from the heat source. Lay the sliced citrus in a single layer on a greased baking sheet. Sprinkle each grapefruit and orange slice with 1 teaspoon turbinado sugar and each tangerine with ½ teaspoon turbinado sugar. Broil immediately until the sugar is hardened and golden brown, 5 to 6 minutes. Transfer to a radicchio-lined serving platter and garnish with mint and extra virgin olive oil.

MAKE IT A MEAL

Serve with generous dollops of your favorite flavor of yogurt for a light, protein-rich lunch. I just love the full-fat Swiss-style vanilla, so that's what I use. (Whoops, there goes the diet. Looks like some people are destined to be Miriam Shira thin, while the rest of us are full-fat forever.)

Alternatively, this salad (without the yogurt!) could also be a refreshing side to Chicken Sausage and Sweet Potato Hash with Baked Eggs (page 145).

PAIR IT CARMEL KAYOUMI WHITE RIESLING

The citrusy tartness of grapefruit goes best with this crisp, dry riesling.

Red Hasselback Potatoes

Kosher Status: Pareve • Prep: 15 minutes • Cook: 60 to 70 minutes •
Total: 1 hour, 25 minutes • Yield: 8 servings

I created these spuds. Okay, that's an overstatement. God created the potatoes and Hasselback potato recipes probably go back to ancient Bolivia or something. I call them accordion potatoes because they remind me of that instrument that, by the way, is only played today at Bar/Bat Mitzvahs.

They really should serve these potatoes at Bar Mitzvahs, too. It's such an elegant way to present a common potato. I make 'em with sliced garlic stuffed into each and every crevice, and then I top them with more garlic for the Transylvanians in the house (that's me). Those Yankees just get a little garlic sprinkle.

Cooking spray

2½ pounds medium red-skin potatoes (about 8), scrubbed

6 garlic cloves, chopped

¼ cup olive oil

2 teaspoons kosher salt

Freshly ground black pepper

1. Preheat the oven to 375°F. Spray a baking sheet with cooking spray.

2. Place each potato in a large wooden spoon. Thinly slice the potato vertically, about every ⅛ inch, being careful not to slice all the way through to the bottom. The shape of the spoon should help prevent it.

3. Place the potatoes on the prepared baking sheet. Sprinkle the garlic evenly over all the potatoes and use your fingers to push it into the slits. Drizzle with the olive oil and sprinkle with the salt and pepper. Bake until tender and browned, 60 to 70 minutes.

VARIATION

For the garlic lovers in the crowd, thinly slice the garlic and place it in the potato slits. You can sub in or add chopped shallots to the garlic in this recipe.

DRESS IT DOWN
• Roasted Red Potatoes •

Cut the potatoes in quarters and toss them with garlic, olive oil, salt, and pepper. Spread the potatoes in a single layer on a baking sheet, and roast at 375°F until tender and browned, about 45 minutes.

MAKE IT A MEAL

I like these with something saucy and elegant, either Coq au Vin with Veal Sausage, Thyme, and Merlot (page 148) or Beer-Braised Holiday Top of the Rib (page 203). But you don't have to go overboard, 'cause this recipe really works well anytime you need a nice-looking, good-tasting, easy-to-pair-with starchy side.

PAIR IT FLAM ROSÉ

With red potatoes, a little acidity would be just right. Go for this crisp rosé from Israel.

Easy Cranberry and Pine Nut Couscous

Kosher Status: Pareve • Prep: 5 minutes • Cook: 10 minutes • Total: 15 minutes • Yield: 6 to 8 servings

I'm crazy for any dish that can be prepped and cooked in fifteen minutes flat. You can make this with rice if you like, but I feel lighter after eating couscous. And anything that makes me feel lighter (or thinner) wins the prize.

Try this out and you'll see that pine nuts and couscous are natural partners. Like Fred and Ginger, Antony and Cleopatra, Hubby and me, Shrek and Fiona.

1⅓ cups instant whole wheat couscous

⅔ cup pine nuts (4 ounces)

1 cup dried cranberries

¼ cup chopped fresh parsley, plus more
   for garnish

¼ cup extra virgin olive oil

Grated zest and juice of 1 lemon, plus
   more zest for garnish

¼ teaspoon ground cumin

½ teaspoon kosher salt

Prepare the couscous according to the package directions. Transfer it to a large bowl. Add the pine nuts, cranberries, parsley, oil, lemon zest and juice, cumin, and salt and stir to mix well. Serve warm or at room temperature, garnished with parsley and lemon zest.

VARIATION

If you love pine nuts, double up—and to bring out their nutty flavor, lightly toast them on a baking sheet in a 375°F oven until golden brown, 5 to 10 minutes, stirring occasionally.

PAIR IT RAMON CORDOVA RIOJA

The sweet cranberries and hearty pine nuts call for a fun and fruity wine.

DRESS IT UP

• Cranberry Couscous Squash Bowls •

Serve this side dish warm in a baked acorn squash bowl.

Cut 5 small acorn squash in half and scoop out the seeds. Bake, cut side down, in a large baking dish or baking sheet with ½ inch water at 400°F, until tender when pierced with a fork, about 50 minutes. Fill each squash half with about ½ cup of the couscous. Top each with 1 tablespoon butter or margarine, return to the baking dish (filled side facing up), and bake until lightly browned, 20 to 25 minutes.

• Cranberry Couscous Eggplant Boats •

Stuff eggplants with the couscous.

Cut 10 small Italian eggplants in half lengthwise, brush the cut sides with olive oil, and sprinkle with salt. Roast on a baking sheet, cut side up, at 400°F until the centers are soft and the tops are golden brown, 30 to 40 minutes. When the eggplants are cool enough to handle, gently scrape out the flesh, being careful not to cut the skins. Reserve the skins; combine the flesh with the couscous. Taste the stuffing and season with salt if needed. Stuff each skin with ¼ cup of the couscous mixture and garnish with more lemon zest and parsley. Keep the remaining couscous in your fridge to sprinkle on a salad or as a healthful snack.

Rice Salad with Toasted Nuts, Apples, and Onion Dressing

Kosher Status: Pareve • Prep: 15 minutes • Cook: 20 minutes • Total: 35 minutes • Yield: 6 servings

Boring old rice becomes instantly alluring in Syrian cooking. I borrowed some of that ancient wisdom for this dressed-up version: rice in a ring mold. Gorgeous! Oh yeah, and it tastes good, too.

DRESSING

½ cup coarsely chopped scallions (white and green parts, about 6 scallions)

¼ cup light mayonnaise

2 tablespoons chopped fresh chives

1 tablespoon chopped fresh basil or 1 teaspoon dried

1 garlic clove

1½ tablespoons apple cider vinegar

¾ teaspoon kosher salt

Juice of 1 lemon

¼ to ⅓ cup extra virgin olive oil

SALAD

1 cup long-grain rice, cooked and cooled

2 cups walnut halves

1 medium Fuji apple, cored and diced

2 tablespoons extra virgin olive oil

1. Prepare the dressing: Combine the scallions, mayonnaise, chives, basil, garlic, vinegar, salt, and lemon juice in a food processor and pulse to coarsely chop. With the processor running, slowly add the oil until the desired consistency is reached. Set aside.

2. Combine the rice, walnuts, apple, and oil in a large bowl and stir. Add the dressing and toss to coat. Serve at room temperature or cold.

VARIATIONS

You can use your favorite rice for this dish. Halved grapes are a nice addition or substitution for the diced apples.

PAIR IT HERZOG RESERVE RUSSIAN RIVER CHARDONNAY

Rice, nuts, and apples call for a full-bodied white. This chardonnay is one of my faves.

• Apple and Nut Rice Ring •

Make a pretty apple-and-nut-topped ring of rice.

Spray a 10- to 12-cup Bundt pan with cooking spray. Spread the walnuts and diced apple evenly over the bottom of the pan. Double the amount of dressing and rice and toss to coat evenly. Tightly pack the rice into the pan and smooth so it's even. Cover the pan with aluminum foil and bake in the center rack of your oven at 350°F for 30 minutes. Invert the Bundt pan onto a rimmed platter and serve the mold warm with a large serving spoon. The ring serves 8 to 10.

Sunday: 9:20 a.m.

Hubby says I'm an incurable hugger.

And you know what, he's right!

I can't help myself.

The second I walk into a room and see someone I like, my arms shoot up, my fingers wiggle, and I start to squeal in a pitch only dogs can hear. Eventually the pitch goes down till the person can discern her name. If she doesn't want to be hugged—*nebach*, she doesn't have a fighting chance.

In fact, when Cassie (my editor) called to let me know we were doing this book together, my voice was so squeaky that she asked, "Are you okay?" and I was gasping, "Yeah, sure, I'm just hugging you through the phone." We could add to the Seinfeld list of people to avoid: the close talker, the anti-dentite, the bad breaker-upper—and now the incurable hugger. If you don't like to be hugged, make sure we never meet. If we do meet, hope that I don't like you.

Mustard Green Beans

Kosher Status: Pareve • Prep: 10 minutes • Cook: 5 minutes • Total: 15 minutes • Yield: 6 servings

My kids actually prefer the dressed-up version—they hold and chomp on the long green and yellow beans like sticks of candy. Oh thank you, God, I must have done something right. Yeah, I know eating green beans with your fingers may not be the best of table manners, but at least they eat green beans—yay—even with the red pepper flakes.

¼ cup extra virgin olive oil

3 tablespoons red wine vinegar

1 tablespoon whole-grain mustard

1 teaspoon red pepper flakes (optional)

½ teaspoon kosher salt

Freshly ground black pepper

2 pounds green beans, trimmed and cut
 into 1-inch pieces

1 red onion, thinly sliced (optional)

1. Whisk together the oil, vinegar, mustard, pepper flakes, if using, salt, and pepper to taste in a small bowl. Set aside.

2. Bring a large pot of water to a boil over high heat. Add the green beans and cook until tender but still crisp, about 5 minutes. Drain and rinse with cold water. Transfer the beans to a large bowl and add the onions (if using). Pour the dressing over the green beans and toss to coat well.

• Colorful Mustard String Beans •

Brighten up this dish.

Keep the beans whole and use 1 pound green beans and 1 pound yellow wax beans. Replace the red onion with 1 cup caramelized pearl onions (or do ½ cup red onion and ½ cup pearl onions) and add ½ cup raw or toasted sliced almonds. Just before serving, toss with the dressing and garnish with 2 tablespoons torn or chopped fresh parsley leaves.

PAIR IT BARON HERZOG PINOT GRIGIO

A light and easy-drinking white wine matches nicely with the crispy, sweet, almost citrus flavor of green beans.

Raw Root Vegetable Salad

Kosher Status: Pareve • Prep: 30 minutes • Cook: 0 minutes •
Total: 30 minutes • Yield: 6 to 8 servings

To get the look of this salad, you have to use a mandoline to slice your veggies paper thin, or as thin as humanly possible.

¼ cup extra virgin olive oil

1 tablespoon toasted sesame oil

1 tablespoon soy sauce

2 teaspoons honey

Grated zest and juice of 1 lime

1 teaspoon grated fresh ginger or 1 pinch
of ground

1 carrot, peeled

1 fennel bulb, trimmed

3 radishes, trimmed

1 medium golden beet, peeled

1 medium red beet, peeled

2 tablespoons coarsely chopped
    hazelnuts

2 tablespoons coarsely chopped
    pistachios

Freshly ground black pepper

1. Prepare the dressing: Whisk together the oils, soy sauce, honey, lime zest and juice, and ginger in a large bowl. Transfer 2 tablespoons of the dressing to a small bowl and set both bowls aside.

2. Thinly slice the carrot, fennel, radishes, and golden beet on a mandoline. Transfer to the large bowl and toss with the dressing. Thinly slice the red beet on the mandoline and toss with the dressing in the small bowl.

3. Arrange the red beet slices on a platter or divide them among plates. Top with the remaining vegetables. Sprinkle with the chopped nuts and pepper to taste and serve.

TIME-SAVER/VARIATION

For a beautiful swap, try candy-striped beets.

If you don't want to start fussing with a mandoline, this dressing is great on cabbage. Just grab a large bag of coleslaw, toss with the dressing to taste, and top with chopped nuts and black pepper before serving.

DRESS IT DOWN
• Asian Roasted Root Vegetables •

Chop the veggies and roast them in the oven for an easy warm side dish.

Chop the peeled beets, carrot, and fennel into 1-inch chunks. Halve the radishes (if they are large, cut them in quarters). Toss the vegetables with the dressing. Roast at 400°F for 45 to 60 minutes; start checking for doneness after 45 minutes. The veggies will be tender (stick a fork in them) with edges that are just starting to crisp and caramelize. Sprinkle with the nuts and pepper before serving.

PAIR IT TEAL LAKE SHIRAZ

Root veggies have a nice earthy flavor, just like a good shiraz.

Sweet Potato Casserole

Kosher Status: Pareve • Prep: 15 minutes • Cook: 35 minutes • Total: 50 minutes • Yield: 6 to 8 servings

Back home, no meal included marshmallows. When it comes to home cooking, of course I mean my grandparents' meals. When they came to our house, they would cook at their place and bring the meal with them. It seems that Eastern Europe suffered from a severe marshmallow shortage because they "didn't know from it."

So the dressed-up version of this dish feels like a real indulgence to me. And the fact that it is considered a legitimate side dish makes it even better. Not a marshmallow fan? Well, first you have to answer to me. I mean, what's not to like about marshmallows? What's the matter with you?

Anyway, if you're not into them, go with the dressed-down, simple sweet potato casserole sans the fluffy whites. Add a dash of dried or minced ginger for a kick.

Cooking spray

2½ pounds sweet potatoes (about
    4 medium), peeled and cubed

¼ cup (4 tablespoons/½ stick) margarine

1 large egg

1 teaspoon pure vanilla extract

½ teaspoon kosher salt

1 cup coarsely chopped pecans

1. Preheat the oven to 350°F. Spray an 8-inch square baking dish with cooking spray.

2. Cover the potatoes with water in a medium pot and bring to a boil over high heat. Simmer until tender, about 15 minutes. Drain well and return the potatoes to the pot. Add the margarine, egg, vanilla, and salt and mash with a fork or potato masher until slightly chunky. Stir in the pecans. Transfer to the prepared baking dish and smooth the top. Bake until golden brown on top, about 20 minutes. Serve immediately.

VARIATION

This is not a sweet casserole, so add sugar or maple syrup if you want it to be sweeter. In the dressed-up version, though, the sugar from the marshmallows melts right into the casserole, making it a nice, sticky, sweet side.

• Marshmallow-Topped Sweet Potato Casserole •

Make a sweet casserole topped with golden pillowy marshmallows.

After baking the casserole, arrange 8 ounces of large marshmallows over the top and bake until golden brown, about 5 minutes.

PAIR IT BARTENURO OVADIA ESTATES DOLCETTO D'ALBA

This one's a fruity Italian that loves food and goes down easy.

Easy Scallion Cornbread

Kosher Status: Pareve • Prep: 15 minutes • Cook: 25 minutes • Cool: 5 minutes •
Total: 45 minutes • Yield: 9 servings

When we're feeling naughty, Hubby and I sneak out to the local bagel shop and order eggs sunny-side up, hash browns well done, fresh buttered croissants, and a hot corn muffin slathered in butter to share. We're splitting the corn muffin 'cause we're also splitting a chocolate chip muffin or a fresh-baked jumbo black and white cookie. This is a scene for cagey negotiations, folks. He likes both the black and white frosting, me only the white. So you'd think he'd be a gentleman, and a prince, and a mensch and offer me the whole white part. But no . . . well, sometimes he does, on my birthday.

I love making this homemade cornbread and eating a warm slice with a giant shmear of salted butter.

¼ cup (4 tablespoons/½ stick) margarine
  or olive oil

1 cup plain soy milk

1 tablespoon fresh lemon juice

1½ cups yellow cornmeal

½ cup all-purpose flour

¼ to ½ cup granulated sugar

1½ teaspoons baking powder

½ teaspoon kosher salt

½ cup soy sour cream

2 large eggs

3 scallions, green parts only, chopped

1. Preheat the oven to 400°F. Place the margarine in an 8-inch square baking dish and place the dish in the oven.

2. Combine the soy milk and lemon juice in a small bowl. Set aside.

3. Place the cornmeal, flour, sugar, baking powder, and salt in a large bowl and whisk to combine. Add the soy sour cream and eggs to the soy milk and whisk to combine. Pour the liquid ingredients into the dry and stir until just combined and moistened; do not overmix. Fold in the scallions and pour the batter into the hot baking dish. Bake until a toothpick inserted into the center comes out clean, about 25 minutes. Let cool 5 minutes before slicing.

Swap the scallions for a handful of dried cranberries, or just omit the scallions for classic cornbread.

DRESS IT UP

• Pretty Cornbread •

Bake the cornbread in a large decorative mold or several individual molds. Grease well to ensure the bread does not stick.

PAIR IT GOOSE BAY CHARDONNAY

This crisp yet buttery wine is a warm complement to the down-home goodness of cornbread.

Thursday: 4:30 a.m., I think

Sleep deprived.

But what can I do? Rockin' my three-month-old back to her sweet slumber in the Pack 'n Play next to my bed. Praying like crazy she'll sleep through till morning. Gave up trying to fall back asleep myself. I might as well work on this book. It's not gonna write itself. Rocking with my left hand, typing with my right.

Yesterday we came across a picture of my oldest daughter, Little Momma (now seven years old), when she was an infant. Hubby and I are holding her, and she's as dressed up as a two-month-old can be. We were going to a cousin's wedding. Just look at me, wearing a pencil skirt eight weeks postpartum. What I wouldn't give to get back into that skirt today.

And I'm thinking, *Who is that girl?* You look at yourself every day in the mirror, and you're sure that you haven't changed much. Yup, day after day, just about the same. Then your sweet little daughter sees a picture of you taken seven years ago, and she keeps repeating how pretty you looked. It's not what she's saying, it's how she's saying it—with surprise—intimating that this is not the mommy she sees every day. What's more, she qualifies her astonishment: "Your face, Mommy, it's glowing." My God, she's right. Where did that come from?

Maybe it's the new mommy glow; maybe it's the glow of getting into that skirt, zipping it and noting that I'm still breathing; maybe I was giving thanks that my first baby inexplicably slept through the night at two months.

But now, I just wonder if the glow is gone forever.

I know sleep would help. Not gonna happen anytime soon.

Avocado Salad with Butter Lettuce and Lemon Dressing

Kosher Status: Pareve • Prep: 15 minutes • Cook: 0 minutes • Total: 15 minutes • Yield: 6 to 8 servings

Are there any words to describe this delicately beautiful, creamy, crunchy, soft and buttery, lightly citrusy simple salad? Well, I tried. Is your mouth watering yet?

¼ cup extra virgin olive oil

1 tablespoon Dijon mustard

Grated zest and juice of 1 medium lemon

½ teaspoon kosher salt

½ teaspoon freshly ground black pepper

2 small heads butter lettuce (Boston or Bibb), large leaves torn into pieces

3 red radishes, trimmed and thinly sliced

¼ cup loosely packed whole small basil leaves

3 ripe avocados, pitted, peeled, and sliced ¼ inch thick

1. Prepare the dressing: Combine the oil, mustard, lemon zest and juice, salt, and pepper in a small bowl; whisk to combine, and set aside. (You can also place the ingredients in a small glass jar with a lid, seal, and shake vigorously.)

2. Combine the lettuce, radishes, and basil in a large bowl. Add the dressing and lightly toss to coat. Add the avocados, and toss gently, being careful not to mush. Serve immediately on salad plates.

VARIATIONS

Change it up: Can't find butter lettuce? Don't love basil? Use about 6¼ cups of your favorite lettuce and toss in 1 cup coarsely chopped mock crab.

For a milder lemon flavor, use the juice of only half a lemon. You can also add 1 finely minced garlic clove to the dressing.

PAIR IT BINYAMINA RESERVE SAUVIGNON BLANC

This white wine has the crisp, refreshing acidity to go well with a light, citrusy salad.

• Mock Crab Salad in Avocados •

Avocados make the perfect edible serving bowl.

Prepare the salad as instructed in the main recipe and add 1 cup chopped mock crab. Carefully halve, pit, and peel an avocado. Fill each peeled avocado half with a generous serving of salad, allowing some salad to spill onto the plate. Repeat according to desired number of servings. Garnish with an additional drizzle of extra virgin olive oil and some freshly ground black pepper. Refrigerate any extra salad to use another time. Alternatively, you can use the avocado skins as your bowls. Remove the avocado flesh from the skins with a large spoon, being careful to keep the skins intact. Dice the avocado flesh and toss with the salad as instructed in the main recipe. Fill each skin with avocado salad.

Yerushalmi Kugel

Kosher Status: Pareve • Prep: 10 minutes • Cook: 45 to 50 minutes • Total: 1 hour • Yield: 8 servings

Yerushalayim is Hebrew for Jerusalem, so Yerushalmi means this dish is Jerusalem-style. It's a sweet and peppery caramelized kugel recipe I got from a friend (who wants to remain nameless) who got it from her mother (who also wants to remain nameless) who got it from a lady (who also wants to remain nameless) who is a native of Jerusalem.

So I'm happy to take all the formal credit for this winner, though I must confess that it wouldn't be authentic if it didn't originate in Jerusalem. If you've never tasted one, you're in for an incredible treat. If you have tasted and/or tried to make one, I can promise you this is the easiest (and best-tasting) recipe for Yerushalmi kugel on earth. No caramelizing sugar necessary, no precooking the noodles. When my friend (the anonymous daughter of the mother whose friend lives in Jerusalem) happened to call me, I had just burned three pots and ruined two bags of noodles trying different wannabe authentic versions of this recipe. To stop my sobbing and whimpering into the phone, she shared this recipe with me.

Cooking spray

2 tablespoons packed light brown sugar

1¼ cups granulated sugar

½ cup (8 tablespoons/1 stick) margarine

2 teaspoons kosher salt

1½ teaspoons freshly ground black pepper

One 12-ounce bag extra fine egg noodles

2 large eggs, beaten

1. Preheat the oven to 350°F. Spray an 8-inch round or square baking dish with cooking spray.

2. Place the sugars, margarine, salt, pepper, and 2 cups water in a medium pot and bring to a rapid boil over medium-high heat, stirring occasionally. Remove from the heat, add the noodles, and mix quickly and vigorously with a wooden spoon to coat and combine. Add the eggs and stir quickly. It's okay if the eggs start to cook; just work fast and pour into the prepared dish. Bake until golden brown and crunchy, about 1 hour. Slice into squares and serve hot, warm, or cold.

• Yerushalmi Raisin Kugel •

Add ¼ cup each regular and golden raisins (or craisins) and bake in a 10- to 12-cup tube pan. Invert onto a round platter and serve slices.

PAIR IT BARON HERZOG OLD VINE ZINFANDEL

Bold enough to stand up to this big kugel, with the ripe fruit flavors to match its sweetness.

Zucchini and Red Bell Pepper Sauté

Kosher Status: Pareve • Prep: 10 minutes • Cook: 15 minutes • Total: 25 minutes • Yield: 8 servings

Since the day I discovered that your everyday vegetable peeler can be used to make gorgeous paper-thin ribbons out of cucumbers, carrots, and zucchini, I ribbon like crazy. Or use a julienne peeler to make zucchini "spaghetti" for a low-carb, pasta-like dish.

4 medium zucchini, ends removed

3 tablespoons olive oil

4 garlic cloves, minced

4 jarred roasted red bell peppers, thinly sliced

1 teaspoon paprika

½ teaspoon kosher salt

1. Use a vegetable peeler to remove a strip lengthwise on one side of a zucchini to make a flat side so the zucchini doesn't roll. Turn the flat side of the zucchini onto a work surface. Use the peeler to remove strips along the top side of the zucchini, forming ribbons, until you get to the bottom and can't cut anymore. Repeat with the remaining zucchini.

2. Heat the olive oil in a large skillet over medium-high heat. Add the zucchini and sauté until slightly softened, 6 to 8 minutes. Add the garlic and sauté 3 minutes more. Add the peppers and sauté until warmed, 5 minutes more. Sprinkle in the paprika and salt; toss to coat.

VARIATION/MAKE IT A MEAL

Add marinara sauce and grated or shaved Parmesan for a light Italian-style lunch.

DRESS IT DOWN
• Zucchini Coins •

Cut the zucchini into ½-inch coins and dice the bell peppers.

PAIR IT PSAGOT CABERNET FRANC

A light red goes with this dish if you prepare it with marinara sauce. Without the sauce, Baron Herzog Chenin Blanc is the perfect choice.

Roasted Brussels Sprouts with Herb "Butter"

Kosher Status: Pareve • Prep: 3 minutes • Cook: 12 minutes • Total: 15 minutes • Yield: 8 servings

Stop the presses! It's a miracle—Hubby and I agree! Kinda . . . sorta. We both love Brussels sprouts, so that's where it starts. But that's also where it ends. He likes his steamed, like all his veggies. Boring. I like mine slathered in this herb "butter," spiced with parsley, thyme, and orange zest. Or I'll take my Brussels sprouts bathed in garlic, like the dressed-down version below. Whenever I make these Brussels sprouts, I make enough for both of us. Well, okay, I set a few aside to steam for him. Better the Brussels sprouts should be steamed than Hubby.

2 pounds frozen Brussels sprouts

2 tablespoons olive oil

2 tablespoons margarine, softened

1 tablespoon chopped fresh parsley or

   1 teaspoon dried

1 teaspoon chopped fresh thyme or

   ¼ teaspoon dried

½ teaspoon grated orange zest

Kosher salt

Freshly ground black pepper

1. Preheat the oven to 425°F.

2. Toss the Brussels sprouts with the olive oil on a large baking sheet. Spread them out in a single layer and roast until tender but still crisp, about 12 minutes.

3. Mix together the margarine, parsley, thyme, and orange zest in a small bowl. When the Brussels sprouts come out of the oven, toss with the herb "butter" to evenly coat and season with salt and pepper. Serve warm.

VARIATIONS

Halve the Brussels sprouts before roasting.

To make real dairy herb butter, simply replace the margarine with butter. (I know that sounds obvious, but when you have pareve brain, you have to be told to use real butter to make butter.)

DRESS IT DOWN

• **Garlic and Thyme Brussels Sprouts** •

Toss Brussels sprouts with the olive oil and thyme, mix in 7 chopped garlic cloves, and season with salt and pepper. Roast as instructed above.

PAIR IT GOOSE BAY SAUVIGNON BLANC

Green veggies, such as Brussels sprouts and asparagus, can make a red wine taste metallic. Something light and tart is the best option.

Wilted Spinach with Crispy Garlic Chips

Kosher Status: Pareve • Prep: 5 minutes • Cook: 12 minutes • Total: 17 minutes • Yield: 6 servings

Yes, for generations my ancestors hailed from Transylvania, but we ain't scared of garlic. Au contraire, Poppy would eat raw garlic like an apple; and the rest of us add it to most everything. Raw garlic is one of the food wonders of the world, and sautéed and roasted garlic are total kitchen miracles. And now that you know how to make these garlic chips, you've got a quick way to dress up any ho-hum veggie.

8 garlic cloves, thinly sliced

½ cup plus 2 tablespoons olive oil

Three 5-ounce bags baby spinach

½ teaspoon kosher salt

Freshly ground black pepper

1. Line a plate with paper towels.

2. Place the garlic and ½ cup of the olive oil in a small saucepan and bring to a simmer over medium-high heat. Reduce the heat to medium-low and cook until the garlic is lightly browned and crispy, 5 to 8 minutes, taking care not to burn it. Transfer the garlic with a fork or slotted spoon to the prepared plate; set aside to drain.

3. Heat the remaining 2 tablespoons olive oil in a large sauté pan over medium-high heat. Add the spinach and cook, stirring continually, until wilted and warm, 2 to 4 minutes. Season with the salt and pepper to taste.

4. Transfer the spinach to a serving plate and garnish with crispy garlic chips.

DRESS IT DOWN
• Garlic Wilted Spinach •

For a quick riff on the main recipe, skip the garlic chips and cook the spinach as instructed above. Season with garlic powder, salt, and pepper.

PAIR IT ELVI CAVA BRUT OR BARON HERZOG CHARDONNAY

Light, crisp, and bubbly work well here. (Or you could just pull out a cool, refreshing beer.)

Latkes with Caviar and Cream

Kosher Status: Dairy • Prep: 15 minutes • Cook: 40 minutes • Total: 55 minutes • Yield: 20 latkes

You see all kinds of ubercreative latke recipes around Chanukah time: apple-parsnip latkes, sweet potato–leek latkes, sweet cheesy latkes, savory cheese and chive latkes (all of which you can find on www.JoyofKosher.com). Truth is, you can't go anywhere in the world of latkes until you've mastered the classic. So first I'll teach you this special recipe from Ma and Uputzi. They always made incredible pureed potato latkes.

I go back and forth between the puree and the shoestring version. You can do whatever you like. No adjustments necessary; just change the food processor blade or the side of the box grater. Of course, Ma and Uputzi grated theirs by hand on the box grater. But when I want to fry up a hundred latkes, I hug my food processor, give it a big kiss, and whisper, "Thank God I have you."

When I have guests, I stick to a classic—then I go wild with toppings, creating a latke topping bar, so your Chanukah party guests can mix and match or try all. Try guac and an over-easy or poached egg, or slices of mozz, tomato, plus a few fresh basil leaves. Oooo, and I love a shmear of brie topped with a dollop of jam, or blue cheese, pear, and arugula piled high. Are you pickin' up what I'm puttin' down here? Endless, endless, endless possibilities.

4 large russet potatoes (about 2½ pounds)

3 large eggs, beaten

2 teaspoons kosher salt

1 teaspoon freshly ground black pepper

Canola oil, for frying

1 medium onion, quartered

¼ cup fine cornmeal or matzoh meal

1¼ cups crème frâiche or sour cream

Caviar, for garnish

1. Fill a large bowl with cold water. Peel the potatoes, cut them into quarters lengthwise, and place them in the bowl of cold water to prevent browning.

2. Combine the eggs, salt, and pepper in a large bowl; set aside.

3. Heat about 1 inch of the canola oil in a large sauté pan over medium-high heat.

4. Put the onion and potatoes in a food processor and pulse until pureed. Transfer the mixture to the large bowl with the eggs. Add the cornmeal and mix to combine.

5. Line a baking sheet with paper towels.

6. Using a ¼-cup measuring cup, scoop up the potato mixture and carefully drop it into the hot oil. Use the back of the measuring cup to flatten the latke. Fill the pan with as many latkes as you can, but do not let them touch. Do not overcrowd your pan, or the latkes will be soggy instead of crispy. Fry until golden brown and crispy, 3 to 5 minutes per side. Drain on the prepared baking sheet. Repeat with the remaining batter.

7. To keep the latkes warm and crispy once fried, spread them in a single layer on a baking sheet and place in a 200°F oven until ready to serve.

8. To serve, place the latkes on a large serving tray and garnish each with a generous tablespoon of crème fraîche and caviar.

QUICK TIP

I can't say it enough times: Remember, don't overcrowd your pan when frying. Make sure the latkes aren't touching and there is room around each for the edges to crisp. That's the perfect latke: soft, fluffy, and creamy on the inside with crispy edges.

DRESS IT DOWN
• Sweet Cinnamon Latkes •

My friend Anita's grandmother used to make her latkes with a pinch of cinnamon. Full disclosure: When she mentioned her grandma's sweet secret, I snagged it for this book.

For a sweeter version, omit the onion and the pepper, reduce the salt to a pinch, and add 2 teaspoons ground cinnamon and 3 tablespoons sugar. Mix 1 cup sour cream with ¼ cup maple syrup and serve it on the side.

PAIR IT DRAPPIER BRUT CHAMPAGNE (CARTE BLANCHE OR CARTE D'OR)

This dish *deserves* bubbly . . . splurge here and go for the champagne.

Creamy Tomato Penne

Kosher Status: Dairy • Prep: 5 minutes • Cook: 17 minutes • Total: 22 minutes • Yield: 6 to 8 servings

I s'pose you know that Hubby taught me how to cook. Someday, just once, I'd love to pull a "student teaches the master" shtick. I try, but he doesn't really go for it. That's because he's a natural. For him, cooking's intuitive. When I cook, it's like a toddler learning how to walk. Never cruising effortlessly, just kinda wobbling around. But everyone is clapping and smiling and screaming "yay!" Maybe 'cause it's so unexpected, or maybe 'cause I somehow manage to make it taste so good.

So I let Hubby teach me little tricks all the time. Like when you break pasta, break it down into the water so the little pieces don't snap all over the cooktop, or, worse, poke out your eye. (Hey, I did it on camera once. Check out my "Pink Linguine" video on www.JoyofKosher.com.) And that a pasta spoon is not for mixing but for serving. Did that with my gorgeous Rosle pasta spoon for the whole world to see (same embarrassing video). So now that I know how to break pasta and use cookware, here's a family-friendly pasta dish. No snapping required.

Kosher salt

One 1-pound box penne rigate

2 tablespoons olive oil

1 large onion, finely diced

4 garlic cloves, minced

One 28-ounce can or two 14-ounce cans
   diced tomatoes

1 cup ricotta

1 cup heavy cream

1 teaspoon dried oregano

½ teaspoon freshly ground black pepper

Grated Parmesan cheese, for garnish

1. In a large pot of salted boiling water, cook the pasta according to the package directions. Drain and set aside.

2. Meanwhile, heat the olive oil in a large sauté pan over medium-high heat. Add the onion and cook until slightly softened, 6 to 8 minutes. Add the garlic and cook 2 minutes more. Add the tomatoes and bring to a simmer. Simmer until the liquid thickens slightly, 5 to 7 minutes. Combine the ricotta, cream, 1½ teaspoons kosher salt, the oregano, and pepper in a small bowl and whisk until smooth. Stir the mixture into the tomato mixture. Add the pasta and toss to coat well. Transfer to a serving bowl, garnish with Parmesan, and serve warm.

VARIATION

If it's hard to get your kids to eat a dish with chunks of tomatoes, use 3 cups of pasta sauce in place of the diced tomatoes.

DRESS IT UP
• Creamy Tomato Basil Nests •
Add fresh herbs and use long noodles.

Use a long pasta such as linguine, spaghetti, or fettuccine. Add ½ cup chopped fresh basil to the sauce right before tossing it with the pasta. Arrange the pasta on plates as nests. Garnish with another ½ cup chopped fresh basil or small whole basil leaves and shaved Parmesan.

MAKE IT A MEAL

This pasta lends itself nicely to add-ins. "Beef" it up with broccoli, sautéed mushrooms, or chopped sun-dried tomatoes for a heartier entrée.

PAIR IT BINYAMINA RESERVE CHARDONNAY

There's creamy and then there's *creamy.* This baby calls for a really rich chardonnay.

Waldorf Salad

Kosher Status: Dairy • Prep: 15 minutes • Cook: 0 minutes • Total: 15 minutes • Yield: 8 servings

So I think I mentioned that when I was a kid, my family would sometimes vacation for a long weekend in New York City, and we sometimes would stay at the Waldorf. (No amusement parks for us. My mom wasn't a theme park girl, more of a Bergdorf's girl.) The night Hubby and I were engaged we went to the Waldorf lobby to discuss our wedding plans. So many happy memories there. I just plain love that place—and their signature salad. The classic creamy dressing is yogurt-based. I added the blue cheese 'cause I love it and it just came on the kosher market. I've been waiting for this.

½ cup mayonnaise

¼ cup sour cream or yogurt

Juice of 1 lemon

1 teaspoon honey

Kosher salt

Pinch of ground allspice

2 Granny Smith apples, unpeeled, cored
   and cut in ¼-inch slices

3 large celery stalks, thinly sliced

1 cup seedless red grapes, halved

½ cup walnut halves

2 heads romaine lettuce, chopped in
   1-inch pieces

Freshly ground black pepper

Make the dressing by whisking the mayonnaise, sour cream (or yogurt), lemon juice, honey, ¼ teaspoon salt, and allspice together in a small bowl. Place the apples, celery, grapes, walnuts, and lettuce in a large bowl. Add the desired amount of dressing; toss to coat well. Season to taste with salt and pepper and serve immediately. Store the remaining dressing in the fridge; it will keep for at least 1 week.

VARIATIONS

Swap in sweet apples, like Red Delicious, for Granny Smith if you don't like the taste and contrast of tart apples. Also swap out some or all of the grapes for a mix of regular and golden raisins.

• Waldorf Salad with Candied Walnuts and Blue Cheese •

Use candied walnuts instead of raw and add blue cheese.

Toss the walnuts with 2 tablespoons granulated sugar, 1 tablespoon olive oil, and ¼ teaspoon salt. Bake in a single layer on a greased baking sheet at 400°F until caramelized, 8 to 10 minutes. Watch closely; the nuts can burn easily. Start checking at 6 minutes. Let cool and add to the salad with ½ cup crumbled blue cheese.

MAKE IT A MEAL

This salad is a great side to Pumpkin Spice Ravioli with Brown Butter (page 236) or the Dress It Down version, Baked Pumpkin Penne (page 238).

PAIR IT PSAGOT CHARDONNAY

Cream loves cream. This chard has a buttery smoothness that works wonders.

Greek Pasta Salad with Creamy Feta Dressing

Kosher Status: Dairy • Prep: 15 minutes • Cook: 8 minutes • Total: 23 minutes • Yield: 8 servings

My marvelous friend Monet craves Godiva chocolates after having a baby. Literally right after. In the hospital. Everybody who comes to visit her knows they can ditch the flowers and teddy bears. Just bring a box of truffles.

Not me. When I have a baby, I crave Greek salad. A perfectly reasonable craving. Oh, and Fiji water—gotta have that, too. There is something about those bottles that just transports me to that South Sea island. Don't you just love the way the water looks so clear in that cool bottle? (I'm a sucker for great packaging.) At the rate I down the stuff, a plane ticket to Fiji might be cheaper.

But I digress. We were talking about postpartum Greek salad. I can always depend on Hubby to stop by the local bagel shop on the way to the hospital and pick up a Greek salad for me. Not when I'm in labor, of course. But right after.

Once I get out of the hospital, I can make my own. Today it's with pasta 'cause I'm in a pasta mood.

Kosher salt

One 1-pound box rotini or gemelli pasta

1 cup finely crumbled feta

¼ cup sour cream

¼ cup chopped fresh dill

1 teaspoon dried oregano

1 garlic clove

Grated zest and juice of 1 lemon

1 teaspoon red wine vinegar, plus more for drizzling

¼ cup extra virgin olive oil, plus more for drizzling

1 English cucumber, cut into ½-inch cubes

15 grape tomatoes, halved

1 small red onion, thinly sliced

¼ pound pitted Kalamata olives

1. In a large pot of salted boiling water, cook the pasta according to the package directions. Drain and set aside.

2. Combine ½ cup of the feta with the sour cream, dill, oregano, garlic, lemon zest and juice, a pinch of salt, and the vinegar in a food processor and pulse a few times. With the processor running, slowly add the olive oil until combined and smooth.

3. Combine the pasta, cucumber, tomatoes, and onion in a large bowl. Add the dressing and toss to coat well. Top with the remaining ½ cup feta and the olives. Drizzle lightly with additional olive oil and red wine vinegar just before serving chilled or at room temperature.

DRESS IT UP
• Fancy and Fresh Greek Pasta Salad •
Use a fancy flat pasta like Rombi by Bionaturae. In place of the chopped cucumbers, use a vegetable peeler to make cucumber ribbons, and replace the tomatoes with 1 pint halved multicolored heirloom cherry tomatoes.

MAKE IT A MEAL

Add 2 cups cooked salmon, in bite-size flakes.

PAIR IT GAMALA CHARDONNAY

Not Greek, but hey, Israel isn't far from Greece, and this Israeli chard is an excellent choice.

Mains

POULTRY

Chicken Sausage and Sweet Potato Hash with Baked Eggs   145

DRESS IT UP *Pastrami and Sweet Potato Hash Cups*

Coq au Vin with Veal Sausage, Thyme, and Merlot   148

DRESS IT DOWN *Quick Coq au Vin*

Sesame Chicken "Sushi" with Hoisin Garlic Sauce   155

DRESS IT DOWN *Asian Roasted Chicken and Vegetables*

Slow Cooker Turkey Spinach Meatloaf   157

DRESS IT UP *Turkey Spinach Meatloaf Stuffed with Red Peppers and Zucchini*

Pretzel-Crusted Chicken Skewers with Herbed Curry Mustard   161

DRESS IT DOWN *Pretzel-Crusted Chicken Nuggets*

Sweet and Sticky Citrus Drumsticks   165

DRESS IT UP *Sweet and Sticky Stuffed Cornish Hens (Meat)*

Sour Mash Whiskey–Glazed Whole Roasted Turkey   168

DRESS IT DOWN *Sour Mash Whiskey–Glazed Turkey Wings and Drumsticks*

Our Family Fricassee   171

DRESS IT DOWN *Fricassee Sloppy Joes*

Moroccan Roasted Chicken   176

DRESS IT DOWN *Slow Cooker Moroccan-Style Chicken*

Crispy Salt and Pepper Chicken with Caramelized Fennel and Shallots   179

DRESS IT DOWN *Salt and Pepper Chicken Wings*

MEAT

Stuffed Veal Rolls with Smoky Tomato Sauce   181

DRESS IT DOWN *Veal Spaghetti and Meatballs*

BBQ Short Rib Sandwiches with Avocado   183

DRESS IT UP *Short Rib Sliders with Flavored Mayo on Garlic Toast*

Jumbo Meatball Garlic Bread Bites   186

DRESS IT UP *Loaded Jumbo Meatball Heroes*

Skirt Steak with Salsa Verde   191

DRESS IT DOWN *Mexican Skirt Steak Salad*

Garlic Honey Brisket   198

DRESS IT DOWN *Honey Brisket Pita Pockets*

Argentinean Brisket with Chimichurri   200

DRESS IT DOWN *Pulled Argentinean Brisket and Rice*

Beer-Braised Holiday Top of the Rib   203

DRESS IT DOWN *Slow Cooker Beer-Braised Top of the Rib*

Loaded Burgers with Special Sauce   205

DRESS IT DOWN *Unloaded Burgers*

Balsamic London Broil   208

DRESS IT DOWN *Oven-Roasted Balsamic London Broil and Potatoes*

Chunky Red Chili   211

DRESS IT UP *Chili Bread Bowls*

Somewhat Sephardic Chulent   214

DRESS IT UP *Puff Pastry Sephardic Chulent Cups*

Daddy's *Mititei* (Romanian Garlic Meat Sausages)   217

DRESS IT UP *Fresh and Fruity Mititei*

"Buttery" Crusted Beef Pot Pie   220

DRESS IT DOWN *Mashed Potato Beef Cottage Pie*

Mediterranean Lamb Skewers   223

DRESS IT DOWN *Mediterranean Lamb Meatloaf*

FISH

Classic Tuna Noodle Casserole (Dairy)   225

DRESS IT UP *Creamy Salmon and Tuna Noodle Pie*

Teriyaki Scallion Rainbow Trout (Pareve)   227

DRESS IT UP *Whole Stuffed Rainbow Trout*

Blackened Tilapia Tacos with Cumin Avocado Sauce (Dairy)   230

DRESS IT UP *Tilapia Tacos with Apple Cabbage Slaw*

Miso-Glazed Salmon (Pareve)   232

DRESS IT UP *Avocado-Stuffed Miso-Glazed Salmon*

Salmon with Lemon Velvet Cream Sauce (Dairy)   234

DRESS IT UP *Side of Salmon with Seared Lemons*

VEGETARIAN

Pumpkin Spice Ravioli with Brown Butter (Dairy) 236

DRESS IT DOWN *Baked Pumpkin Penne*

Poppy and Grandma's Layered *Rakott Crumpli* (Dairy) 239

DRESS IT DOWN *Rakott Crumpli* Bake

Roasted Summer Squash Lasagna (Dairy) 241

DRESS IT UP *Roasted Vegetable Summer Lasagna*

Butternut Squash Mac 'n' Cheese (Dairy) 243

DRESS IT DOWN *Butternut Mac 'n' Cheese Muffin Cups*

Blue Cheese, Pear, and Arugula Pizza (Dairy) 245

DRESS IT DOWN *White Pizza*

Country Spinach, Tomato, and White Bean Soup (Pareve) 248

DRESS IT UP *Easy Cheese Twists (Dairy)*

Cold Soba Noodles with Sweet Sesame Tofu (Pareve) 250

DRESS IT UP *Soba, Sweet Sesame Tofu, and Vegetables*

Monday: 5:00 p.m.

Doing time . . .

I am not the planning type. Not at all.

It's something in my DNA. Today we're allowed to blame everything on our DNA.

But it's true that when I'm forced to plan, I break out in hives, or at least into a cold sweat. Something about it seems unnatural, as if I'm defying my inner being or something. My inner being has quite a mind of its own, really. It will tell me to eat a whole box of truffles, but then it will *force* me to step on that bathroom scale. Gotcha. That's the kind of inner being I've got. Most nights it will seduce me into staying up really late, like I don't have a gaggle of kids to get to school in the morning. Time, what's that?

Now Hubby, on the other hand, aside from being a great cook, is uberorganized, always on time, and prepared for every eventuality—a real Boy Scout. And the contrast is glaring: it's cold out and he's standing at the door (looking at his watch) in his coat, hat, and gloves, while I'm still searching for my jacket, or at least a scarf, or my keys. My driver's license, phone, umbrella—I never have 'em when I need 'em. It's a good thing that Hubby always keeps quarters in the car for parking meters. I often use that change to pay tolls (when I can't find my E-Z Pass) or to tip the delivery guy, because God knows I can't find my wallet. Of course, he kinda looks at me funny when I tell him to wait while I run out to the car, but I always come back with a few bucks' worth of quarters.

So even with my avowed talent for running up against the clock, you'd think I'd know when dinnertime is coming . . . at least once. I mean, it happens every day, but it still creeps up on me like a stray cat that keeps coming back even though you think it's gone. How do all of them find their way to my house, anyway? It's not like I put out bowls of milk and call "Here, kitty, kitty . . ." Is there a secret society of stray cats that publishes "best garbage in town" addresses? Is this what social networking has come to?

Anyway, lately I've been so *farmisht*. (I know you expect a translation of that word. You might say frazzled, only more so.) So when late afternoon comes around, I'm feeding The Baby, screaming at Bruiser to get off the dining room table ("And put down that vase—*gently!*"), telling Angel Face to stop drawing on the wall, then screaming again at Bruiser—who dutifully got off the table and is now *in* the kitchen sink—"Turn off the hot water!" All the while, I'm trying to explain to Little Momma why you don't pronounce the *k* in "know" and showing Miss Bouncy, who's learning the alphabet, the difference between lowercase *c* and *e*.

All of a sudden, some kid (it doesn't matter which one, sometimes it's all of them) will ask, "What's for dinner?"

Um, yeah. Dinner.

Chicken Sausage and Sweet Potato Hash with Baked Eggs

Kosher Status: Meat • Prep: 8 minutes • Cook: 40 minutes • Total: 48 minutes • Yield: 4 servings

Warning: Don't try anything too tricky—even eggs—if it's late and you're running on no sleep (up with the baby all night or cramming for exams), or your clothes dryer just broke, or your kid is in his fifth day of refusing to take a bath. Case in point: I was making over-easy eggs the other night for dinner, and one of the yolks broke midflip. I had a meltdown, almost cried—until Hubby said, "Now everybody, give Mommy some space," and pulled me back off the ledge.

I really am crazy about breakfast for dinner. Back in the day, my mom used to take us to the diner around the corner, and she'd let us order Belgian waffles. For dinner. The waitress would look at us like we were holding the menu upside down, but who cares?

So while eggs, sausage, and potatoes may be considered "breakfast food," this is my book and I say they are certainly acceptable as dinner fare. (Tell me I'm right.)

2 tablespoons olive oil

2 small sweet potatoes, peeled and cut into ½-inch cubes

1 medium onion, sliced

1 medium red bell pepper, ribs and seeds removed, cut into ½-inch cubes

1 medium green bell pepper, ribs and seeds removed, cut into ½-inch cubes

4 cooked chicken sausage links, sliced ¼ inch thick

1 teaspoon ground cumin

1 teaspoon kosher salt

½ teaspoon paprika

4 large eggs

Freshly ground black pepper

1. Preheat the oven to 400°F.

2. Heat the olive oil in a large ovenproof skillet over medium-high heat. Add the sweet potatoes and sauté until browned, about 12 minutes. Add the onion and bell peppers and sauté until slightly softened, 6 to 8 minutes. Add the sausages, cumin, salt, and paprika; sauté 4 minutes. Make 4 wells in the mixture and crack an egg into each well.

3. Transfer the skillet to the oven and bake until the sweet potatoes are tender and the eggs are set but the yolks are still soft, 10 to 12 minutes. Divide the mixture evenly among four plates, giving each person one egg with some hash. Sprinkle with pepper.

VARIATION

Use one or two russet potatoes in place of the sweet.

DRESS IT UP

• Pastrami and Sweet Potato Hash Cups •

This dressed-up version is fun for the kids, but impressive enough for a fancy family brunch or any breakfast/dinner party you may be hosting.

Omit the sausage from the recipe and bake the hash in pastrami cups in a jumbo muffin tin. Spray the tin with cooking spray. Line the walls of each cup with 2 thin slices of pastrami. Fill the cups halfway with the cooked sweet potato hash, make a well, and crack an egg into the well. Bake at 400°F until the eggs are set but the yolks are still soft, 10 to 12 minutes. Let rest 5 minutes before running a knife around the edge of the cup to remove.

MAKE IT A MEAL

Serve with Belgian waffles or Birthday Pancake Towers (page 265) for dessert.

PAIR IT BARKAN RESERVE MERLOT

The dressed-up version might like a bolder red wine, but without the pastrami, I'd stick with this fruity red.

Coq au Vin with Veal Sausage, Thyme, and Merlot

Kosher Status: Meat • Prep: 5 minutes • Cook: 1 hour, 55 minutes • Total: 2 hours • Yield: 4 servings

This is the first fancy chicken recipe I ever cooked. Well, okay, I didn't actually cook it all by my lonesome. A week after my wedding, Hubby's mom took pity on me and came over to teach me his favorite dish. I watched her in disbelief, thinking, This will never *be me. She was so tactful, too—she totally ignored the fact that when she asked for a saucepan, I handed her a stockpot.*

I have a Speedy Coq au Vin recipe in my first book, and this recipe is a great upgrade—still quick, but thanks to Aunt Rachey and Grandma Martha, we've added veal sausage. It's one of those inspired additions that makes a quick dish taste like a complex, flavorful patchka *(a big, big fuss).*

2 tablespoons olive oil

One 3½-pound chicken cut into 8 pieces

½ teaspoon kosher salt

½ teaspoon freshly ground black pepper

3 veal, chicken, or beef sausage links
   (about 6 ounces total), fresh or frozen,
   cut in 1-inch pieces

1 cup peeled pearl onions

2 garlic cloves, minced

2 tablespoons tomato paste

One 750ml bottle merlot

1 small bunch fresh thyme or 1 tablespoon
   dried

1 bay leaf

1 cup cremini mushrooms, halved

1. Preheat the oven to 375°F.

2. Heat a large Dutch oven over medium-high heat and pour in the olive oil. Season the chicken with the salt and pepper. Brown the chicken on all sides, cooking for 10 to 15 minutes total, and transfer to a large plate. Add the sausage to the drippings in the pot and cook until browned, 6 to 8 minutes; transfer to the plate with the chicken. Add the onions to the drippings and sauté them until browned, about 6 minutes. Add the garlic and cook for about 3 seconds, until fragrant. Stir in the tomato paste and cook 2 minutes. Add 1 cup water, the wine, thyme, bay leaf, and reserved chicken and sausage. Bring to a simmer, cover, and transfer to the oven. Bake 30 minutes.

3. Add the mushrooms, re-cover, and bake until the chicken is tender, about 30 minutes more.

4. Transfer the chicken, sausage, and all the vegetables with a fine-mesh strainer or slotted spoon to a bowl and keep warm. Remove and discard the bay leaf and the thyme sprigs so just sauce remains in the pot. Bring to a boil, and simmer until reduced by half, about 20 minutes. Return the chicken and vegetables to the sauce and stir to coat well and heat through. Serve immediately on a rimmed platter, passing any extra sauce in a gravy boat.

QUICK TIP

If you tie the thyme sprigs and bay leaf together in a square of cheesecloth, it will be easy to fish them out at the end.

DRESS IT DOWN

• Quick Coq au Vin •

Make a speedy stovetop variation.

Sauté 1 cup each sliced onions and sliced mushrooms in 2 tablespoons olive oil over medium heat until golden, about 5 minutes, stirring and being careful not to burn them. Remove from the pan and set aside. Season 4 boneless, skinless chicken breasts (about 2 pounds) with salt and pepper. Sear the chicken and cut-up sausages in the pan with an additional tablespoon of olive oil until brown on all sides, about 6 minutes. Return the onions and mushrooms to the pan. Make an easy wine sauce by adding ½ cup dry red wine, ¼ cup water, and ½ teaspoon dried thyme. Cover and simmer on the stovetop until the chicken is cooked through and the liquid is reduced, 15 to 20 minutes.

MAKE IT A MEAL

Serve it alongside simple mashed or baked potatoes.

PAIR IT PSAGOT MERLOT

The recipe gets a bottle of merlot, and so should you. Psagot Merlot tastes like a $50 bottle at about half the price.

Tuesday: 4:05 p.m.

....

Idea Man

Hubby is the yin to my yang, a natural cook who knows how to handle just about any food; and he's full of ideas. He comes from a family of caterers, so his mind automatically turns a pineapple into a stunning peacock centerpiece, or a baby carriage, or an umbrella. (My mind automatically turns everything into laundry.) I can't always count on his creative genius, though. The other day I asked him how I could dress up a meatloaf, and he answered, "Put a bow tie on it."

Ho, ho. What I don't need in my kitchen is a comedian. I have to admit that sometimes he pulls me right through a kitchen crisis with a well-timed line, reminding me that life is supposed to be fun. I know he's right; but to me, coming up with a new recipe is serious business. Cookbooks may look easy to write, but there are a thousand traps along the way.

Of course, Hubby disagrees, because cookbooks "come naturally to Gellers." He tells me—about twice a day—that as a charming child with straw-blond hair, he graced the cover of a cookbook fashioned by his mother. It was a project of The Mother's Center, a place for mothers to get together out on The Island (that's what we New Yorkers call Long Island). So my mother-in-law, Karen, spearheaded the supersuccessful *Mother's Center Cookbook* and filled it with Geller classics, along with a few hundred recipes contributed by the other mothers. And that was the official beginning of the Geller Family Cookbook Dynasty. Never mind that I authored a couple of cookbooks myself without the benefit of Geller genes. In our kitchen, Hubby's book is strategically positioned in front of mine, just to remind me who is the teacher and who is the student.

When I started my first cookbook (Hubby's idea, come to think of it), he was right there with me in the guise of collaborator, confidant, and cheerleader. He even coaxed his mom to jump in on the fun, essentially to help her stressed-out cookbook novice of a daughter-in-law get on with the job.

We had no clue what we were getting into. We measured pans with a ruler so we could figure out their sizes when I referenced them in recipes. Ever notice that pans don't come with the measurements written on the bottom? Pretty annoying. How is a girl supposed to write up recipes if the pans don't tell you how big they are?

Our naïveté was hilarious. We set up two laptops in our apartment. Then on one long Sunday, we wrote and edited, chose fonts and colors (as if this were the version the public would see), did data entry, and went to Staples to print and bind our masterpiece. To be honest, my *shviger* (translation: mother-in-law, but oh, so much more) and I did all the work, and Hubby contented himself by being the "idea man." He'd pop in now and then, and, noting my harried face, chide me that "stress is a wasted emotion." Then, with his signature line, "My work is done here," he'd dance out of the room.

Oh, we laugh about "idea man" now . . .

Anyway, the copy that I decided to print on pink paper at Staples is not the one that hit the market, thank the Lord. By the time my first real cookbook was released, I had learned a thing or two about the world of publishing.

Oh, we were talking about Hubby's great ideas. Sesame Chicken "Sushi" is one of his best.

Sesame Chicken "Sushi" with Hoisin Garlic Sauce

Kosher Status: Meat • Prep: 15 minutes • Cook: 18 minutes • Total: 33 minutes • Yield: 6 servings

A gem of a recipe from Hubby's catering days. Every time I made my Chicken Pastrami Roll-Ups, he would tell me to try his "sushi" version. So I did. And he was right. It's gorgeous, tasty, and a delectable upgrade of my standby recipe.

Cooking spray

6 chicken cutlets, pounded ⅛ inch thick

1 tablespoon rice vinegar

1 tablespoon toasted sesame oil

½ teaspoon kosher salt

¼ teaspoon freshly ground black pepper

1 small zucchini, cut into 4-inch-long julienne

1 medium carrot, peeled and cut into 4-inch-long julienne

½ red bell pepper, ribs and seeds removed, cut into 4-inch-long julienne

1½ teaspoons black sesame seeds

½ teaspoon white sesame seeds

HOISIN GARLIC SAUCE

¼ cup hoisin sauce

2 tablespoons soy sauce

Juice of ½ lime

¼ teaspoon garlic powder

1. Preheat the oven to 350°F. Spray a baking sheet with cooking spray.

2. Lay the cutlets on the baking sheet and sprinkle them evenly with the vinegar, sesame oil, salt, and pepper. Distribute the zucchini, carrot, and pepper evenly on the cutlets,

laying them in a thin line lengthwise down the center of each. Carefully roll up the cutlets along the long edge, ending with the seam sides down. Sprinkle each with the black and white sesame seeds. Bake until done but still juicy, 15 to 18 minutes.

3. Whisk together the hoisin, soy sauce, lime juice, and garlic powder in a small bowl until well combined.

4. To serve, slice the cutlets into ½-inch-thick pieces and lay the slices on their sides, like sushi. Serve with a small bowl of dipping sauce and chopsticks.

VARIATIONS

Not in the mood to julienne your veg? Use small broccoli florets to stuff your chicken. Less work, and it will still be a thing of beauty.

The Hoisin Garlic Sauce is also great on roasted chicken on the bone and on salmon steaks and fillets.

DRESS IT DOWN

• Asian Roasted Chicken and Vegetables •

Quickly make an easy Asian-inspired chicken dinner with oven-roasted veg.

Place the cutlets and half the Hoisin Garlic Sauce in a resealable plastic bag, massage around to coat the chicken evenly, and set aside. Cut 2 medium carrots, 2 small zucchini, and 1 red pepper into 1-inch cubes. Toss the vegetables with the remaining half of the Hoisin Garlic Sauce and spread them in a single layer on a baking sheet lined with foil and sprayed with cooking spray. Roast at 350°F for 12 minutes. Remove the baking sheet from the oven, lay the cutlets in a single layer on top of the vegetables, and continuing roasting until the chicken is tender and juicy and the vegetables are soft, about 16 minutes.

MAKE IT A MEAL

Serve the chicken over sticky sushi rice tossed with black sesame seeds and toasted sesame oil.

PAIR IT COVENANT LAVAN CHARDONNAY

Real sushi calls for a light, fresh wine. For this chicken "sushi," go richer.

Slow Cooker Turkey Spinach Meatloaf

Kosher Status: Meat • Prep: 5 minutes • Cook: 3 hours • Total: 3 hours, 5 minutes • Yield: 8 servings

Drum roll, please. I would like to publicly thank a true American hero: Irving Naxon, the guy who invented the slow cooker. I would set off fireworks and give everyone a day off in honor of his birthday, if I knew when that was, 'cause having a slow cooker is like having another hand in your kitchen—one that actually knows how to cook without burning everything. For crazy-busy people like me who throw a few ingredients into the pot, turn it on, and forget about it till dinnertime, it's a godsend. So Irving, from the bottom of my heart, a shaynem dank. (Thanks a heap, really.)

MEATLOAF

Cooking spray

2 pounds ground turkey

3 large eggs, beaten

⅔ cup dry bread crumbs

1 cup frozen chopped spinach, thawed
   and squeezed dry

2 tablespoons balsamic vinegar

1 teaspoon dried oregano

1 teaspoon kosher salt

½ teaspoon garlic powder

½ teaspoon red pepper flakes (optional)

SAUCE

1 tablespoon olive oil

1 garlic clove, minced

1 cup canned crushed tomatoes

½ cup chicken broth, such as
   Manischewitz All Natural Chicken
   Broth

1 tablespoon honey

1 tablespoon tomato paste

½ teaspoon kosher salt

½ teaspoon dried basil

1. Spray the inside of a slow cooker with cooking spray. Combine the turkey, eggs, bread crumbs, spinach, vinegar, oregano, salt, garlic powder, and red pepper flakes, if using, in a large bowl; mix well. Form into an evenly thick rectangular loaf and place in the prepared slow cooker. Cook on high for 3 hours. Cool loaf before cutting.

2. Make the sauce about 30 minutes before the meatloaf is done: Heat the oil in a medium saucepan over medium-high heat. Cook the garlic until fragrant, about 2 minutes. Stir in the tomatoes, broth, honey, tomato paste, salt, and basil; bring to a boil. Reduce the heat to a simmer and cook until the sauce is slightly reduced, 12 to 15 minutes. Pour the sauce into a blender or food processor and blend until smooth. Serve slices of the meatloaf with the sauce drizzled over the top.

QUICK TIP

Some people find ground turkey to be a little dry; that's why we've got a nice sauce in this here recipe. But you could easily replace the turkey with ground chicken, beef, veal, or a combo.

VARIATION

To set it and forget it, add a few tablespoons of chicken broth to the slow cooker and cook on low for 6 hours.

• Turkey Spinach Meatloaf Stuffed with Red Peppers and Zucchini •

Shred 1 large zucchini and combine it with 1 cup diced roasted red peppers. Set aside. Spray a loaf pan with cooking spray and press in half of the meatloaf mixture. Top with a layer of the mixed peppers and zucchini and press the remaining meatloaf mixture on top. Bake at 350°F for 1 hour and 30 minutes. Allow to cool slightly before carefully slicing and plating.

MAKE IT A MEAL

Serve with spaghetti or steamed green beans. Make a double portion of the tomato sauce to drizzle over all.

PAIR IT HARKHAM SHIRAZ

The deep, slow-cooked flavors of turkey are balanced by this fruity, spicy shiraz.

Pretzel-Crusted Chicken Skewers
with Herbed Curry Mustard

Kosher Status: Meat • Prep: 15 minutes • Cook: 6 to 10 minutes in the pan or
18 to 20 minutes in the oven • Total: 25 to 35 minutes • Yield: 8 skewers

When I developed this recipe, I had kids in mind—and not just my kids.

Your kids.

My neighbors' kids.

Every kid in the universe.

We love schnitzel in this house, but it's easy for it to get boring. So I started to think what I can do creatively here. I mean, everybody has tried crushed corn flakes. Then I walked by the takeout counter at my supermarket and saw Rice Krispie–crusted chicken and potato chip–crusted chicken. And this idea popped into my head: pretzel-crusted chicken. Crunchy salty heaven. It's my all-time favorite idea, till the next one.

½ cup honey mustard

2 tablespoons chopped fresh dill

2 tablespoons chopped fresh parsley

½ teaspoon curry powder

1 large egg, beaten with 1 tablespoon
water

2½ cups small salted pretzels

1 teaspoon paprika

1 teaspoon dry mustard

2 large boneless, skinless chicken cutlets
(1 pound)

3 tablespoons olive oil or cooking spray

EQUIPMENT

Eight 6-inch skewers (soak wooden skewers in water for 1 hour before use)

1. Combine the honey mustard, dill, parsley, and curry powder in a small bowl. Set aside.

2. Place the egg wash in a rimmed plate. Crush the pretzels to medium fineness in a food processor or in a plastic bag, using a mallet. Stir together the pretzel crumbs, paprika, and dry mustard in a rimmed plate.

3. Place a chicken cutlet on a work surface or cutting board. Lay your hand on top of the cutlet and cut it in half, slicing parallel to the cutting board. Repeat with the second cutlet; you will have 4 thin cutlets. Then cut each piece lengthwise into 2 strips, so

that you have 8 strips. Thread each strip onto a skewer, keeping it flat, and place it on a baking sheet.

4. Set up an assembly line: chicken, egg wash, and pretzel crumbs.

5. Holding the skewer, coat each chicken strip in egg wash, letting any excess drip back into the plate. Dip the strip into the pretzel coating, turning and pressing gently to coat it evenly. Gently shake off any excess coating, and return the skewer to the baking sheet.

6. If pan-frying, heat the olive oil over medium heat in a sauté pan large enough to fit all or several skewers lying flat. Pan-fry the skewers in a single layer, turning once, until the crust is golden and the chicken is cooked through, 3 to 5 minutes per side. You may have to cook the skewers in batches. Alternatively, place the skewers on a baking sheet sprayed with cooking spray. Spray the chicken with additional cooking spray, and bake at 350°F for 8 to 10 minutes. Remove the baking sheet from the oven, flip the skewers, spray again, and bake until the chicken is cooked through, 8 to 10 minutes more.

7. Serve the skewers immediately with the honey mustard sauce on the side.

QUICK TIPS

If you are not comfortable thinning the cutlets, buy four extra-thin cutlets from your butcher.

When pan-frying skewers, take special care that the heat is on medium so that the chicken has time to cook through and the crust doesn't burn.

If your chicken cutlets are not all the same thickness, you can pound them to a uniform thickness so that the skewers cook through evenly.

DRESS IT DOWN

• Pretzel-Crusted Chicken Nuggets •

For kid-friendly finger food, make these.

Don't slice the cutlets horizontally; instead, cut them into bite-size nuggets. Toss the nuggets in the egg wash, then into the pretzel coating. Pan-fry as instructed for about 3 minutes per side. Great with ketchup or barbecue sauce!

Serve with Baked Sweet Potato Chips (page 66). Hold the dollops of sour cream; instead, double (even triple) the Herbed Curry Mustard. You'll be dipping the chips and the chix in that sweet herby sauce.

PAIR IT PACIFICA OREGON PINOT NOIR

The pretzel-crusted chicken is for the kids, but the wine is for you. Treat yourself to the raspberry and cherry flavors in this satisfying wine.

Sweet and Sticky Citrus Drumsticks

Kosher Status: Meat • Prep: 5 minutes • Marinate: 3 hours • Cook: 30 minutes • Total: 3 hours, 35 minutes • Yield: 8 drumsticks

Mommy loves no-utensil meals + kids love drumsticks = this fab meal. Big kids, like Hubby and me, never outgrow loving these drumsticks with a bright, sassy kick. I have to buy the "family pack" of chicken when I make these. Even if you don't have a busload of kids, you'll need the family pack too 'cause they're soooo good.

One 12-ounce jar orange marmalade

3 tablespoons honey

1 tablespoon extra virgin olive oil

1 tablespoon Dijon mustard

Juice of 1 lemon

Juice of 2 limes

½ teaspoon garlic powder

½ teaspoon kosher salt

¼ teaspoon ground white pepper

8 chicken drumsticks (about 2 pounds)

1 small orange, thinly sliced

Cooking spray

1. Make the marinade by mixing the marmalade, honey, olive oil, mustard, lemon and lime juices, garlic powder, salt, and pepper in a small bowl; whisk to combine.

2. Place the marinade, drumsticks, and orange in a large resealable plastic bag and massage around the chicken to coat evenly. Refrigerate for 1 to 3 hours.

3. Preheat the oven to 450°F. Line a baking sheet with foil and spray with cooking spray.

4. Transfer the drumsticks, sauce, and oranges to the prepared baking sheet. Bake until the chicken is golden and cooked through, 25 to 30 minutes.

TIME-SAVER

In a pinch, simply pour on the marinade and bake.

VARIATION

This marinade works great on a roasted chicken, whole or cut into 8 pieces, as well.

• Sweet and Sticky Stuffed Cornish Hens (Meat) •

Pour this marinade over elegant stuffed Cornish hens.

Sauté 1 pound ground beef with 1 medium onion, diced, and 1 tablespoon chopped fresh rosemary (or 1 teaspoon dried) in a little olive oil until brown. Mix in 1 cup cooked rice and set aside. Prepare the glaze, omitting the salt and pepper. Season four 1½-pound Cornish hens with salt and pepper. Stuff the hens with the meat-rice filling, and tie the legs together. Pour and brush half of the glaze over the hens. Bake at 350°F for 30 minutes. Brush the remaining glaze over the hens, and bake until both the meat and the stuffing register 165°F on an instant-read thermometer, an additional 20 minutes.

MAKE IT A MEAL

Rice pilaf or steamed or sautéed snow peas go great here. Better yet, toss the pilaf with the snow peas for an all-in-one complementary side.

PAIR IT CHÂTEAU FOURCAS DUPRÉ LISTRAC-MÉDOC BORDEAUX BLEND

Ruby red, balanced with fruity aromas and woody notes, this blend is a great starter French wine.

HOW TO USE A MEAT THERMOMETER

Using a meat thermometer is the best way to be sure your meat and poultry are done. Instant-read thermometers are quick, easy to use, and my preference for gauging temperature. Follow these steps for perfect roasting every time!

- Read the instructions that came with your thermometer.
- Prepare the meat or poultry according to the recipe instructions.
- Test doneness by pulling the roasting pan *out* of the oven and inserting the instant-read thermometer into the thickest part of the meat, without touching the bone. Wait a few seconds for the reading to appear.
- Remove the thermometer and put the meat back into the oven if more cooking time is needed.
- Repeat until the meat is at the correct temperature.

Sour Mash Whiskey–Glazed Whole Roasted Turkey

Kosher Status: Meat • Prep: 5 minutes • Cook: 2 to 2½ hours • Rest: 15 to 20 minutes •
Total: 2 hours, 20 minutes to 2 hours, 55 minutes • Yield: 13 to 16 servings

The ultimate entrée for a crowd. It's got a slightly sweet and edgy kick, and is a juicy, delicious beauty, this bird.

1 cup Jack Daniel's Tennessee Whiskey

½ cup soy sauce

½ cup red wine vinegar

½ cup Dijon mustard

½ cup packed light brown sugar

One 15-pound whole turkey, rinsed and patted dry

Kosher salt

Freshly ground black pepper

½ cup (8 tablespoons/1 stick) margarine, softened

4 cups chicken broth, such as Manischewitz All Natural Chicken Broth

2 tablespoons all-purpose flour

1. Preheat the oven to 375°F.

2. Make the glaze: Whisk together the Jack Daniel's, soy sauce, vinegar, mustard, and brown sugar in a medium bowl; set aside.

3. Place the turkey, breast side up, on a rack in a large roasting pan. Season all over with salt and pepper. Tuck the wings underneath the body and tie the legs together. Spread a thick layer of margarine all over the turkey. Pour the chicken broth into the bottom of the roasting pan.

4. Roast the turkey for 30 minutes. Pour and brush about half the glaze all over the turkey and return it to the oven. Roast for 30 minutes more. Pour and brush the remaining glaze over the turkey and return it to the oven. Roast for another 60 minutes. Check the temperature with a thermometer inserted into the thickest part of the thigh. Continue roasting until the temperature registers 165°F on an instant-read thermometer. Remove the turkey from the roasting pan, and let it rest on a cutting board, loosely tented with foil, for 15 to 20 minutes before carving.

5. While the turkey is resting, prepare the gravy: Pour the accumulated pan juices into a bowl or a fat separator. Let sit for a minute or two to allow the fat to separate and rise to the top. If you are using a bowl, carefully tilt it and skim off the fat from the pan juices with a large spoon, reserving 2 tablespoons and discarding the rest, or use a fat separator. Set aside the pan juices. Return the 2 tablespoons fat to the roasting pan. Whisk in the flour slowly to prevent lumps from forming. Cook on top of the stove over medium heat, stirring up any browned bits, until the flour is incorporated and the mixture is smooth. Gradually add 2 to 3 cups of the pan juices to the pan, stirring continually. Cook until the gravy is thickened, about 5 minutes. If you'd like it a little thinner, add up to 1 additional cup of the pan juices. Season with additional pepper, if desired. Strain the gravy through a fine-mesh sieve.

VARIATION

Pour this glaze on a brisket—go low and slow and braise it at 300°F, 1 hour per pound.

DRESS IT DOWN

• Sour Mash Whiskey–Glazed Turkey Wings and Drumsticks •

When you're not expecting fifteen for dinner, pour this glaze on turkey parts.

Halve the glaze recipe above. Place 4 wings and 4 drumsticks in a foil-lined baking dish and pour and brush with half the glaze. Roast at 350°F for 60 minutes. Flip the turkey parts and pour and brush the remaining glaze all over. Bake for 20 to 25 more minutes.

MAKE IT A MEAL

For a lighter side, go with Mustard Green Beans (page 106); or to out-and-out party, serve with Sweet Potato Casserole (page 110).

PAIR IT PACIFICA OREGON PINOT NOIR

Fruity and light, this pinot noir goes great with turkey. If you prefer a white wine with your bird, go for chardonnay.

Our Family Fricassee

Kosher Status: Meat • Prep: 15 minutes • Cook: 2 hours •
Total: 2 hours, 15 minutes • Yield: 6 to 8 servings

Thank you, Judy (Hubby's stepmom), for all your amazing recipes! This one was torn from the pages of her local West Hempstead, New York, community cookbook. Hubby always wants his food exactly as Judy made it, and this dish is no exception. I could never get up the nerve to make this because the classic recipe calls for pupiks! Ahhh, clueless about that? They're chicken tummies (aka gizzards). In Yiddish, a pupik is also a belly button. (As a rule, not a term you'd use in polite conversation, but I don't mind admitting that the last time I was pregnant I couldn't see past my pupik to my pumps.) Now maybe in some foreign shtetl, pupiks are considered a delicacy, but I just couldn't stomach stomaching those. So I ignored Hubby's pleas for fricassee for more than seven years, until I got this recipe from Judy. Turns out, she doesn't even use pupiks.

There are those who make this dish using the real thing, but thankfully I don't have to be one of them.

Two 8-ounce cans sliced mushrooms,
   drained

½ red bell pepper, ribs and seeds
   removed, diced

½ green bell pepper, ribs and seeds
   removed, diced

½ yellow bell pepper, ribs and seeds
   removed, diced

1 medium onion, diced

2 garlic cloves, minced

1 pound ground beef

¼ cup marinara sauce (homemade or
   store-bought)

2 tablespoons seasoned dry bread
   crumbs

2 pounds chicken wings (or a combo of
   necks, wings, and pupiks)

1¼ teaspoons hot sauce

One 8-ounce can tomato sauce

1 tablespoon paprika

2 teaspoons dried parsley

2 teaspoons garlic powder

2 teaspoons onion powder

2 teaspoons kosher salt

½ teaspoon freshly ground black pepper

One 6-ounce box rice pilaf, cooked
   according to the package directions,
   for serving

1. Pour 1½ cups water into a medium stockpot; add the mushrooms, bell peppers, onion, and garlic. Place the ground beef, marinara, and bread crumbs in a large bowl. Using your fingertips, lightly mix to combine, and form into 1-inch meatballs. Add the meatballs to the vegetables along with the chicken, hot sauce, tomato sauce, paprika, parsley, garlic and onion powders, salt, and pepper. Stir gently to combine.

2. Cook, covered, over low heat for 1 hour. Stir and continue cooking, covered, until the chicken is falling off the bone, 1 hour more. Using a slotted spoon, transfer to a plate of rice pilaf. Serve warm.

VARIATION

Some people howl when I suggest using canned mushrooms, but I happen to have a wild fascination with mushrooms from a can—just love 'em on pizza, love 'em a lot, even straight out of the can. You may, of course, sauté sliced fresh mushrooms (about two 8-ounce cartons) if you don't share my obsession.

DRESS IT DOWN
• Fricassee Sloppy Joes •

Make it hearty. Pile the fricassee on a whole wheat bun, sloppy Joe–style.

Lose the bread crumbs and the rice. Replace the chicken parts with 2 pounds ground chicken. Brown the meats, using a wooden spoon to break them into very small pieces. Use chopped mushrooms. Increase the marinara to ½ cup and add it to the pot. Add the rest of the ingredients to the meats and cook until the vegetables are tender, 20 to 30 minutes. Pile the fricassee high on a bun and top it with coleslaw and a few slices of avocado and tomato.

PAIR IT HERZOG SPECIAL RESERVE CABERNET/ZINFANDEL/SYRAH

Match the wide assortment of meats and flavors in this dish with a perfect blend.

Sunday: 12:00 noon

Play Date, Lunchtime

I like to think my kids have somewhat sophisticated palates. On the other hand, you don't want a five-year-old reeking with sophistication, either.

Case in point: When Little Momma was in kindergarten, she had a friend over to play on a Sunday. Lunchtime comes along, and I ask, "Sandwiches?" I offer PB&J, grilled cheese, or tuna. You expected me to serve them duck à l'orange? Come on, it's Sunday and I'm not whipping up a cookbook recipe for a couple of five-year-olds. (So now your illusions that Sunday lunch in my house is any different from yours have been correctly shattered for life.) The friend answers, "No."

I ask, "Noodles with cheese or ketchup?" (Blech. I can't handle it, but the kids go for it every time.)

She says, "No." My daughter now pipes up that her friend only eats sushi and brings it to school for lunch—every day. "Chopsticks and all?" I ask. They nod.

Go figure.

Moroccan Roasted Chicken

During the developing and testing process for this book, this dish became Hubby's new favorite. Totally unexpected—I was sure he'd steal a line from the kids and say, "Thank you anyway, but this is not my taste." (We taught them to say that instead of "Ooo, yick!") It's just not the usual stuff and spices he goes for, but apparently the combination was soooo his taste. And mine, too. It's one of those winner recipes that will make you dance around your kitchen. You may hug me now.

Cooking spray

2 tablespoons honey

¼ cup olive oil

2 teaspoons ground cumin

2 teaspoons ground turmeric

½ teaspoon ground cinnamon

4 garlic cloves, chopped

One 3½-pound chicken, cut into 8 pieces

2 medium red onions, quartered

1 pound small red-skin potatoes, scrubbed and halved

1 cup dried apricots

½ cup golden raisins

½ cup coarsely chopped pistachios

2 tablespoons chopped fresh cilantro

1. Preheat the oven to 350°F. Line a baking sheet with aluminum foil; spray the foil with cooking spray.

2. Mix together the honey, olive oil, cumin, turmeric, cinnamon, and garlic in a small bowl. Place the chicken, onions, and potatoes in a large bowl. Toss with three-quarters of the honey mixture and arrange in a single layer on the prepared pan. Toss the apricots and raisins with the remaining honey mixture and set aside.

3. Bake the chicken, onions, and potatoes for 35 minutes. Add the apricots and raisins and bake until the chicken is cooked through, 15 to 20 minutes more. Garnish with the pistachios and cilantro.

DRESS IT DOWN/MAKE IT A MEAL
• **Slow Cooker Moroccan-Style Chicken** •

Make this a slow cooker meal.

Use 4 chicken leg quarters (thigh with leg attached), and toss all the ingredients except the pistachios and cilantro in the slow cooker with 3 cups chicken broth, such as Manischewitz All Natural Chicken Broth. Cook on low for 6 hours. Serve over whole wheat couscous and garnish with the pistachios and cilantro.

PAIR IT CARMEL KAYOUMI SHIRAZ

A yummy, spicy shiraz enhances the rich flavors in this dish.

Crispy Salt and Pepper Chicken with Caramelized Fennel and Shallots

Kosher Status: Meat • Prep: 5 minutes • Cook: 45 minutes • Total: 50 minutes • Yield: 4 servings

Cooking doesn't have to be difficult or complicated, and it doesn't need to use lots of ingredients to be perfect. The better cook you are, the quicker you learn that. Here's one recipe that proves it.

Cooking spray

One 3½-pound chicken, cut into 8 pieces

¼ cup all-purpose flour

2 large fennel bulbs, trimmed and cut into 1½-inch slices

4 shallots, halved if large

4 garlic cloves, smashed

3 tablespoons olive oil

2 teaspoons kosher salt

¾ teaspoon freshly ground black pepper

¾ teaspoon ground white pepper

2 tablespoons chopped fresh parsley

1. Preheat the oven to 400°F. Spray a baking sheet with cooking spray.

2. Place the chicken pieces and flour in a large resealable plastic bag and toss to coat evenly. Shake off any excess flour. Place the chicken, fennel, shallots, and garlic in a single layer on the prepared baking sheet. Drizzle with the olive oil and sprinkle with the salt and black and white peppers. Bake until the chicken is cooked through and the skin is crispy, 40 to 45 minutes. Sprinkle with the parsley before serving.

QUICK TIP

Fennel, sometimes called anise, can be found in the produce section of your supermarket. It looks kind of like celery and smells like licorice and even has a hint of that taste. It's one of my favorite veggies to enjoy raw, thinly sliced in a salad. It's also great sautéed, braised, and roasted.

VARIATION

For especially crispy chicken, after tossing it with the flour, pan-sear it in hot oil until golden, about 5 minutes per side, then roast with the vegetables.

• **Salt and Pepper Chicken Wings** •

Toss 2 pounds chicken wings and/or drumettes in 2 tablespoons olive oil, 1 teaspoon salt, and ½ teaspoon each black and white pepper. Place in a single layer on a baking sheet and roast at 450°F for 30 minutes, flipping halfway through. Serve with your favorite dip.

MAKE IT A MEAL

Serve with hot "buttered" wide egg noodles. Toss drained hot noodles with margarine and salt and pepper to taste. Optionally, you can add poppy seeds or chopped fresh parsley.

PAIR IT BARONS EDMOND ET BENJAMIN DE ROTHSCHILD HAUT-MEDOC

A licorice flavor is sometimes detected in French Bordeaux. The anise in this recipe makes this one a great choice.

Stuffed Veal Rolls with Smoky Tomato Sauce

Kosher Status: Meat • Prep: 20 minutes •
Cook: 40 minutes • Total: 1 hour • Yield: 6 servings

Another Hubby request from Judy's reper-toire—with her around, at least I don't have to really think, just know how to copy down reci-pes. This is an art in itself, believe me. Great cooks like Judy just assume you know what in the world they're talking about. You can try to bluff it, taking it down exactly as they say it, and then blow it in the kitchen. Or you can ask sly questions at the confusing points, trying not to sound like a dummy. "Um, adding the wine sounds really good. How do you prefer to do that?"

But this isn't Judy's recipe. It's from her friend Betty. She deserves the credit. Turns out, Judy also knows how to copy down a good recipe or two.

Cooking spray
1 tablespoon olive oil
1 small red onion, diced
1 garlic clove, chopped
2½ teaspoons kosher salt
¼ teaspoon dried oregano
½ cup dry bread crumbs
1 large egg, beaten

3 cups marinara sauce (homemade or
  store-bought)
Juice of 1 lemon
¼ cup dry white wine
2 teaspoons sweet or hot smoked paprika
Twelve ¼-inch-thick slices veal scaloppini
  (about 2 pounds)
¼ teaspoon freshly ground black pepper

1. Preheat the oven to 350°F. Spray a 9 x 13-inch baking pan with cooking spray.

2. Heat the olive oil in a medium sauté pan over medium-high heat. Add the onion and sauté until translucent, about 6 minutes. Add the garlic, 1½ teaspoons of the salt, and the oregano; sauté 2 minutes more. Remove from the heat and transfer to a medium bowl. When slightly cooled, add the bread crumbs and egg; stir well.

3. To make the smoky tomato sauce, in a medium bowl, whisk together the marinara, lemon juice, white wine, and paprika. Spread half the sauce on the bottom of the pan.

4. Season the veal with the remaining 1 teaspoon salt and the pepper. Place a heaping tablespoon of the stuffing on the end of each slice of veal and roll. You may need to secure the rolls with toothpicks. Place the veal rolls seam side down in the pan.

5. Pour the remaining sauce over the rolls, cover with foil, and bake until veal is tender and cooked through, about 30 minutes. Both the veal and the stuffing should be at 165°F on a instant-read meat thermometer.

DRESS IT DOWN/MAKE IT A MEAL

• Veal Spaghetti and Meatballs •

Instead of scaloppini, make meatballs with ground veal.

Combine 2 pounds ground veal with ½ cup dry bread crumbs, 1 teaspoon dried oregano, and 2 large eggs. Mix lightly with your fingertips so that the meatballs will be fluffy, not tough. If the meat mixture is too soft to form into balls, refrigerate for 30 minutes to 1 hour. Roll the mixture into 2-inch balls and bake them on a greased baking sheet at 400°F for 35 to 40 minutes. Serve over long noodles with warm smoky tomato sauce (if you're serving to kids, either eliminate the wine or cook down the sauce for 15 to 20 minutes).

PAIR IT ALEXANDER WINERY RESERVE MERLOT

The general rule is to put the same bottle on the table as the one you use in the recipe. But some rules are made to be broken. So sip the white wine while you're cooking, but serve the veal with this full-bodied merlot. It's a bit fruity and a great match for light meat.

BBQ Short Rib Sandwiches with Avocado

Kosher Status: Meat • Prep: 15 minutes • Cook: 4 hours, 30 minutes • Assembly: 30 minutes •
Total: 5 hours, 15 minutes • Yield: 4 big sandwiches (4 to 6 cups meat)

We have a few favorite restaurants, Hubby and I—none that we agree on, of course. When he wants steak and fries, I want blue cheese, pear, and arugula pizza, so I started making it for myself (page 245). He's a Chinese-right-out-of-the-carton, standing-up-at-the-counter kinda guy; I just love being waited on, love a beautifully set table, love fancy napkins and those waiters with white gloves. Makes me feel like a duchess dining at my magnificent ancestral estate. "That will be all, Charles."

But anyway, we do have one place in New York City, The Prime Grill, that we both adore, and even one dish we order right away to split: their Short Ribs Sandwich. Okay, to be honest, we usually order a main for each of us, plus the sandwich to share. (I can't believe I'm actually confessing this in print.) Since we crave this dish more often than we can trek to the city, I decided to try it at home. Good thing I don't frustrate easily. Not too easily, anyway. It took about 15 pounds of meat, but I finally, finally perfected this version of our fave sandwich. This is fall-off-the-bone, melt-in-your-mouth meat. After two cookbooks and over 400 original recipes, Hubby said this sandwich is the best thing I ever created. Woo-hoo, the ultimate compliment! Once in a while, Hubby gets it right.

2 teaspoons kosher salt

2 teaspoons onion powder

2 teaspoons garlic powder

2 teaspoons paprika

2 teaspoons freshly ground black pepper

1 teaspoon cayenne pepper

1 teaspoon ground ginger

1 teaspoon dry mustard

5 pounds bone-in flanken short ribs

6 tablespoons canola oil

2 medium onions, chopped

10 garlic cloves, smashed

3 cups barbecue sauce

3 tablespoons Worcestershire sauce

1 baguette, cut into 4 pieces

4 tablespoons mayonnaise

2 medium avocados, pitted, peeled, and
  sliced

1. Preheat the oven to 325°F.

2. In a large bowl, combine the salt, onion powder, garlic powder, paprika, pepper, cayenne, ginger, and dry mustard. Add the short ribs and rub in the spice mixture until the meat is well coated on all sides.

3. Heat 5 tablespoons of the canola oil in a Dutch oven or large heavy-bottomed ovenproof pot over medium-high heat. Sear the short ribs, in batches, on both sides until nicely browned, about 4 minutes per side. Remove the meat from the pot. Add the remaining 1 tablespoon oil, the onions, and the garlic and sauté until caramelized, 8 to 10 minutes. Return the short ribs to the pot. Cover with the barbecue sauce, 2 cups water, and the Worcestershire and bring to a boil. Cover the pot and transfer it to the oven. Cook until the meat is falling off the bone, about 4 hours.

4. Remove the meat from the pot and place it in a large bowl. Discard the bones. Shred the meat into small pieces using two forks. Use a ladle or large spoon to skim the fat from the sauce. Add enough of the sauce to the meat to moisten it well (reserve the rest of the sauce for another use if you like).

5. To assemble the sandwiches, slice the baguette sections in half to form sandwiches and spread each with 1 tablespoon mayonnaise. Top with 1 cup meat and one-quarter of the avocado slices.

It's already a meal (especially with all the meat I'm stuffing into these buns), but go the extra mile and top with **Crispy Fried Red Onions:** Thinly slice 2 red onions and toss them in a resealable plastic bag with ⅓ cup all-purpose flour, 1 teaspoon kosher salt, ½ teaspoon black pepper, and 1 to 2 teaspoons cayenne, if desired. Seal the bag and toss to coat. Heat 2 inches canola oil in a deep heavy pot to 360°F. Shake the excess flour off the onions and fry in batches until golden brown and crispy, 4 to 6 minutes. Remove the onions from the oil with a slotted spoon and drain them on paper towels. Serve immediately. Also great as a topping for burgers, hot dogs, or grilled steak.

DRESS IT UP

• Short Rib Sliders with Flavored Mayo on Garlic Toast •

Instead of 4 sandwiches, make 12 sliders on garlic toast with 3 flavored mayo sauces.

Smear each slider bun with a pat of margarine and a few dashes of garlic powder, then broil on high, cut side up, for a minute to toast. Assemble as directed above, but instead of using plain mayo, create three spicy mayo varieties: Mix 2 tablespoons sweet red horseradish with 2 tablespoons mayo; 2 tablespoons wasabi sauce with 2 tablespoons mayo; and finally, 2 tablespoons spicy white horseradish with 2 tablespoons mayo. Add a little shredded cabbage or Crispy Fried Red Onions (recipe above) for some crunch and serve one of each slider variety per serving.

PAIR IT BINYAMINA RESERVE ZINFANDEL

The unique ripe fruit flavors of a zin go really well with BBQ sauce.

Jumbo Meatball Garlic Bread Bites

Kosher Status: Meat • Prep: 30 minutes • Cook: 25 minutes • Assembly: 5 minutes •
Total: 1 hour • Yield: 6 sandwiches

Yum beyond yum! Got this idea from Jeff Mauro the Sandwich King, an Italian chef on the Food Network. (Gastronomically, of course, Italians are like Jews—we both have mamas standing over us urging, "Mangia! Mangia!" "Ess, ess, mein kindt.")

Hubby will grab meatballs from the fridge, slice each in half, and place them on a long garlic bread hero—and when he's feeling crazy, he'll add a layer of mashed potatoes. I guess he's been doing this for a while, but since he was using up my leftover meatballs, mash, and frozen garlic bread, I never considered it a recipe. Until now.

Know what? This is the kind of sandwich you look at and say, "Oh baby!" At least, that's what Hubby says, but he's not talking to me; he's talking to the sandwich. After he finishes eating, though, he thanks God that I learned how to cook.

Cooking spray

2 slices soft white bread

1 cup plain soy milk

1 pound ground beef

1 tablespoon Worcestershire sauce

2 large eggs

1 teaspoon dried basil

1 teaspoon dried oregano

½ teaspoon onion powder

¼ cup plain dry bread crumbs

1 teaspoon kosher salt

½ teaspoon freshly ground black pepper

1½ teaspoons garlic powder

⅓ cup extra virgin olive oil

1 loaf Italian bread, about 21 inches long
(or shorter loaves that add up to 21
inches)

1 cup marinara sauce, warmed

1. Preheat the oven to 425°F. Liberally spray a baking sheet with cooking spray.

2. Tear the white bread into 1-inch pieces and place them in a medium bowl. Mix in the soy milk and soak for 20 minutes.

3. In a large bowl, combine the beef, Worcestershire, eggs, basil, oregano, onion powder, bread crumbs, salt, and pepper.

4. Gently squeeze the soy milk from the soaked bread and discard the milk. Add the bread to the beef mixture. Mix gently with your fingertips to incorporate all the ingredients,

but don't overhandle the meat. Divide the mixture into 6 equal parts; form each into a large round ball. (If the mixture is too loose to form into balls, cover with plastic wrap and refrigerate for 30 minutes.)

5. Place the meatballs on the prepared baking sheet and bake, turning after about 10 minutes, until no longer pink inside, about 25 minutes total.

6. Meanwhile, whisk together the garlic powder and olive oil in a small bowl. Split the loaf, not all the way through, to open like a book, then cut it into six 3½-inch lengths. Place the mini rolls, open but not separated, on a baking sheet, cut side up.

7. When the meatballs are done, remove them from the oven and set the broiler to high. Toast the rolls lightly under the broiler, 1 to 2 minutes, watching carefully so as to not let them burn. Give the garlic oil a quick stir and brush it onto the cut sides of the rolls. Place 1 meatball on each roll and top with 2 to 3 tablespoons of the marinara sauce.

DRESS IT UP

• **Loaded Jumbo Meatball Heroes** •

Make mega meatball sandwiches.

Make 12 smaller meatballs and bake them for 15 minutes. Split and toast 4 hero rolls and brush with the garlic oil. Stuff each hero with 3 meatballs, drizzle with marinara, and layer on sliced roasted red bell peppers and a handful of fresh arugula.

PAIR IT CHÂTEAU ROLLAN DE BY BORDEAUX BLEND

If you gave up French wines because you found them too dry, try this new one. It's a charming traditional blend of cabernet sauvignon, merlot, and cab franc that can really stand up to hearty meat dishes.

Thursday: 3:45 a.m.

The Skirt Steak

Angel Face just knocked on my bedroom door and said, "I think someone's in the house . . ."

Uhm, scary . . .

But he always thinks someone is in the house. We keep telling him the furnace clanks and makes funny noises, but he won't buy it, so we go through the flashlight thing, searching the corners of the house, the doorways, the windows. That part is for our benefit, because once someone wakes you up at 3:00 a.m. and says, "I think someone's in the house," you can't sleep either till you've checked.

So now I'm up and can't sleep. Ya know, it does sound like somebody's in the house. The Baby is fussing, too, so I'm writing and rocking . . . and listening for footsteps.

Writing with the right hand, rocking with the left—women have to be ambidextrous. It's a life skill. Last Tuesday, Hubby watched me open the oven and reach in with my right hand while holding The Baby in my left arm. For some reason, he got all nervous. "Jamie, let me take her, please."

I thought it was impressive, juggling The Baby and the brisket. And I was emulating a long line of Geller woman, too—all the way back to GG (Great-Grandma Martha). Legend has it that she always cooked with a baby in one hand. So it's a rite of passage, of sorts.

Okay, it's probably not the safest thing in the world. And it's certainly easier to have two hands when typing or cooking. But that's the least of my worries. It's my head—I'm always so distracted. Here I am, trying to make dinner and wondering what I'm missing at the office, while Angel Face is playing with the kitchen faucet and breaking the soap pump, and Miss Bouncy just asked me for scissors and glue for the fortieth time, and it's time to flip the skirt steak, and Bruiser has set up his parade of police cars, ambulances, fire engines, and dump trucks right in the middle of the kitchen floor, and Little Momma is reviewing her math out loud next to me: "1 + 10 is 11, 2 + 10 is 12, 3 + 10 is 13, 4 + 10 is 15 . . ." and I say, "Great," and she answers, *"No, Mommy, it's not!* It's 14. 5 + 10 is 15, 6 + 10 is 16 . . ."

Quick! Gotta flip the steak. Now you know why I cook like this: I have to. I always dream about casual, relaxed cooking with creative headspace on a calm, breezy spring day. It's gonna happen.

One day.

Not one day soon, though.

And certainly not today.

Skirt Steak with Salsa Verde

Kosher Status: Meat • Prep: 15 minutes • Cook: 20 minutes •
Rest: 5 minutes • Total: 40 minutes • Yield: 4 servings

I needed a dinner that would cook fast. And since I had skirt steak in the freezer, I came up with an idea for Skirt Steak with Salsa Verde. We like it sorta medium, so about 5 minutes per side does the trick, with a nice, slightly spicy (and I do mean slightly spicy) crust on the steak.

1 large onion, quartered

1 jalapeño chile, seeded and quartered

1 green chile (poblano, ancho, Anaheim— whatever you like), seeded and halved

10 medium tomatillos, husks removed, scrubbed and quartered

6 garlic cloves, smashed

6 tablespoons olive oil

Kosher salt

Juice of 2 limes

⅓ cup torn fresh cilantro, or 1½ tablespoons dried, plus additional fresh cilantro, for garnish (optional)

½ cup vegetable broth

1 teaspoon ground cumin

1 pound skirt steak

Freshly ground black pepper

1 lime, cut into 4 wedges, for garnish (optional)

Warm flour tortillas, for serving

1. Preheat the oven to 400°F.

2. To make the salsa verde, combine the onion, jalapeño, green chile, tomatillos, and garlic on a large baking sheet. Drizzle 5 tablespoons of the olive oil and sprinkle 1 teaspoon salt on the vegetables; toss to coat. Roast until the veggies are softened and slightly charred, 15 to 20 minutes. Transfer to a blender or food processor and add the lime juice, cilantro, broth, and cumin. Process until smooth, adding a little water to thin it down if the consistency is too thick. Set aside.

3. Heat a large sauté pan over high heat. Rub the steak with the remaining 1 tablespoon olive oil and lightly season it with salt and pepper. Sear the steak until nicely browned, 5 minutes per side for medium, or to your desired doneness. Let it rest 5 minutes.

4. Slice the steak ¼ inch thick, against the grain and on a slight diagonal. Fan the steak slices out on a serving board and garnish with the lime wedges and cilantro, if desired. Serve the warm tortillas and sauce on the side.

———————
VARIATION

Add an extra jalapeño for a kick.

DRESS IT DOWN

• **Mexican Skirt Steak Salad** •

Toss 1 cup corn kernels (thawed frozen or drained canned), 1 cup cooked black beans (rinsed and drained), 10 halved cherry tomatoes, and 3 cups chopped romaine with the sliced skirt steak and salsa verde to taste.

Another simple and complementary dressing idea is **Sweet Cilantro Dressing:** Whisk together 3 tablespoons extra virgin olive oil, 3 tablespoons lime juice, 2 tablespoons chopped fresh cilantro, and honey, salt, and pepper to taste.

———————
MAKE IT A MEAL

Serve the sliced steak over Spanish rice with the Mexican Salad on the side.

———————
PAIR IT HERZOG SPECIAL RESERVE ALEXANDER VALLEY CABERNET SAUVIGNON

Steak and cab just go well with each other—don't let the "verde" throw you off. The flavors in this wine aren't super ripe, so it will work nicely here.

Sunday: 10:20 a.m.

A Love Story

I've got a real love story to tell you.

No, not the one about how Hubby and I met and married in five minutes.

It's a different kind of love story: about my love affair with brisket.

As a beginner, I learned to love brisket because it will never do you wrong. You can do anything to it. Put it in the oven and forget about, leave it alone for hours on end, don't text, don't call, and it will never get back at you. It will stay sweet and obliging. Brisket has made me look like a good cook over and over and over again, even when I didn't deserve it. That's love.

There was only one time that I felt let down by brisket, and that made me sad—I'm talking moaning and tears, crawl-under-the-covers-I-can't-face-the-world kinda sad. I don't hold it against brisket. We've all fought with the loves of our lives at least once, right? Real love makes you do crazy things.

In this case, I let my brisket burn. Didn't mean to, but even brisket couldn't forgive. I must have blocked out the memory, details are somewhat hazy. The problem was really me, not the brisket . . .

First of all, I didn't follow a recipe. You can't even begin to know how many brisket recipes I have now, but this story happened a long time ago. I was young and stupid.

Arrogant, too. I didn't think I needed a measuring cup or spoon. I discovered, too late, that it's not a good idea to open a jumbo spice container and just turn the thing over into the food. So in the end, it was crazy overspiced. Then I emptied an entire bottle of some great wine in there, squirted in some ketchup, added some water, wrapped that baby up, stuck it in the oven, and then forgot about it. I mean literally, really, forgot about it. Or maybe I left it uncovered the entire time? Can't quite remember. It's too horrible.

I thought brisket loved me as I loved it. That it could never be hurt. With other meats, you have to stand by the oven, set four timers in the kitchen and then a few others in the rooms you may wander into, in case you can't hear the kitchen timer. You're married to your meat thermometer 'cause if you miss that moment of medium rare (or however you like it), all the dough you splurged on the roast might as well have gone up in flames with the meat.

Not brisket. It will wait for you. But if you forget your brisket entirely, and wake up the next morning with the smell of charcoal in the air, you can't expect it to be there for you as if nothing happened. It's like a date—there's only so long he'll wait for you before he figures out that you've stood him up.

Now this particular brisket debacle happened on the holiday of Purim. We were invited to a Purim party by our friends Shai and Aliza. They said they were expecting twenty-five people, and I said I'd bring the brisket. So here it is, Purim morning, and I just remembered the brisket I put in the oven last night. Smoke came out of the oven as I opened the door. Little brisket was lying there, forlorn, hard, and shrunken. All of its wine and sauce had evaporated. I cried, I looked at Hubby, he cried (about the money, not the brisket), and then he said, gently, "Don't worry, we'll buy some takeout."

"But I'm a cookbook author! How can I bring takeout to the party?" So Hubby came up with a clever story about how I'm pregnant and wasn't feeling well enough to cook meat, but we really wanted to bring something, so we bought it instead . . . and we convinced each other that it was not really a lie because, in fact, I *was* pregnant (so maybe my hormones messed with the brisket) and raw meat did majorly gross me out. *Shoin!* We had our excuse and that was that.

We decided to go ahead with our normal Purim route, first schlepping forty miles from our home in Monsey, New York, to Queens for a brunch Purim party at my stepmom-in-law's place. Then we'd be off to Aliza's for the afternoon Purim party. So after a lavish brunch, we drove home and headed to our favorite takeout place. Closed. So we went to another place, then another, then another, then a kosher supermarket, and they were *all* closed. They closed early for Purim!!! I am near convulsions. OMG, there's nowhere to even buy raw meat (another cut that I could cook quickly, or chicken, something, anything). Somebody, hand me a brown bag so I can breathe!

Hubby says to call Rabbi K, our neighbor, who runs the most popular takeout in town. Even if the store is closed, maybe, just maybe, he's still there and can open it just for us. He says no, they closed *hours* ago. He's at his own party, and a little tipsy. He yells to his wife, "Do we have any brisket left?" Then he comes back to the phone, jubilantly announcing that they have four or five slices, and we're welcome to them. Lovely man—but four or five slices? Just four or five? Doesn't he know I have to feed twenty-five people, for goodness' sake!

I'm near collapse, the clock is ticking, and Hubby suggests that we go home and doctor up our burned little meatball. When we took it out of the fridge, it looked even drier than we remembered it. I came up with a scientific plan to rejuvenate it with new sauce. We threw together more wine, more ketchup, some flour, more spices. It all pooled around the dry brisket, which still looked terrible. I tell Hubby I'm not going, I can't go.

But Aliza is relying on us to bring the main. So Hubby says, "Tell them I made it!" I was incredulous. He was willing to take the fall. What a man!

I guess this is also a love story about Hubby.

So I made a couple of bags of coleslaw, we wrapped up our twenty dry, wrinkled slices of brisket in bad sauce, and we headed over to Aliza's house. I couldn't even say anything to her. I didn't want to ruin her party. As I dumped the package on the counter, Hubby nonchalantly—and all smiles—pops his head into the kitchen and says, "Oh, I made the brisket . . . hope you like it . . . it was my first try!" Then, with a wink, he went off to mingle.

Well, as Hubby reminds me now, not a bite of that brisket was left over! I maintain that was because there was simply not enough food, not that it was so good. People will eat anything when they're hungry and a bit bombed.

This year, we're invited to Aliza's again, and I just have to redeem myself. I'm not sure if she'll let me volunteer to bring the brisket, but if she does, I'm going to bring the Garlic Honey Brisket you see here. My baby, my brisket, as long as you and I follow the instructions, and I don't go rogue, pregnant, or crazy again, we can do no wrong.

Garlic Honey Brisket

Kosher Status: Meat • Prep: 10 minutes • Marinate: 1 to 24 hours • Cook: 3 hours, 5 minutes •
Rest: 15 minutes • Total: 3 hours, 30 minutes, plus marinating time • Yield: 8 servings

*I developed this for Rosh Hashanah, pouncing on the chance to add honey to brisket.
It's a tender, rich entrée for the holiday, but not overly sweet. This is destined to be one
of your favorite briskets recipes; turn to it like an old friend whenever you need a good
showing.*

1 cup honey

½ cup Dijon mustard

8 garlic cloves, minced

¼ cup fresh orange juice

1 tablespoon fresh lemon juice

½ teaspoon red pepper flakes

½ teaspoon dried thyme

1 teaspoon kosher salt

½ teaspoon freshly ground black pepper

One 4-pound brisket

2 tablespoons olive oil

½ teaspoon all-purpose flour

1. Combine the honey, mustard, garlic, orange and lemon juices, red pepper flakes, thyme, salt, and pepper in a medium bowl, whisking to blend well. Place the brisket in a resealable plastic bag. Add the marinade, seal, and refrigerate at least 1 hour or up to 24 hours.

2. Preheat the oven to 350°F. Remove the brisket from the refrigerator 30 minutes before cooking to allow it to come to room temperature.

3. Heat the olive oil in an ovenproof Dutch oven over medium heat. Remove the brisket from the marinade, reserving the marinade. Add the brisket to the oil and sear it until nicely browned, about 5 minutes per side. Pour the reserved marinade over the brisket, cover, place it in the oven, and bake for 2 hours. Remove the lid and continue to cook until tender, 30 minutes to 1 hour more. Transfer the brisket to a cutting board and let rest at least 15 minutes before slicing against the grain.

4. Return the Dutch oven to the stovetop and bring the pan juices to a simmer. (Skim off some fat if there's more than 1 to 2 tablespoons in the pan.) Whisk in the flour and simmer until thickened, 3 to 5 minutes. Pour the gravy over the sliced brisket and serve.

DRESS IT DOWN
• Honey Brisket Pita Pockets •

Stuff slices of brisket in warmed pita bread with chopped crisp lettuce and drizzle with sauce.

PAIR IT BARKAN ALTITUDE SERIES + 624 RESERVE CABERNET SAUVIGNON

Deep garnet color, kind of intense, a bit sweet, sorta spicy—in short, a fab high-end cab to go with this elegant dish.

Argentinean Brisket with Chimichurri

Kosher Status: Meat • Prep: 15 minutes • Cook: 2 hours, 10 minutes • Rest: 15 minutes •
Total: 2 hours, 40 minutes • Yield: 6 to 8 servings

Originally from Argentina, chimichurri is a popular herb sauce used across Latin cook-ing. Basic "green" chimichurri is made from parsley, garlic, olive oil, oregano, and white or red vinegar. Tweak the sauce to your liking with some additional flavorings, such as cilantro, paprika, cumin, thyme, and lemon. It's traditionally served with grilled meat, but I also like it with white-fleshed fish or chicken, or by the spoonful. You know me by now, so you can't be surprised.

BRISKET

2 tablespoons paprika

2 tablespoons ground cumin

1 tablespoon kosher salt

1 tablespoon dried oregano

1 tablespoon garlic powder

1 teaspoon cayenne pepper

One 3½-pound brisket

3 tablespoons canola oil

1 cup beef broth, such as Manischewitz
   All Natural Beef Broth

2 tablespoons red wine vinegar

CHIMICHURRI

1½ cups chopped fresh parsley leaves

1 tablespoon dried oregano

3 garlic cloves, smashed

Grated zest and juice of 1 lemon

1 tablespoon red wine vinegar

1 teaspoon kosher salt

½ teaspoon freshly ground black pepper

1 teaspoon red pepper flakes (optional)

½ cup extra virgin olive oil

1. Preheat the oven to 375°F.

2. In a small bowl, combine the paprika, cumin, salt, oregano, garlic powder, and cayenne; mix well. Rub the mixture all over the meat. Heat the canola oil in a Dutch oven over medium-high heat and sear the meat for 3 to 5 minutes on each side. Add the broth and vinegar, cover, and transfer to the oven. Roast until tender, about 2 hours.

3. Transfer the brisket to a cutting board and let rest at least 15 minutes before slicing.

4. To make the chimichurri sauce, combine the parsley, oregano, garlic, lemon zest and juice, vinegar, salt, black pepper, and red pepper flakes, if using, in a food processor. Pulse to coarsely chop, stopping to scrape down the sides. With the processor running, slowly add the olive oil in a stream until you have a fairly smooth but still slightly chunky sauce.

5. Slice the brisket ¼ inch thick against the grain, transfer it to a serving plate, and drizzle the chimichurri sauce on top.

VARIATION

I use a lot of dried herbs because in a kosher kitchen, fresh herbs and some vegetables must be stringently checked for infestations. Most kosher supermarkets offer washed and checked parsley, so I use it often throughout the book. If you want to check your own oregano, you can omit the dried oregano from the sauce, use ½ cup fresh oregano leaves instead, and reduce the amount of fresh parsley to 1 cup.

QUICK TIP

If you're not serving the brisket immediately but want to slice it, store it in the fridge, and rewarm it later, add 1 cup water and one 8-ounce can tomato sauce and double the beef broth to 2 cups and vinegar to ¼ cup before baking so you will have a sauce to submerge your sliced brisket in.

DRESS IT DOWN/MAKE IT A MEAL

• **Pulled Argentinean Brisket and Rice** •

Shred the meat and toss with chimichurri and 2 cups cooked rice. Serve with warmed flour tortillas.

PAIR IT FLECHAS DE LOS ANDES GRAN MALBEC

Make this Argentinean dish feel right at home with this super Argentinean wine.

Beer-Braised Holiday Top of the Rib

Kosher Status: Meat • Prep: 10 minutes • Cook: 4 hours • Rest: 15 minutes •
Total: 4 hours, 25 minutes • Yield: 8 to 10 servings

I'm a big fan of meat cuts you can't mess up. (No snide cracks, please. I'm only being honest.) As a superforgiving piece of meat, top of the rib is right up there with brisket. Like twins—some people can tell them apart, but you can swap one for the other in any recipe without making adjustments. So it's my second-best friend in the meat aisle.

Like brisket, top of the rib is even better when cooked in advance. Let the meat and veg cool in the pan. Slice the meat against the grain, submerge it in the sauce, cover, and refrigerate or freeze. Bring it to room temperature before reheating, covered, in a 350°F oven until warmed through, about 30 minutes.

1 tablespoon sweet or hot smoked
  paprika

1 tablespoon dark brown sugar

1 tablespoon ground cumin

1 tablespoon instant coffee granules

1 teaspoon kosher salt

1 teaspoon freshly ground black pepper

½ teaspoon onion powder

½ teaspoon garlic powder

One 5-pound top of the rib

3 tablespoons olive oil

Three 12-ounce cans or bottles dark lager
  beer

1 garlic head, halved horizontally

1 pound small parsnips, peeled and
  halved lengthwise

1 pound peeled baby carrots with greens

1. Preheat the oven to 325°F.

2. Combine the paprika, brown sugar, cumin, coffee, salt, pepper, onion powder, and garlic powder in a small bowl and stir to mix. Pat the meat dry with paper towels and rub the spice mixture all over.

3. Heat the olive oil in a large Dutch oven over medium-high heat. Sear the meat until nicely browned, 4 to 6 minutes per side. Pour the beer over the meat, cover, and transfer to the oven.

4. Roast for 2 hours. Flip the meat over. Add the garlic, parsnips, and carrots. Cover and roast until the meat and vegetables are tender, about 1½ hours more. Transfer the meat to a cutting board and let rest at least 15 minutes before slicing. Transfer the vegetables and garlic to a platter, reserving the pan sauce.

5. The fat should easily separate and rise to the top of the pan sauce. Skim off and discard all but a tablespoon or two of the fat with a large spoon. Reduce the pan sauce over medium-high heat until thickened, 10 to 15 minutes.

6. Slice the meat thinly, against the grain. Arrange the slices on the platter with the vegetables. Drizzle with the sauce. Serve immediately with remaining sauce in a gravy boat on the side.

QUICK TIPS

When applying spice rubs, lay meat on butcher's paper or a large piece of foil on your counter for easy application and cleanup.

It's not always easy to find the baby carrots with the greens. You can replace them with 1 pound baby carrots without the greens or 1 pound small carrots, peeled and halved lengthwise.

If you want beautiful thin slices and don't want the meat to shred on you, you need a nice sharp knife, and you must let the meat rest and cool for at least 15 minutes. If you're not serving the meat immediately, allow to cool completely, or even in the fridge overnight, before slicing.

VARIATION

Add a few tablespoons of tomato paste for more depth of flavor.

DRESS IT DOWN

• Slow Cooker Beer-Braised Top of the Rib •

Omit the veggies.

After searing the meat, transfer to a slow cooker and cover with 3 cups (2 cans) beer. Cook on high for 4 hours or low for 8 hours. Transfer to a cutting board and let rest for at least 15 minutes before slicing. Transfer the braising liquid to a medium saucepan, skim off the fat, and cook the liquid over medium-high heat until thickened, 10 to 15 minutes. Pour over the brisket to serve.

PAIR IT YATIR RED BLEND

A ripe, juicy red for this saucy meat.

Loaded Burgers with Special Sauce

Kosher Status: Meat • Prep: 15 minutes • Cook: 30 minutes • Rest: 5 minutes •
Total: 50 minutes • Yield: 8 burgers

The king of your BBQ, this jumbo baby is a two-hander. I used to put the onion rings on the side—but that's a thing of the past! Hubby always loads them right onto his burger, and now everyone else—even the kiddies who can't open their mouths wide enough—do it, too.

Dressing a burger is a very personal matter, you know. Whenever we take the family out and order burgers, it's a real scene: We all open our "standard" burgers and create a central toppings bar. Little Momma and I split the tomatoes; I take all the onions; lettuce is going in and out; Hubby and I go crazy adding tons of mayo. Everyone indulges in whatever specific topping means "perfect burger" to them.

I just noticed that I take everything. Oh, and the kids want extra ketchup and fries to pile on their burgers (just like Hubby), but that doesn't count—they're kids.

2 tablespoons olive oil	Freshly ground black pepper
1 medium onion, diced	2 to 3 tablespoons canola oil
½ cup mayonnaise	8 sesame buns, split and toasted
½ cup sweet pickle relish	8 Boston lettuce leaves
½ cup ketchup	8 heirloom tomato slices
½ cup pareve ranch dressing	2 large dill pickles, thinly sliced
3 pounds ground beef	8 large frozen onion rings, prepared
Kosher salt	according to package directions

1. Heat the olive oil in a medium sauté pan over medium-high heat. Add the onion and sauté until caramelized and translucent, 10 to 12 minutes. Let cool slightly.

2. While the onion is cooking, make the special sauce: In a large bowl, combine the mayonnaise, pickle relish, ketchup, and dressing. Stir to mix well.

3. Preheat the grill to high.

4. Place the onions, ground beef, and ½ cup special sauce in a large bowl. Mix lightly with your fingertips to combine. Divide the mixture into 8 equal portions and form them

into patties. Season both sides lightly with salt and pepper and brush them with oil. Cook the burgers for 3 to 4 minutes per side for medium rare, or to desired doneness. Remove the burgers from the grill and let rest for 5 minutes. (To cook on the stovetop, heat a grill pan over high heat, brush the burgers with oil, and cook as directed, or heat the oil until shimmering in a sauté pan or griddle over high heat and cook as instructed.)

5. To assemble, place each burger on the bottom half of a bun. Top with 1 lettuce leaf, 1 to 2 tablespoons special sauce, 1 tomato slice, pickle slices, 1 onion ring, and the top of the bun. Serve immediately.

6. Store any remaining special sauce in a resealable container in the refrigerator for up to 1 week.

DRESS IT DOWN

• **Unloaded Burgers** •

If the burger is good enough, it can speak for itself.

No need to overaccessorize perfection if you're in the mood for something simpler, more manageable. Make this an everyday burger by serving a patty straight up on a bun with lettuce, tomato, and special sauce.

MAKE IT A MEAL

Serve with a hefty side of Baked Sweet Potato Chips (page 66).

PAIR IT HERZOG SPECIAL RESERVE NAPA VALLEY CABERNET SAUVIGNON

The ripe fruit flavors in this beautiful cabernet sauvignon will bring out the best in juicy burgers.

Balsamic London Broil

Kosher Status: Meat • Prep: 10 minutes • Marinate: 3 to 6 hours • Cook: 50 minutes •
Rest: 5 minutes • Total: 4 to 7 hours • Yield: 8 to 10 servings

---

Oooh, this is one beautiful recipe. Just look at the photo and let your mouth water. That shiny, vinegary sear on the meat is a magnificent gift to your thousands of little tiny taste buds. You have about 10,000 taste buds, in fact. Really. But they aren't all on your tongue. Some are under the tongue, or on the roof of your mouth, even in your cheeks, and on your lips. Could I make this up?

No, I'm not like one of those Jeopardy! *types, with all kinds of random facts memorized (I used to watch* Jeopardy! *with Uputzi all the time, but apparently I had zero retention.)*

Google is great.

One 2½-pound London broil

5 garlic cloves, minced

¾ cup balsamic vinegar

¼ cup plus 1 tablespoon olive oil

2 medium red onions

2 medium yellow onions

8 medium shallots

Kosher salt

Freshly ground black pepper

1. Combine the meat with the garlic, vinegar, and ¼ cup of the olive oil in a large resealable plastic bag. Marinate in the refrigerator for 3 to 6 hours.

2. Preheat the oven to 400°F. Remove the meat from the refrigerator so it can come to room temperature.

3. Cut the onions into quarters and halve the shallots. On a large rimmed baking sheet, toss together the onions, shallots, and the remaining 1 tablespoon olive oil. Season with salt and pepper and roast until tender, 40 to 50 minutes.

4. After the veggies have been roasting for 20 minutes, pour off and discard the marinade from the meat. Pat the meat dry and season it all over with salt and pepper. Heat a large ovenproof skillet over medium-high heat and sear the meat until nicely browned, about 5 minutes per side. Transfer the skillet to the oven and cook alongside the vegetables

until an instant-read thermometer inserted into the meat reads 130°F for medium rare, 12 to 18 minutes. Remove the meat and veggies from the oven. Let the meat rest for 5 minutes before slicing.

5. To serve, place the sliced meat on a large platter surrounded by the roasted onions.

DRESS IT DOWN

• Oven-Roasted Balsamic London Broil and Potatoes •

For a more informal meal, cut up the London broil to roast it.

Line 2 baking sheets with foil and spray with cooking spray. Preheat the oven to 400°F. Cut the London broil into 2 x 1-inch pieces. Toss with half the marinade in a large bowl and spread in a single layer on a prepared baking sheet. Toss the onions and 1 pound halved fingerling potatoes with the remaining marinade in the same large bowl. Spread in a single layer on the second prepared baking sheet. Roast the onions and potatoes until the potatoes are tender, 35 to 45 minutes. About 10 minutes before the potatoes are done, roast the London broil 6 minutes for rare, 8 minutes for medium, or 10 to 12 minutes for well. Time it so the meat, onions, and potatoes are all done at the same time.

PAIR IT TZUBA METSUDA RESERVE BLEND

Red meat loves red wine! This merlot and cab blend is just right.

Chunky Red Chili

Kosher Status: Meat • Prep: 10 minutes • Cook: 2 hours, 20 minutes •
Total: 2½ hours • Yield: 8 servings

I like soup in a bread bowl, not just 'cause it looks good, but also 'cause I love eating the soup-soaked bread at the end, like dessert after the meal. And here's a peek into how my mind works: Just love soup in a bread bowl, hmmm, stew would also be good in a bread bowl, wait . . . how about chili? *and voilà—this baby made its debut in a boule! Watch how the bowl makes this dish decidedly cozy, uncomplicated, and quite presentable.*

This chili is nice and thick; for a soupier chili, don't drain the plum tomatoes.

For a quick, casual lunch or dinner, serve the chili with your favorite tortilla chips. For a treat we love Tostitos Scoops, great for chili and dip delivery, bought by the big bagful at Costco. Of course there are always carrot sticks, but it's not so easy to balance your chili on a stick.

3 tablespoons olive oil

1 pound ground beef

1 pound beef stew meat, cut into ½-inch
  chunks

1 large onion, coarsely chopped

1 medium green bell pepper, ribs and
  seeds removed, coarsely chopped

One 28-ounce can whole plum tomatoes,
  drained

One 8-ounce can tomato sauce

One 15½-ounce can red kidney beans,
  rinsed and drained

One 15½-ounce can black beans, rinsed
  and drained

3 tablespoons packed light brown sugar

2 tablespoons Worcestershire sauce

2 tablespoons red wine vinegar

1 tablespoon chili powder

2 teaspoons dried basil

2 teaspoons ground cumin

2 teaspoons kosher salt

2 bay leaves

Tortilla chips, for serving (optional)

1. Heat 1 tablespoon of the olive oil in a large pot or Dutch oven over medium-high heat. Add the ground beef and cook, breaking up the beef, until nicely browned, about 8 minutes. Remove the ground beef with a slotted spoon and set aside in a large bowl

or plate. Pour another tablespoon of oil into the pot; when hot, add the stew meat and cook until nicely browned on all sides, about 8 minutes. Remove the stew meat with a slotted spoon and add it to the ground beef. Pour off the fat and any accumulated juices from the pot.

2. Heat the remaining 1 tablespoon oil in the pot. Add the onion and pepper, and cook until slightly softened, about 4 minutes. Return the meats to the pot and add the tomatoes, tomato sauce, kidney beans, black beans, sugar, Worcestershire, vinegar, chili powder, basil, cumin, salt, and bay leaves. Stir well to mix, breaking up the whole tomatoes with the back of a wooden spoon. Bring to a boil, reduce the heat to a simmer, and cook, covered, until the stew meat is soft, about 2 hours. Remove and discard the bay leaves. Divide the chili among 8 bowls and serve warm, with chips on the side, if you like.

DRESS IT UP

• Chili Bread Bowls •

Serve the chili in a sourdough bread bowl.

Cut ¼ inch off the top of a small boule and scoop out the insides, leaving about ½ inch all around for stability. Fill the boule with the chili, and garnish with a dollop of soy sour cream and chopped scallions.

VARIATION

Add a chopped jalapeño chile for some kick.

MAKE IT A MEAL

Heap the chili into taco shells with shredded lettuce, diced avocado, a dollop of soy sour cream, and some hot sauce or jarred sliced jalapeño chile rings if you can stand it.

PAIR IT SEGAL'S FUSION RED BLEND

You'll need a cool head with this dish. This is an easy-drinking red blend.

Somewhat Sephardic Chulent

Kosher Status: Meat • Prep: 15 minutes • Cook: 12 hours, 15 minutes to 18 hours •
Total: 12½ hours to 18 hours • Yield: 10 to 15 servings

Plan ahead: Chulent cooks for the better part of a day, so if you're not making this for Shabbos you'll have to schedule your weekday craving.

I believe I was Sephardic in a past life. If you're reading this book in order, you know that I've said that before. I'll probably say it again, too. Who reads a cookbook in order, anyway?

And I really believe this, so you need to know it. Do I have proof? Well, my Romanian/Hungarian grandfather had a sorta olive complexion, so that's one proof. And I picked up Spanish pretty well in high school—that's my second proof. And I love the food.

But I must call this Somewhat *Sephardic Chulent 'cause in this life I am totally Ashkenazic. Chulent in Ashkenaz culture is essentially a European beef stew including beans, barley, potatoes, and onions seasoned with S + P. Variations in ingredients and spicing are usually determined by which shtetl your family called home and the preferences of the cook. Sephardic chulent, known for its spiciness and distinctive flavor profile—including garlic, cumin, cinnamon, allspice, and ginger—often includes a combo of rice, wheat berries, and chickpeas in place of beans and barley, chicken instead of meat, and the addition of whole raw eggs (in the shell!). Though the basic recipe was given to me by my authentically Sephardic friend Miriam (who, like most Sephardim, can count back every generation of her ancestry to Moses), it did pass through my hands. Who knows what Ashkenazic energy I may have unwittingly imparted along with my addition of brown rice? Now that I've tampered with it, Miriam officially wants no part of this recipe . . .*

1 tablespoon olive oil

1 large onion, chopped

4 garlic cloves, chopped

2 large sweet potatoes, peeled and cut in
  2-inch pieces

2 pounds flanken, cut into large chunks
  between the bones

1½ teaspoons kosher salt

1 teaspoon freshly ground black pepper

4 veal marrow bones (about 1 pound)

1 cup brown rice

1 cup dried chickpeas

1 teaspoon paprika

1 teaspoon ground turmeric

½ teaspoon ground cumin

½ teaspoon cayenne pepper

½ teaspoon ground cinnamon

½ teaspoon ground allspice

4 large eggs in their shells, washed

1 quart chicken broth, such as Manischewitz All Natural Chicken Broth

1. Heat the olive oil in a large sauté pan over medium heat. Add the onion and sauté until golden brown and very soft, about 15 minutes. Add the garlic and sauté until fragrant and soft, 1 to 2 minutes. Remove from the heat.

2. Line the bottom of a slow cooker with the sweet potatoes. Season the meat with the salt and pepper and place on top of the potatoes. Add the marrow bones and the sautéed onion and garlic. Sprinkle in the rice and gently shake the slow cooker so that the rice settles into all the crevices. Add the chickpeas and repeat the gentle shake. Sprinkle with the paprika, turmeric, cumin, cayenne, cinnamon, and allspice. Gently nestle in the eggs. Pour in the chicken broth; add water if necessary to just cover everything.

3. Cook on low for 12 to 18 hours. If the liquid all gets absorbed and it looks as if your chulent is burning or drying out, or the top is not cooking, add boiling water as necessary to keep the contents barely covered.

4. Just before serving, remove and peel the eggs. Scoop the chulent into individual bowls or a covered serving dish. Cut the eggs into quarters and arrange them on top of the chulent or in a bowl alongside.

TIME-SAVER

You can skip sautéing the onions and garlic and just add them raw to the slow cooker.

VARIATION

Swap in russet potatoes for the sweet potatoes—or use one of each. Add chicken legs in place of some or all of the flanken.

• Puff Pastry Sephardic Chulent Cups •

Place individual chulent servings in puff pastry shells.

Bake the shells according to the package directions. Just before serving, fill each warm shell with a few spoonfuls of chulent and top with half a hard-cooked egg sliced on the diagonal or a single egg slice. Garnish with chopped fresh cilantro leaves, if desired. To make ahead: Once baked, the puff pastry shells will keep for 24 to 48 hours at room temperature in a tightly covered container. Warm them in an oven, in a warming drawer, or on a hot plate, loosely covered, just before filling and serving.

MAKE IT A MEAL

I love heavy sticky chulent with a light fresh salad. A totally unexpected and nontraditional side, but a great contrast and complement to the chulent: Raw Root Vegetable Salad (page 108). If you're asking me, that's what I would want. Or you could always go a safer route and pair it with the Pastrami-Fry Salad (page 86)—that's what Hubby would want.

PAIR IT DOMAINE NETOFA RED

Okay, full disclosure: Sephardim don't call this dish chulent, Ashkenazim do. The Ashkenazic word is derived from an Old French term *chaloir* (to warm) and further derived from the modern French *chaud* (warm, hot) and *lent* (slow), because this stew is set to cook prior to Shabbos on Friday and kept simmering until it's served on Shabbos afternoon. The Sephardim call it *chamin*, which also means hot in Aramaic, the language of the Talmud.

Whether you call it chulent or chamin, you want to pair its hearty flavors with a full-bodied red wine, so let's go with a wine modeled after authentic French Rhône red blends.

Daddy's *Mititei* (Romanian Garlic Meat Sausages)

Kosher Status: Meat • Prep: 20 minutes • Cook: 15 to 20 minutes • Marinate: 24 hours to 48 hours • Total: 40 minutes, plus marinating time • Yield: 15 sausages

I really should stop griping about being disadvantaged when it comes to cooking DNA. Fact is, Daddy is one of the best cooks on the planet. What gives his Mititei *authentically Transylvanian flavor is the loads and loads of garlic—not at all for the faint of heart.*

Warning: If you don't like garlic, this recipe is not for you. If you just kinda like garlic, this recipe is not for you.

If you love garlic, you will hug this book, hug me when you see me, tear out this recipe and frame it on your wall, ask for my dad's number so you can call him, thank him, and arrange for a time to meet him in person, and hug him, too.

When I was growing up in Philly, we had Indian neighbors, Sudah and Jayraj. Vegetarians. But they abandoned their principles whenever Daddy cooked Mititei. *Mommy would call them in advance, so they could mentally and emotionally prepare for the experience.*

My (Grand)Ma loved these sausages, too, which was a real surprise because she was a superb cook who rarely liked anybody else's food. Daddy's Mititei *and his Potato Kigel (page 91) were the exceptions.*

The secrets to this dish are the club soda (for fluffiness), ground caraway, loads of garlic, and letting the meat marinate overnight. Did I mention the garlic?

By the way, tradition dictates that these are served with mustard, not ketchup.

2 pounds ground beef (not too lean)

2½ teaspoons ground caraway

¼ teaspoon kosher salt

¼ teaspoon freshly ground black pepper

1 large garlic head

½ teaspoon baking soda

2 cups club soda or seltzer

Canola oil

Spicy mustard, for serving

1. Place the beef in a large bowl. Add the caraway, salt, and pepper. Crush the garlic cloves with a garlic press and add them to the bowl.

2. Combine the baking soda with 1 cup of the club soda or seltzer in a small bowl and whisk to dissolve. Add to the meat and mix well by hand to fully incorporate. Once fully

absorbed, mix in an additional ½ cup club soda or seltzer. Once that is fully incorporated, add the remaining ½ cup. Continue to mix by hand for 5 minutes.

3. Cover the bowl with plastic wrap and let marinate in the refrigerator for at least 24 hours or up to 48 hours.

4. When you are ready to cook, preheat the grill to high.

5. Oil your hands, scoop ⅓ cup of the meat mixture, and form it into an oblong sausage about 3 inches long by 1 inch wide. Place the sausage on a plate or baking sheet. Repeat with the remaining meat mixture to form 15 sausages total. Lower the heat to medium and place the sausages on the grill. Grill for about 15 minutes, gently flipping and turning them often so they don't burn and are evenly cooked through, until an instant-read thermometer registers the temperature at 160°F. (To cook on the stovetop, heat a grill pan over high heat, brush the *Mititei* with canola oil, lower the heat to medium, and cook as directed, or heat about 2 tablespoons canola oil until shimmering in a sauté pan or griddle over high heat, lower the heat to medium, and cook as directed.)

6. Serve with mustard.

VARIATION

My dad says, ideally, for "real" *Mititei*, use ground neck meat with 200 grams (in English that's a little less than half a pound) of beef fat added in. Since I can't even begin to go there, I just buy 2 pounds of ground beef for the pride of Romanian cuisine.

MAKE IT A MEAL

Serve it with my father's other specialty, Daddy's Deep-Dish Potato Kigel/Kugel (page 91).

PAIR IT SHILOH LEGEND

Tame the garlic beast with a fruity, refreshing, yummy red blend.

• Fresh and Fruity *Mititei* •

Sweeten the pot.

Serve the *Mititei* with **Peach Salsa:** Combine 4 ripe peaches or nectarines, pitted and diced (about 1½ cups); 1 small red onion, thinly sliced; 20 cherry tomatoes, halved; the juice of 1 lemon; 2 tablespoons extra virgin olive oil; 2 tablespoons torn fresh basil leaves or 2 teaspoons dried; 2 tablespoons torn fresh mint leaves (optional); 1 tablespoon honey; and ½ teaspoon kosher salt in a medium bowl. Toss well and serve on top or on the side of the warm *Mititei*.

"Buttery" Crusted Beef Pot Pie

Kosher Status: Meat • Prep: 15 minutes • Cook: 50 minutes • Total: 1 hour, 5 minutes • Yield: 9 servings

Sometimes shortcuts are better than the long way, and this toast crust is a perfect example. It's crunchy and melt-in-your-mouth all at the same time—really incredible. This pot pie is one of the ultimate comfort foods of our time, made easy.

Cooking spray

2 tablespoons olive oil

1 large onion, diced

2 medium carrots, peeled and diced

2 medium parsnips, peeled and diced

1 large russet potato, peeled and diced

1½ pounds ground beef

¼ cup tomato paste

1 garlic clove, chopped

1 cup frozen peas, thawed and drained

1 cup beef broth, such as Manischewitz
   All Natural Beef Broth

2 teaspoons kosher salt

1½ teaspoons freshly ground black
   pepper

1½ tablespoons margarine

Nine ½-inch baguette slices

1. Preheat the oven to 400°F. Spray an 8-inch square baking dish with cooking spray.

2. Heat the oil in a large sauté pan over medium-high heat. Sauté the onion, carrots, parsnips, and potato until lightly browned, about 10 minutes. Add the beef and sauté until browned, about 8 minutes more. Drain the excess fat. Add the tomato paste and garlic and sauté 2 minutes more. Stir in the peas, broth, salt, and pepper and remove from the heat.

3. Transfer to the prepared baking dish. Spread the margarine on the bread (add more slices if they'll fit!). Lay the bread on top of the beef mixture, "buttered" side up. Bake until the bread is golden brown, 25 to 30 minutes. To serve, scoop so each serving has a slice of crusty bread and a nice portion of beef filling.

VARIATION

This could also be fun and easy, dressed up in individual ovenproof bowls, topped with a slice of "buttery" bread—kinda looks like French onion soup, sans the cheese of course.

QUICK TIP

I like to do a small (½-inch) dice on my veg; they cook nicely and uniformly and look great, too. The pieces aren't too big, won't overwhelm the ground beef, and closely match the size of the peas.

DRESS IT DOWN/MAKE IT A MEAL
• Mashed Potato Beef Cottage Pie •

It's already a meal, but for a more informal comfort-food dinner, top the pie with mashed potatoes instead of crusty bread.

Omit the potato from the recipe. Peel and dice 2 pounds of potatoes and boil until tender. Drain and mash with 6 tablespoons margarine and 1 teaspoon kosher salt, or more to taste. Spread the mashed potatoes over the beef mixture and bake until the potatoes are golden brown on top, 25 to 30 minutes.

PAIR IT GAMLA RESERVE CABERNET SAUVIGNON

This one's a fave of *Wine Enthusiast* magazine, and it's my fave with this beefy dish.

Mediterranean Lamb Skewers

Kosher Status: Meat • Prep: 25 minutes • Cook: 35 minutes • Total: 1 hour • Yield: 15 skewers

Remember Chanie's Ktzitzot recipe (page 33)? This dish is its cousin, mostly because of the cumin and cinnamon. Westerners think of cinnamon as mainly a dessert spice (think buns, cake, cookies). Yet with true Middle Eastern flair, Moroccans like to pair cinnamon with meat—and in Israel you see it a lot with chicken, lamb, and beef schwarma. Took me a while, but I got comfy with that concept, adding cinnamon to ground lamb to create these uberflavorful, utterly beautiful kebabs.

2 slices whole wheat bread

1 pound ground lamb

1 small red onion, diced

¼ cup chopped fresh parsley

1 tablespoon red wine vinegar

1 teaspoon ground cumin

½ teaspoon ground cinnamon

½ teaspoon dried oregano

½ teaspoon kosher salt

½ teaspoon grated lemon zest

2 tablespoons olive oil

Hummus or tahini, for serving (optional)

EQUIPMENT

Fifteen 6-inch bamboo or wood skewers, soaked in water for 1 hour

1. Place the bread in a small bowl, completely cover with water, and soak for 20 minutes.

2. Remove the bread from the water and squeeze out as much water as possible. Place the bread in a large bowl and add the lamb, onion, parsley, vinegar, cumin, cinnamon, oregano, salt, and lemon zest. Mix lightly with your fingertips until well combined. Divide into 15 portions and shape each into a ball. Press each ball around a skewer, gently shaping it into a 2- to 3-inch-long tube.

3. Heat the olive oil in a large sauté pan over medium-high heat. Brown the skewers on all sides. If all the skewers won't fit in one pan, use two pans rather than cooking in batches. Reduce the heat to medium. Continue cooking, turning often, until nicely browned and cooked through, 8 to 10 minutes. Serve with a dollop of hummus or tahini, if you like.

Use ground beef in place of the lamb.

DRESS IT DOWN
• Mediterranean Lamb Meatloaf •

Mix all the ingredients (except the olive oil) with 1 large egg. Shape into a 6 x 3-inch loaf on a greased baking sheet. Bake at 400°F for 35 minutes. Let rest 5 minutes before slicing and serving with hummus or tahini.

MAKE IT A MEAL

Perfect with **Pine Nut–Raisin Couscous:** Combine 2½ cups cooked whole wheat couscous with ¼ cup toasted pine nuts, ¼ cup raisins, 2 tablespoons chopped fresh chives, and 2 tablespoons chopped fresh parsley in a large bowl. Toss with 2 tablespoons red wine vinegar and 2 tablespoons extra virgin olive oil. Serve at room temperature with warm kebabs or a slice of meatloaf.

PAIR IT BINYAMINA RESERVE SHIRAZ

The earthy flavors of the lamb and shiraz make them a natural pairing.

Classic Tuna Noodle Casserole

Kosher Status: Dairy • Prep: 10 minutes • Cook: 45 minutes • Total: 55 minutes • Yield: 10 servings

I just like this dish—it reminds me of the tuna casserole at summer camp. I see warm tuna and I think lakes, campfires, and color wars. The dish was too American to be found in my house, and certainly not in my grandparents' kitchen (though they did embrace Thanksgiving). No hot lunches at my school, so I had to wait for summer camp for this delicacy. Would you ever think this would be called a delicacy? Eat it with a big bag of chips for fine dining.

Cooking spray

One 1-pound box rotini or bow tie pasta, cooked al dente and drained well

Two 6-ounce cans chunk tuna in water, drained and flaked

1 cup frozen peas, thawed

6 tablespoons (¾ stick) unsalted butter

¼ cup all-purpose flour

3 cups whole milk

One 8-ounce bag shredded cheddar cheese (about 2 cups)

¾ cup sour cream

3 tablespoons country Dijon mustard

1 teaspoon kosher salt

1½ teaspoons onion powder

1½ teaspoons paprika

½ teaspoon freshly ground black pepper

½ teaspoon garlic powder

½ cup seasoned dry bread crumbs

½ cup shredded Parmesan cheese

1. Preheat the oven to 350°F. Spray a 3-quart casserole dish with cooking spray.

2. Toss the pasta, tuna, and peas in a large bowl.

3. Melt 4 tablespoons of the butter in a medium saucepan over medium heat. Gradually whisk in the flour until smooth. Cook until the mixture turns light brown and is bubbly around the edges, about 3 minutes. Add the milk in a slow, steady stream, whisking continually. Continue to stir over medium heat until the sauce begins to thicken, 8 to 10 minutes. Add the cheddar and cook, stirring continually, until a smooth sauce comes together, about 2 minutes. Remove from the heat and stir in the sour cream, mustard, salt, onion powder, paprika, pepper, and garlic powder.

4. Pour the cheese sauce over the pasta mixture and stir until well combined. Transfer to the prepared casserole dish. Combine the bread crumbs, Parmesan, and remaining 2 tablespoons butter in a small bowl and sprinkle on top of the casserole. Bake until golden brown and bubbly, 25 to 30 minutes.

DRESS IT UP

• Creamy Salmon and Tuna Noodle Pie •

Substitute one 6-ounce can drained and flaked salmon for 1 can of tuna and one 4-ounce log goat cheese (for a bit of tang!) for the sour cream. Omit the onion powder. Add 1 cup sliced cremini mushrooms, 2 tablespoons chopped fresh dill, and ½ small red onion, diced and sautéed. For a pretty pie presentation, bake in a 9-inch springform pan and serve in wedges.

MAKE IT A MEAL

This dish needs a light fresh side like a simple green or tomato salad drizzled with olive oil, lemon, and salt and pepper.

PAIR IT ALEXANDER LIZA CHARDONNAY

Whenever you've got cheesy, buttery, or creamy in a recipe, think chardonnay. This one's a yum.

Teriyaki Scallion Rainbow Trout

Kosher Status: Pareve • Prep: 10 minutes • Cook: 35 minutes • Total: 45 minutes • Yield: 6 servings

I learned about trout from Uputzi, who would make rainbow trout for us as a special treat. My initial recipe list for this book ran about twenty-five recipes too long. So I had a few friends look it over, each suggesting which recipes to cut. Until one of my supposed friends suggested I nix the trout recipe—said she'd never eaten it. Say it ain't so! I'm not even sure how to talk to someone who's never tasted trout. I refused to rethink including a trout recipe that I firmly feel should make regular appearances at your dinner table. In fact, I'm making it tonight for my family. It's one of my staples, and my kiddies love it!

½ cup all-purpose flour

Six 8-ounce skin-on rainbow trout fillets

1 teaspoon kosher salt

4 tablespoons olive oil

10 scallions, green parts, coarsely chopped

3 garlic cloves, minced

1 cup teriyaki sauce

1 lime, cut into wedges, for garnish

1. Preheat the oven to 200°F.

2. Spread the flour onto a large plate. Season the fillets with the salt and coat them with a thin layer of flour on both sides.

3. Heat 1 tablespoon of the olive oil in a large skillet over medium heat. Add 2 fillets and cook until a nice golden crust forms, about 4 minutes. Flip and cook 4 minutes more. Transfer the fillets to a large platter and keep warm in the oven. Wipe out the skillet with a paper towel. Repeat twice, heating the oil before adding the fillets each time.

4. Once all the fish is cooked and in the warm oven, wipe out the sauté pan and add the remaining tablespoon oil. Reduce the heat to medium-low. Add the scallions and sauté until just wilted, about 4 minutes. Add the garlic and sauté until fragrant, 15 to 30 seconds. Add the teriyaki sauce and cook until warm, about 5 minutes. Pour the sauce over the fish and serve with the lime wedges.

Just drizzle the fried fillets with warm teriyaki sauce and garnish with fresh chopped scallions.

• **Whole Stuffed Rainbow Trout** •

Present a whole fish to really get the attention of your guests.

Stuff a cleaned whole trout with thinly sliced red onion, thin lime rounds, whole cilantro sprigs, and salt and pepper. Place on a well-greased baking sheet and drizzle teriyaki sauce on top. Sprinkle with minced garlic and grated fresh ginger. Bake at 400°F until the fish is opaque, 20 to 25 minutes.

A beautiful, fruity white that goes down easy with fish.

Blackened Tilapia Tacos
with Cumin Avocado Sauce

Kosher Status: Dairy • Prep: 15 minutes • Cook: 15 minutes • Total: 30 minutes • Yield: 8 tacos

When you're writing a cookbook, you eat funny things like glazes and fish tacos for breakfast. Really, they were so good that I woke up dreaming about them and could find no good reason not to have them instead of cereal. I'm sure in some part of the world I would fit right in.

CUMIN AVOCADO SAUCE

½ cup sour cream

1 teaspoon ground cumin

½ teaspoon kosher salt

½ teaspoon freshly ground black pepper

Juice of 1 lime

1 medium avocado, pitted, peeled, and chopped

TILAPIA

2 teaspoons paprika

2 teaspoons onion powder

2 teaspoons garlic powder

2 teaspoons dried oregano

2 teaspoons cayenne pepper

2 teaspoons kosher salt

2 teaspoons freshly ground black pepper

Four 8-ounce tilapia fillets, cut in half lengthwise

1 tablespoon olive oil

8 small flour tortillas

1. For the sauce, puree the sour cream, cumin, salt, pepper, lime juice, and avocado in a blender. With the blender running, slowly add ¼ to ⅓ cup water to achieve a dip-like consistency. Refrigerate until serving.

2. On a flat plate, mix together the paprika, onion and garlic powders, oregano, cayenne, salt, and black pepper. Press the fish fillets into the spice rub to evenly coat on both sides.

3. Heat the olive oil in a large sauté pan over medium-high heat. Add the fish and cook until blackened and cooked through, 5 to 6 minutes per side. Place each fillet in a warmed tortilla and top with a generous dollop of the sauce.

The sauce can be made up to 48 hours in advance and refrigerated; if the sauce browns, just remove the top layer.

DRESS IT UP/MAKE IT A MEAL

• Tilapia Tacos with Apple Cabbage Slaw •

Fish tacos have a fresh and super-satisfying appeal.

Add my apple slaw and you, too, will be eating this for breakfast, lunch, and dinner. Toss together 2 cups shredded green cabbage, 1 small shredded or diced Fuji apple, 2 tablespoons apple cider vinegar, and 1 tablespoon chopped fresh cilantro. Pile each tortilla with a tilapia fillet, a handful of slaw, and a generous dollop of sauce.

VARIATION

Toast the tortillas right over your stovetop until crunchy and slightly charred. Use a pair of tongs to flip—watch carefully as they can burn quickly.

MAKE IT PAREVE

Sub in soy sour cream for the dairy version.

PAIR IT HAGEFEN BRUT CUVÉE

A delish sparkling wine.

Miso-Glazed Salmon

Kosher Status: Pareve • Prep: 5 minutes • Marinate: 2 hours • Cook: 16 minutes •
Total: 2 hours, 21 minutes • Yield: 4 servings

Just one of those easy Japanese restaurant classics that makes me wonder why I pay for it when I can make it just as good at home.

¼ cup sake

¼ cup mirin (sweet Japanese rice wine)

¼ cup white miso paste

¼ cup honey

2 tablespoons reduced-sodium soy sauce

1 tablespoon toasted sesame oil

Four 6-ounce skin-on salmon fillets

1 tablespoon olive oil

1 tablespoon sesame seeds, for garnish

1. Whisk together the sake, mirin, miso, honey, soy sauce, and sesame oil in a small bowl. Place the fish in a rimmed dish and cover with the sauce. Cover with plastic wrap and refrigerate for at least 2 hours or overnight, flipping the fillets halfway through marinating.

2. Heat the oil in a large sauté pan over medium heat. Remove the fish from the sauce. Discard the marinade. Place the fillets around the outer rim of the pan, leaving the middle empty. Sear the fish until just done, 5 to 8 minutes per side. Garnish with the sesame seeds.

3. Alternatively, place the fish on a greased baking sheet and drizzle 1 tablespoon of the marinade over each fillet. Bake at 400°F until the salmon flakes with a fork, 20 to 25 minutes.

PAIR IT WEINSTOCK CELLAR SELECT ALICANTE BOUSCHET

This light-bodied French varietal is perfect with salmon.

• Avocado-Stuffed Miso-Glazed Salmon •

A super simple way to doll up salmon.

After the salmon is marinated, butterfly the fillets and stuff each with ¼ avocado, sliced. Fold the fish over to enclose the avocado and place on a greased baking sheet. Drizzle 1 tablespoon marinade over each fillet and bake at 400°F until the salmon is cooked through, 15 to 20 minutes. Garnish with sesame seeds.

Avocado-stuffed salmon is also great with store-bought teriyaki sauce instead of miso glaze.

Salmon with Lemon Velvet Cream Sauce

Kosher Status: Dairy • Prep: 5 minutes • Cook: 25 minutes • Total: 30 minutes • Yield: 6 servings

This creamy sauce, bright from a blast of citrus, is fantastic on any fish or pasta.

Cooking spray

Six 6- to 8-ounce skin-on salmon fillets

Kosher salt

2 tablespoons (¼ stick) unsalted butter

2 tablespoons all-purpose flour

1 cup milk

½ cup heavy cream

Grated zest and juice of 1 lemon

2 tablespoons dry white wine

1 tablespoon chopped fresh dill or
   1 teaspoon dried

Freshly ground black pepper

1. Preheat the oven to 425°F. Lightly spray a baking sheet with cooking spray.

2. Place the salmon on the prepared baking sheet and sprinkle with 1 teaspoon salt. Bake until just opaque in the center, 20 to 25 minutes.

3. While the salmon is baking, melt the butter in a medium sauté pan over medium heat. Add the flour and stir until it becomes a smooth paste. Add the milk, whisking constantly, and cook over medium heat until the sauce begin to boil and thicken. Simmer over low heat, whisking constantly, for 5 minutes. Stir in the heavy cream, lemon zest and juice, wine, dill, and salt and pepper to taste. Remove from the heat.

4. Transfer the salmon to a serving platter and pour the sauce over it to serve.

TIME-SAVER

A full side of salmon is a winner when entertaining. In a pinch, slather salmon with teriyaki or BBQ sauce and serve with seared lemons or limes for a pretty presentation.

MAKE IT A MEAL

Flake the salmon and toss with Lemon Velvet Cream Sauce and your favorite pasta.

• Side of Salmon with Seared Lemons •

It's always impressive to present a side of salmon.

Season a whole 2-pound side of salmon with 1 teaspoon salt. Bake it on a greased baking sheet at 400°F for 30 minutes for medium to medium-well; transfer to a large platter. Cut 4 lemons in half and sear them, cut side down, in a medium sauté pan over medium heat, until nicely browned, about 5 minutes. Serve the salmon garnished with fresh dill and surrounded by the seared lemons. Drizzle some Lemon Velvet Cream Sauce over the top and serve any extra in a gravy boat on the side.

PAIR IT YATIR VIOGNIER

A rich, fatty fish like salmon can handle a light red wine, but the cream sauce in this recipe calls for a rich white.

Pumpkin Spice Ravioli with Brown Butter

Kosher Status: Dairy • Prep: 18 minutes • Cook: 7 minutes • Total: 25 minutes • Yield: 4 servings

Oh, brown butter, how I love thee.

So I have a real thing for brown butter. A while back, when I was pregnant, I tried brown butter, and my life changed forever. Never try eating anything new during a pregnancy—it could result in a lifelong obsession. Now I have to have it always. Last fall, when I bought out the supermarket's canned pumpkin section (sorry if you were looking for some) to make this ravioli, I tripled the brown butter so I would have some to drink with my meal.

Kosher salt

½ cup canned pure pumpkin (not
   pumpkin pie filling)

¼ cup grated Parmesan cheese, plus
   some shaved for garnish

¼ cup ricotta cheese

2 tablespoons shredded mozzarella
   cheese

Pinch of nutmeg

Pinch of garlic powder

2 to 4 tablespoons heavy cream

36 round wonton wraps

8 tablespoons (1 stick) unsalted butter

4 fresh sage leaves, optional

Freshly ground black pepper

1. Fill a large pot three-quarters full with salted water and bring to a boil.

2. Combine the pumpkin, Parmesan, ricotta, mozzarella, ½ teaspoon salt, nutmeg, and garlic powder in a medium bowl and stir well. Add enough of the cream to smooth out the filling but not thin it out. You want a thick filling, not a sauce.

3. Lay 18 wonton wrappers on a cutting board; place 1 tablespoon of the filling in the center of each. Brush the edges with a little water. Place a second wonton wrapper on top, sealing the edges with your fingers or the tines of a fork, pressing out any air bubbles around the filling and leaving about an ⅛-inch border all around.

4. Drop the ravioli into the boiling water. Cook until the ravioli float to the top, 2 to 3 minutes. Remove the ravioli from the water with a slotted spoon and drain well on kitchen towels. Try to keep them from touching; they will stick together.

5. Melt the butter in a large sauté pan over medium-low heat until it foams. Increase heat to medium-high and add the sage leaves, if using, and pepper to taste. Cook until the sage becomes crispy and the butter begins to brown, 2 to 4 minutes. Remove from the heat and carefully add the ravioli. Spoon the butter over the ravioli to coat. Divide among 4 plates. Garnish with shaved Parmesan.

VARIATION

Swap pureed butternut squash in equal parts for the canned pumpkin.

MAKE IT A MEAL

We *need* a green here. Pair it with steamed broccoli or Brussels sprouts topped with a squeeze of fresh lemon juice and pretty curls of lemon zest. Season with salt and pepper and a drizzle of extra virgin olive oil, if desired.

PAIR IT SHILOH BARBERA

Light and luscious, Barbera is an Italian grape that's right at home with ravioli. This wine was given the royal treatment at Shiloh, a boutique winery in Israel built near the site of ancient winepresses.

• Baked Pumpkin Penne •

Make an autumnal family-style baked pasta.

Omit the butter and sage. Increase the pumpkin in the filling to one 15-ounce can, the mozzarella to ½ cup, and the heavy cream to ½ cup. Combine with the rest of the filling ingredients. Toss well with 1 pound cooked (al dente) and drained penne pasta. Transfer to a 9 x 13-inch greased baking dish and sprinkle with 1 cup shredded mozzarella. Bake at 350°F until the cheese is bubbly and melted, 15 to 20 minutes.

Poppy and Grandma's Layered *Rakott Crumpli*

Kosher Status: Dairy • Prep: 25 minutes •
Cook: 1 hour, 15 minutes • Cool: 10 minutes •
Total: 1 hour, 50 minutes • Yield: 8 servings

*Both Poppy and Grandma and Ma and Uputzi
made this indulgent Hungarian casserole. They
used to do layers upon layers upon layers of potatoes, sour cream (full-fat!), sliced hard-boiled
eggs, bread crumbs, and butter. I got lazy and just
pulled out a 2-quart baking dish for two fabulous
layers. Bake it until it's sort of creamy and golden-crunchy. I've heard of people spicing
this with paprika, which, as you can imagine, is oh so Hungarian, but we didn't. I don't
even remember black pepper, so I added white for good measure.*

*Thanks again to my friend, recipe editor and tester Paula Jacobson, who taught me
how to make perfect hard-cooked eggs.*

4 medium russet potatoes (about
  1½ pounds), scrubbed

Kosher salt

3 tablespoons unsalted butter, at room
  temperature

Two 16-ounce containers sour cream

1 cup milk

10 large eggs, hard-cooked and peeled
  (see page 54)

Ground white pepper

1 cup seasoned dry bread crumbs

1. Place the potatoes in a large pot and cover with lightly salted cold water to 2 inches
   above the potatoes. Bring to a boil. Boil until just tender, about 20 minutes. Drain and
   rinse with cold water. Once the potatoes are cool enough to handle, peel away the skins.

2. Preheat the oven to 350°F. Grease the bottom and sides of a 2-quart oven-to-table baking dish with the butter.

3. In a large bowl, mix the sour cream and milk to a pourable consistency.

4. Slice the potatoes into ¼-inch-thick rounds. Place half of the potatoes on the bottom of the baking dish. Slice the eggs ¼ inch thick. Place half of the eggs in a layer over the potatoes. Top with half of the sour cream mixture. Season with 1 teaspoon salt and white pepper to taste. Sprinkle with half of the bread crumbs. Repeat the layers, ending with the bread crumbs. Bake until just starting to crisp around the edges, 35 to 45 minutes. Allow to cool for 5 to 10 minutes. Bring to the table and use a large spoon to scoop and serve.

VARIATION

Not classic, but I've seen it done—a layer of sautéed onions. Thinly slice 2 large Vidalia onions and sauté in butter in a large pan over medium heat until soft and just starting to caramelize, 10 to 15 minutes. Add the onions between the potato and egg layers.

QUICK TIP

I use my egg slicer, and it makes slicing the eggs a cinch. I love it.

DRESS IT DOWN

• *Rakott Crumpli* Bake •

The authentic version calls for thinly sliced and layered eggs and potatoes. But you can coarsely chop and mix it all up when you're in a rush and want the flavor without all the work.

MAKE IT A MEAL

This is screaming (can you hear it?) for a light green leafy salad on the side.

PAIR IT GOOSE BAY SAUVIGNON BLANC

This baby complements both the *Rakott Crumpli* and the salad.

Roasted Summer Squash Lasagna

Kosher Status: Dairy • Prep: 15 minutes • Assembly: 10 minutes • Cook: 1 hour, 15 minutes •
Cool: 10 minutes • Total: 1 hour, 50 minutes • Yield: 10 servings

Fontina is a cow's milk Italian cheese. Fairly acidic, it melts nicely and imparts a delicate flavor to the dish you are cooking. Gruyère, Emmental, Edam, and Gouda may all be substituted for Fontina. All are available with kosher certification.

Cooking spray

2 large green zucchini, trimmed and cut lengthwise, ¼ inch thick

2 large yellow summer squash, trimmed and cut lengthwise, ¼ inch thick

2 tablespoons olive oil

2 teaspoons kosher salt

One 15-ounce container whole milk ricotta cheese

1 pound shredded mozzarella cheese

1 cup shredded Fontina cheese

1 large egg, beaten

1 tablespoon dried basil

1 teaspoon dried oregano

½ teaspoon freshly ground black pepper

1 pound oven-ready lasagna noodles

One 28-ounce or two 14.5-ounce cans diced tomatoes, drained

1 cup shredded Parmesan cheese

1. Preheat the oven to 425°F. Lightly spray 2 baking sheets with cooking spray.

2. Arrange the zucchini and yellow squash in an even single layer on the prepared baking sheets. Brush with the olive oil and sprinkle with 1 teaspoon of the salt. Roast until tender and browned, 25 to 30 minutes. Remove from the oven and set aside to cool.

3. Reduce the oven temperature to 350°F. Spray a deep 9 x 13-inch lasagna pan with cooking spray.

4. Combine the ricotta, half of the mozzarella, the Fontina, egg, basil, oregano, pepper, and the remaining 1 teaspoon salt in a large bowl. Stir well.

5. To assemble: Cover the bottom of the pan with one-quarter of the noodles, overlapping them slightly. Spread half of the ricotta mixture over the noodles. Follow with half of the roasted squash, and top with a layer of noodles. Spread with half of the tomatoes

and half of the remaining mozzarella. Top with another layer of noodles, the remaining ricotta mixture, the remaining squash, and another layer of noodles. Finish with the remaining tomatoes, the rest of the mozzarella, and the Parmesan. Lightly spray one side of aluminum foil with cooking spray. Cover the lasagna with the foil, sprayed side down, so that the melted cheese won't stick. Bake 30 minutes, remove the foil, and continue baking until golden brown and bubbly, 10 to 15 minutes. Let rest 10 minutes before slicing.

DRESS IT UP

• Roasted Vegetable Summer Lasagna •

Make it a vegetable extravaganza.

Add 1 large eggplant sliced ¼ inch thick, 1 large red onion sliced ¼ inch thick, and 8 ounces sliced mushrooms to the squash for roasting. Layer in the same way, but use ½ cup chopped fresh basil in place of the dried herbs. Garnish with additional fresh basil right before serving.

PAIR IT BARTENURA OVADIA ESTATES MORELLINO DI SCANSANO

Italian all the way. This one is fruity and goes down nice 'n' easy.

Butternut Squash Mac 'n' Cheese

Kosher Status: Dairy • Prep: 5 minutes • Cook: 35 minutes • Total: 40 minutes • Yield: 10 servings

Saw this idea on the cover of Cooking Light. *It looked ooey-gooey-cheesy and orange, which is how I like my mac 'n' cheese.* Neon *orange. Exactly like that processed, powdered out-of-a-box Wacky Mac I had growing up as a kid. (Still love it. Maybe I'll make some for dinner tonight and split it with the kids and Hubby—he loves it, too. There! We agree on something!)*

This butternut squash gives me that classic unnatural color but without the chemical-laden cheese powder. Wish I had thought this one up myself.

Cooking spray

3 cups shredded cheddar cheese

½ cup panko bread crumbs

½ cup grated Parmesan cheese

½ teaspoon dried thyme

4 tablespoons (½ stick) unsalted butter

¼ cup all-purpose flour

2 cups whole milk

½ cup vegetable broth, such as Manischewitz All Natural Vegetable Broth

1 teaspoon dry mustard

½ teaspoon paprika

½ teaspoon garlic powder

10 dashes hot sauce

1 egg, beaten

1 cup shredded Gruyère cheese

One 10-ounce box frozen butternut or winter squash, thawed

Kosher salt

Freshly ground black pepper

One 1-pound box cavatappi, spiral, elbow, or similar pasta, cooked al dente and drained well

1. Preheat the oven to 400°F. Lightly spray a 9 x 13-inch baking dish with cooking spray.

2. Combine 1 cup of the cheddar, the panko, Parmesan, and thyme in a small bowl and set aside.

3. To make the sauce, melt the butter in a large saucepan over medium-low heat. Sprinkle in the flour and whisk constantly until smooth and melty, about 5 minutes. In a slow, steady stream, pour in the milk, then the broth, whisking constantly. Add the dry mustard, paprika, garlic powder, and hot sauce. Cook, whisking constantly, until thickened, about 5 minutes.

4. Temper the egg by slowly whisking in ¼ cup of the warm sauce. Add the egg mixture to the sauce and whisk. Add the remaining 2 cups cheddar and the Gruyère and whisk to melt and form a thick cheese sauce. Remove from the heat. Stir in the squash until smooth and season to taste with salt and pepper. Add the pasta and toss to coat well.

5. Pour into the prepared dish. Sprinkle the reserved cheddar-panko mixture over the pasta. Bake until golden and bubbly, about 20 minutes.

DRESS IT DOWN

• **Butternut Mac 'n' Cheese Muffin Cups** •

Go fun and handheld.

Spoon the mac into muffin tins lined with lightly greased cupcake papers and sprinkle with panko topping if desired. Bake at 400°F for 15 minutes. Easy to eat—no utensils required.

MAKE IT A MEAL

I love my mac 'n' cheese with applesauce. I think it's because the mac 'n' cheese TV dinner we always ate growing up came with a small compartment of applesauce and another compartment stuffed with a chocolate brownie for dessert. For the dressed-up version, I would serve my company Mustard Green Beans (page 106) and a chunky applesauce side to satisfy my cravings. No question that the dressed-down version goes with a smooth and sweet applesauce.

PAIR IT ELVI ADAR CAVA BRUT

Better than beer, and twice as good with this dish. A delish Spanish bubbly.

Blue Cheese, Pear, and Arugula Pizza

Kosher Status: Dairy • Prep: 8 minutes • Cook: 10 minutes • Total: 18 minutes • Yield: Two 10-inch pizzas

I went out to celebrate something one day with my bud Tamar. Can't remember what we were celebrating, maybe just the end of a long day at the office. So it's around 8:00 p.m., we're both far from home, and by golly, we'd already missed bedtime with the kiddies. I guessed Hubby was managing without me.

So we treated ourselves and checked out Basil, a new kosher restaurant in Brooklyn. Maybe we were just giddy, but everything we tried was insanely delish. I mean, three of the four dishes we had that night inspired recipes in this book. We're talking that good.

I just had to re-create them at home because Basil is too far from my house to go back every day to satisfy my new cravings. But unlike the restaurant chef, I'm a sneaky shortcut kinda cook; I use store-bought pizza dough.

Fine yellow cornmeal

All-purpose flour

One 1-pound prepared pizza dough

2 Bartlett pears, unpeeled, halved, cored, and sliced ⅛ inch thick

3 tablespoons extra virgin olive oil, plus more for drizzling (optional)

1 teaspoon kosher salt

½ teaspoon freshly ground black pepper

⅔ cup crumbled blue cheese

½ to 1 cup baby arugula

1. Preheat the oven to 450°F. Sprinkle 2 large baking sheets with a light dusting of cornmeal. Lightly flour the work surface.

2. Separate the pizza dough into 2 equal pieces. Roll out each piece of dough into a 10-inch circle and transfer it to a prepared baking sheet. Layer the sliced pears evenly on the 2 pizzas, leaving a ½-inch border all the way around. Drizzle the olive oil evenly over the pizzas and sprinkle the salt and pepper over the top. Bake until the crust is just starting to turn golden brown, about 10 minutes. Sprinkle the crumbled blue cheese all over and top with the arugula and an additional drizzle of oil, if desired. Serve immediately.

DRESS IT DOWN

• White Pizza •

Make delicious, simple mozzarella and ricotta pies.

Instead of using the blue cheese, pears, and arugula, drizzle each dough round with 1½ tablespoons olive oil and ¼ teaspoon salt. Top each with ¾ cup shredded mozzarella and dot all over with ½ cup ricotta (about 10 dollops). Bake for 8 to 10 minutes. Variation: I can't help myself from dressing up this dressed-down version with slices of sautéed garlic and fresh torn basil leaves.

PAIR IT DRAPPIER CARTE D'OR CHAMPAGNE

Never thought of champagne with pizza? Think again!

Country Spinach, Tomato, and White Bean Soup

Kosher Status: Pareve • Prep: 8 minutes • Cook: 27 minutes • Total: 35 minutes •
Yield: 8 cups soup (about 4 servings)

Yes, this is a soup, but a hearty one, kinda bordering on stew. Fills you up, and then some. You can congratulate yourself on serving a really delish and healthful meal, full of fiber, iron, and vitamin C. Until you add the cheese twists, that is. But hey, the cheese twists add lots of—um—protein (not to mention fun).

2 tablespoons olive oil

1 large onion, coarsely chopped

2 medium carrots, coarsely chopped

1 celery stalk, coarsely chopped

2 garlic cloves, chopped

One 14-ounce can diced tomatoes

One 15-ounce can cannellini beans, rinsed and drained

1 quart vegetable broth, such as Manischewitz All Natural Vegetable Broth

1 tablespoon fresh thyme or 1 teaspoon dried

1 bay leaf

One 5-ounce container whole fresh baby spinach leaves or 2 cups frozen chopped spinach

1 teaspoon kosher salt

½ to 1 teaspoon red pepper flakes (optional)

Freshly ground black pepper

Heat the olive oil over medium-high heat in a large pot. Add the onion and cook until it begins to soften, about 5 minutes. Add the carrots, celery, and garlic, and cook 5 minutes more, stirring often. Add the tomatoes and their juice, beans, broth, thyme, and bay leaf and bring to a boil. Reduce the heat to a simmer and cook, stirring occasionally, until the vegetables are tender, about 15 minutes. Stir in the spinach, salt, red pepper flakes (if using), and black pepper to taste. Cook just until the spinach is wilted, 2 minutes more. Remove and discard the bay leaf. Ladle the soup into bowls and serve warm.

PAIR IT CARMEL APPELLATION SAUVIGNON BLANC

Herbal and refreshing, this white wine is perfect with vegetable stew.

• **Easy Cheese Twists (Dairy)** •

Serve the soup with cheese sticks on the side.

Spray a work surface with cooking spray or lightly dust with flour. Lay out 1 thawed sheet of frozen puff pastry, spray with cooking spray, and sprinkle with ½ cup shredded cheddar, ¼ cup shredded or grated Parmesan, and 1 teaspoon dried oregano, pressing lightly into the dough. Cut the dough into 8 strips and gently twist them. Place on a greased parchment-lined baking sheet and press down the ends to secure. Bake at 400°F until golden, 18 to 20 minutes.

Cold Soba Noodles with Sweet Sesame Tofu

Kosher Status: Pareve • Prep: 8 minutes • Cook: 22 minutes • Total: 30 minutes • Yield: 4 servings

I'm a sucker for this. Honestly—entire thing—I can eat it myself. Two of my kids love "tofuf," as they say. I don't care what they call it. I'm just thrilled we can all share a package. This one goes out to all you tofu lovers.

One 8-ounce package soba noodles

½ cup fresh orange juice

¼ cup smooth peanut butter

2 tablespoons rice vinegar

1 tablespoon low-sodium soy sauce

½ teaspoon garlic powder

⅓ cup plus 1 tablespoon canola oil

1 pound extra-firm tofu, patted dry and cut into 1-inch cubes

1 tablespoon light brown sugar

1 tablespoon black sesame seeds, for garnish

2 scallions (green parts only), thinly sliced, for garnish

Toasted sesame oil, for serving

1. Cook the soba noodles according to the package directions. Rinse with cold water and drain well. Allow to cool completely and transfer to a large bowl.

2. Combine the orange juice, peanut butter, vinegar, soy sauce, garlic powder, and the ⅓ cup canola oil in a food processor. Blend until smooth. Pour over the noodles and toss to coat. Refrigerate until serving.

3. Line a plate with paper towels. Heat the remaining 1 tablespoon canola oil in a large nonstick sauté pan over medium-high heat. Add the tofu and sauté until it starts to turn golden, 8 to 10 minutes. Add the brown sugar and cook 3 to 5 minutes more, stirring often. Drain on the prepared plate.

4. Divide the cold noodles among 4 shallow bowls and top with tofu. Garnish with sesame seeds and scallions and finish with a drizzle of toasted sesame oil.

VARIATIONS

Top with chopped toasted peanuts, fresh torn cilantro, and red pepper flakes. Halved snow peas also go great here.

It already is a complete protein and total meal in one. Serve with iced green tea spiked with grated fresh ginger and the sweetener of your choice.

DRESS IT UP

• Soba, Sweet Sesame Tofu, and Vegetables •

Add ½ cup thinly sliced red bell pepper, ½ cup shredded carrots, and ¾ cup shelled edamame to the cold noodles. Slice the tofu into ¼-inch-thick matchsticks, and gently sauté over medium-high heat with brown sugar for 3 to 5 minutes.

PAIR IT CARMEL KAYOUMI WHITE RIESLING

There's a hint of sweetness in this riesling, just enough to bring out the sweet flavors in this dish.

Desserts

PAREVE

Sorbet Cups with Strawberry Kiwi Salsa   255
DRESS IT DOWN *Sorbet and Salsa*

Nutty Caramel Brownies   257
DRESS IT UP *Toasted Marshmallow Nutty Caramel Brownies*

Spiced Pumpkin Mousse   260
DRESS IT UP *Cocoa Cream Pumpkin Mousse Trifles*

Sweet Potato Cake   262
DRESS IT UP *Peaches and Jam Sweet Potato Cake*

Birthday Pancake Towers   265
DRESS IT UP *Birthday Pancake Cutouts*

Holiday Carrot Honey Cake   267
DRESS IT DOWN *Carrot Honey Loaf*

Tart Green Apple Pie à la Mode   270
DRESS IT DOWN *Green Apple Crumble*

Caramel Apples with Crushed Nuts   273
DRESS IT UP *Caramel Fruit Bites*

Big Chewy Dark Chocolate Chunk Cookies   277
DRESS IT UP *Chocolate Chip Cookie and Cream Stacks*

Salted Almond and Pistachio Bark   279
DRESS IT DOWN *Kiddie Candy Bark*

Olive Oil Dark Chocolate Mousse   285
DRESS IT UP *Olive Oil Dark Chocolate Mousse Shots*

Cherry Bourbon Hand Pies   287
DRESS IT DOWN *Warm Cherry Topping*

Gooey Chocolate Cherry Cake   292
DRESS IT UP *Red Wine Chocolate Cherry Heart Cake*

DAIRY

Cardamom-Scented Chanukah Cookies   295
DRESS IT UP *Black and White Chocolate–Dipped Chanukah Cookies*

Chocolate Hazelnut Milk Shake Martinis   298
DRESS IT DOWN *Chocolate Hazelnut Milk Shakes*

Funnel Cakes   303
DRESS IT UP *Funnel Cakes with Basil Ice Cream*

Orange-Scented Cheesecake   305
DRESS IT UP *Candied-Orange Cheesecake*

Black and White Ice Cream Bombe   308
DRESS IT UP *Black and White Sundae Bar*

Cannoli Egg Rolls with Chocolate Sauce   311
DRESS IT UP *Cannoli Cones*

Sorbet Cups with Strawberry Kiwi Salsa

Kosher Status: Pareve • Prep: 15 minutes • Cook: 0 minutes • Freeze: 3 hours •
Total: 3 hours, 15 minutes • Yield: 4 servings

This is possibly one of the most gorgeous, refreshing desserts on the planet. Back in high school, I used to hit a real Italian restaurant and I always ordered authentic Italian sorbet served in the fruit it was made from. That was way back when we were just scared of fat, not sugar—you know, the whole fat-free cake phase. I gladly ate the whole cake 'cause, well, it was fat free. So, anyhoo, I love fat-free fruity sorbet, and now with this jewel—which kinda looks like sparkly fruit salsa—it's beyond terrific. Anyone can do this and make it look amazing. No special skills, no food styling secrets, no oven—you're gonna love it!

4 medium oranges, such as navel, tangelo, or Cara Cara, rinsed

¼ cup plus 2 tablespoons granulated sugar

1 pint sorbet, your favorite flavor

1 cup hulled, diced strawberries

½ cup peeled, diced kiwi (about 2)

Grated zest and juice of 1 lime

½ teaspoon coconut extract (optional)

1 cup nondairy whipped "cream" (see Quick Tip)

1. Slice ½ inch off the top of each orange and reserve for garnish, if desired. Cut a thin slice off the bottom of each orange just so that the oranges can stand steady and upright. Carefully cut around the flesh and scoop out the insides of the oranges with a small sharp knife or grapefruit spoon (save the orange segments for fruit salad or smoothies). Moisten the outside of the orange shells with a little water and roll them in ¼ cup sugar to lightly coat. Fill the shells with the sorbet and level off the tops so you have a flat surface. Freeze until solid, 2 to 3 hours.

2. Make the salsa: Combine the remaining 2 tablespoons sugar with the strawberries in a small bowl and let sit until juicy, about 15 minutes. Add the kiwi and lime juice and stir well.

3. Gently fold the lime zest and coconut extract, if using, into the whipped "cream" in a large bowl.

4. Before serving, remove the oranges from the freezer and let them soften for 5 minutes. Plate the oranges and top them with the fruit salsa, sprinkling extra salsa around the orange. Garnish with a dollop of the flavored whipped "cream."

DRESS IT DOWN

• **Sorbet and Salsa** •

Serve the sorbet in bowls with Strawberry Kiwi Salsa on top.

VARIATION

Try extra-large lemons as your sorbet shells. Mix and match lemons and oranges filled with different colors and flavors of sorbet for a gorgeous table.

PREP AHEAD

The orange cups can be prepared up to 4 days in advance, the salsa up to 24 hours in advance. Assemble by topping the cups with the "salsa and cream" just before serving.

QUICK TIP

Nondairy whipped "cream" is available in tubs in the freezer section of your supermarket; it is usually called "whipped topping." If you prefer to make your own, try this recipe. **Nondairy Coconut Whipped Cream:** Chill two 13-ounce cans full-fat coconut milk, a mixing bowl, and beaters overnight in the fridge. Turn the cans of chilled coconut milk upside down. Open the cans from the bottom and drain off the clear liquid; reserve it for other uses, such as smoothies or homemade popsicles. Using a rubber spatula, transfer the chilled coconut "cream" left in the can to the chilled bowl. Beat with an electric mixer until thick, creamy, and fluffy. Beat in ¼ teaspoon pure vanilla extract, then confectioners' sugar, 1 tablespoon at a time, to taste. Do not overbeat. If preparing the coconut cream in advance, remove it from the fridge 1 hour before serving because it will harden a bit when refrigerated.

PAIR IT HERZOG LATE HARVEST ORANGE MUSCAT

Sweet foods can make dry wines taste bitter. Choose late harvest wines (they combine sweet and tart qualities) as a super match for sweet desserts.

Nutty Caramel Brownies

Kosher Status: Pareve • Prep: 8 minutes • Bake: 28 minutes • Total: 36 minutes • Yield: 9 brownies

Total decadence in an 8-inch square pan. As in, decadent enough that you can tell your-self and your guests, "Oh, just eat one square"—but you can't. When this baby came out of the oven, Hubby and I had two forks in the pan at once, fencing over one square. So I cut a few more squares and we each had two brownies, somberly vowing to leave the rest for the kids. Under cover of darkness, after the kids and Hubby were asleep, I tiptoed into the kitchen and snagged another brownie (okay, two). But I must have left a trail of crumbs behind me, 'cause in the morning Hubby wanted to know if I was leaving a path so I could find my way home. Why wouldn't he believe that I was walking in my sleep?

Cooking spray

¾ cup all-purpose flour

2 tablespoons unsweetened cocoa powder

¼ teaspoon baking soda

¼ teaspoon kosher salt

4 ounces semisweet chocolate, coarsely chopped

2 teaspoons canola oil

½ cup packed light brown sugar

¼ cup granulated sugar

2 tablespoons light corn syrup

2 teaspoons pure vanilla extract

1 large egg

½ cup walnuts, coarsely chopped

¼ cup store-bought caramel sauce

1. Preheat the oven to 350°F. Spray an 8-inch square baking pan with cooking spray.

2. Whisk together the flour, cocoa powder, baking soda, and salt in a medium bowl. Combine the chocolate and canola oil in a microwave-safe bowl. Melt carefully in the microwave in 20-second intervals, stirring after each interval, until smooth. Add the sugars, corn syrup, and vanilla and stir until combined. Add the egg and mix well. Add the chocolate mixture to the flour and stir until smooth and combined. Fold in the walnuts, and transfer the batter, which will be quite thick, to the prepared pan. Drizzle the caramel all over the top.

3. Bake until the center is firm and a toothpick comes out clean when inserted in the middle, 25 to 28 minutes. Let cool completely before cutting into 9 squares.

• **Toasted Marshmallow Nutty Caramel Brownies** •

A campfire cliché? As we say in New Yawk, "Fuhgetaboudit." These gooey toasted marsh-
mallows immediately make these brownies intriguing enough for your next dinner party.

After the brownies have cooled for about 20 minutes, cover the top with 2 cups mini marshmallows. Broil on high until the marshmallows are golden brown and gooey, 3 to 5 seconds (or more, depending on the position of your oven rack and strength of your broiler). Just before serving, drizzle 2 to 3 tablespoons store-bought hot fudge or chocolate sauce on top—add an extra 2 to 3 tablespoons caramel sauce for a superdecadent treat!

PREP AHEAD

Marshmallow-topped brownies can be made and stored in an airtight container up to 2 days in advance (they won't have that hot, gooey, just-out-of-the-oven texture, but they'll still be wicked good). Drizzle the sauces on just before serving.

TIME-SAVER

Doctor up your favorite store-bought brownie batter with nuts and caramel sauce before baking and top with toasted marshmallows and caramel and chocolate sauces just before serving.

PAIR IT SHILOH FORT DESSERT WINE

A fab combo for brownies, this port-style wine is rich, sweet, and robust.

Spiced Pumpkin Mousse

Kosher Status: Pareve • Prep: 7 minutes • Cook: 3 minutes • Chill: 2 hours •
Total: 2 hours, 10 minutes • Yield: 4 cups mousse

This can best be described as pumpkin pudding-mousse-pots-de-crème-esque. In short, it's lush and it's vegan: Do I get points for that?

And . . . it doesn't take long to set. If you're crazy for pumpkin, it's a nice, light up-grade from pumpkin pie, which just happens to be my first (or was it second, or third?) dessert love.

1 cup vanilla soy milk

½ cup granulated sugar or 1 cup pure
   maple syrup

One 15-ounce can pure pumpkin puree

Pinch of ground allspice

¼ teaspoon pumpkin pie spice

1 pound silken tofu, drained

½ teaspoon pure vanilla extract

1. Combine the soy milk in a small pot with the sugar and bring to a simmer over medium heat until the sugar dissolves, stirring occasionally, taking care not to burn the mixture, about 3 minutes.

2. Remove from the heat. Add the pumpkin puree, allspice, and pumpkin pie spice and mix until smooth.

3. Process the tofu and the pumpkin mixture in a blender until completely smooth. Stir in the vanilla; taste and adjust for flavor, adding more vanilla if desired.

4. Chill in a big bowl or individual bowls, covered tightly with plastic wrap, for at least 2 hours or overnight. Serve chilled.

PREP AHEAD

This mousse can be made up to 48 hours in advance.

QUICK TIP

To make your own nondairy whipped cream from coconut milk, see page 256.

• Cocoa Cream Pumpkin Mousse Trifles •

Serve the mousse in a variety of vintage goblets—mismatched is fun!—for an elegant presentation.

Garnish each with a dollop of **Cocoa Cream:** Whisk ½ teaspoon vanilla extract, 1 tablespoon cocoa powder, and 1 tablespoon confectioners' sugar into ½ cup non-dairy whipping cream. Whip until the "cream" holds stiff peaks. Alternatively, sift cocoa and sugar and gently fold together with vanilla into 1 cup already whipped "cream." Top each dollop of cream with a small decorative store-bought cookie.

PAIR IT BARON HERZOG JEUNESSE BLACK MUSCAT

Any of the Jeunesse sweet dessert wines would work here.

Sweet Potato Cake

Kosher Status: Pareve • Prep: 20 minutes • Bake: 45 minutes • Cool: 15 minutes • Total: 1 hour, 20 minutes • Yield: 6 to 8 servings

My grandmother's cakes were the kind of perfection that can be achieved only by a Hungarian-born baker. Folks from those parts are known for their confectionery skills. I don't have any of her recipes, but I know for a fact that at least one of her famous desserts called for schmaltz (rendered chicken fat). Inspired by her moist, spongy concoctions, I came up with this.

And it's darn good. So soft and moist—yes, I am proud. I don't always trust my brood for opinions—they're slightly biased. So I tested this on my friend Hadassah and her four grown boys, and it's been universally declared a winner. Hubby went looking for the last bite, but I got there first. Ha!

1 pound sweet potatoes, peeled and
   diced

Cooking spray

1½ cups all-purpose flour

1 teaspoon ground cinnamon

1 teaspoon ground ginger

1 teaspoon baking soda

1 teaspoon baking powder

½ teaspoon ground nutmeg

½ teaspoon kosher salt

1 cup granulated sugar

½ cup canola oil

2 large eggs

1. Steam the sweet potatoes until tender, about 15 minutes. Mash them into a smooth texture and set aside 1 cup; reserve any remaining sweet potatoes for another use.

2. Preheat the oven to 325°F. Spray a 9 x 5-inch loaf pan with cooking spray.

3. Combine the flour, cinnamon, ginger, baking soda, baking powder, nutmeg, and salt in a large bowl and whisk well. Combine the 1 cup sweet potatoes, sugar, and canola oil in the bowl of an electric mixer and beat with the paddle until smooth. Add the eggs, one at a time, beating well to incorporate after each addition. Add the flour mixture in two additions, mixing by hand just until combined. Transfer the batter to the prepared pan. Bake until a toothpick inserted in the center comes out clean, 40 to 45 minutes. Cool in the pan 15 minutes and then let cool completely on a wire rack.

• **Peaches and Jam Sweet Potato Cake** •

Cut the loaf horizontally in thirds. Spread the top of the bottom layer with raspberry jam, top with peach slices and then the middle layer of the cake. Repeat with more jam and peaches and place the top layer of the loaf on top. Can be served immediately or prepared a few days in advance. (Store wrapped tightly in plastic wrap, on a cake platter with a top, or in a container with a tight-fitting lid.)

Try whipped cream in place of the jam and use different fruits like kiwis, strawberries, or bananas (sliced lengthwise) in place of the peach slices.

PAIR IT MORAD DANUE PASSION FRUIT WINE

Stay sweet here. Sweet potato + passion fruit = pure magic.

Birthday Pancake Towers

Kosher Status: Pareve • Prep: 10 minutes • Cook: 40 minutes • Total: 50 minutes •
Yield: 24 pancakes, to make 8 servings

I always marvel at mommies who know how to frost a birthday cake with fancy swirls and flowers, not to mention a perfect portrait of their child's face made from piped colored icing. They mastered the art in that rigorous ten-week cake-decorating course they took in their "spare time." Spare time. Yeah, right. The last time I had spare time was in the hospital after my first kid was born.

So if you didn't take the class, or haven't the skill, heart, time, desire, or patience for it all (like me), here's your solution. So cute and obviously kiddie-friendly, it's a super-special easy way to say "I love you." This is such a novelty, and it's as easy as making pancakes. Now, that I can do.

One 16½-ounce box yellow cake mix

1 teaspoon baking powder

2 large eggs

1 to 1½ cups soy milk

¼ cup rainbow sprinkles

Cooking spray

1 cup confectioners' sugar

½ teaspoon pure vanilla extract

1. Preheat the oven to 200°F.

2. Combine the cake mix and baking powder in a large bowl and whisk. Combine the eggs and 1 cup soy milk in a small bowl and whisk. Add the wet ingredients to the dry ingredients and stir well until smooth. Add the remaining ½ cup soy milk a little at a time until pancake batter consistency is reached—not too thick, not too thin, a little bit lumpy. Stir in the sprinkles and set aside for 5 minutes.

3. Preheat a skillet or griddle over medium heat. Spray with cooking spray.

4. Pour ¼ cup batter for each pancake onto the hot griddle. Cook until bubbles form on the top and the edges look done, 2 to 3 minutes. Flip with a large spatula and cook 2 minutes more. Transfer the pancakes to a baking sheet and keep warm in the oven until all the pancakes are made.

5. Whisk the confectioners' sugar and vanilla with about 2 tablespoons water in a small bowl until a thin glaze is formed. To make each serving, stack 3 pancakes and drizzle the glaze on top.

DRESS IT UP

• **Birthday Pancake Cutouts** •

Use cookie cutters to make fun-shaped pancakes.

Make pancakes as instructed above and then use cookie cutters to cut out shapes. Snack on the scraps while you work. Stack three like shapes per person and serve with the glaze, fresh berries, and sliced bananas.

PAIR IT WALDERS VODKA & VANILLA

Serve chocolate milk to the kiddies; spike it with this creamy liqueur for the grown-ups.

Holiday Carrot Honey Cake

Kosher Status: Pareve • Prep: 15 minutes • Bake: 50 minutes • Cool: 1 hour, 10 minutes • Total: 2 hours, 15 minutes • Yield: 10 servings

There are things that are your thing, and things that are not your thing. Then there are things that are so not your thing. Honey cake is one of those so-not-my-thing things. Of course, Hubby loves it.

It's a tradition to make honeyed foods for Rosh Hashanah, the Jewish New Year, and this dessert is one of them. I had to find a way to make a honey cake I could actually eat. As the aroma of this cake filled our home, the kids all drifted into the kitchen, pleading for a slice. "No, you're not going to like this," I warned them.

"Just a taste!"

"Trust me. You'll hate it."

"Puhleeease?" So I gave in and gave them each a slice. Then they wanted another slice, and another. The next morning, my picky eater Angel Face wandered into the kitchen, searching for "more of that brown cake." Ahhh, just like his father!

Hubby told me (although I knew it already) that it's not traditional to bake this in a Bundt pan, so I decided to do it anyway. I think it's super pretty like this, perfect for the holidays. When I decided to add carrots (another symbolic New Year food), he groaned, "Oooh, nooo," but when he tasted it he said, "Oooh, goood." Oh, the glaze is also not traditional, but I like the cake better with it. And the nuts are a bit controversial. Sephardic Jews eat them on Rosh Hashanah, but Ashkenazis don't. Go figure. So to be safe, use the coconut flakes when serving this for Rosh Hashanah and the nuts when entertaining year-round.

Cooking spray

1 tablespoon instant coffee granules

1 cup hot water

3 large eggs

¾ cup canola oil

1½ cups honey

½ cup packed light brown sugar

2 teaspoons pure vanilla extract

One 4-ounce jar carrot baby food

½ cup fresh orange juice

3½ cups all-purpose flour

2 teaspoons baking powder

2 teaspoons baking soda

1 teaspoon ground cinnamon

½ teaspoon ground nutmeg

½ teaspoon ground cloves

½ teaspoon ground allspice	1 cup confectioners' sugar
½ teaspoon kosher salt	¼ to ½ cup slivered almonds, chopped
2 cups shredded carrots (optional)	pecans or walnuts, or coconut flakes

1. Preheat the oven to 350°F. Spray an 8- to 10-cup Bundt pan with cooking spray.

2. Combine the coffee and hot water in a small bowl; stir until dissolved. Combine the eggs, canola oil, and honey in the bowl of an electric mixer and beat at medium speed until well blended. Stir in the dissolved coffee, sugar, vanilla, carrot baby food, and juice.

3. Whisk the flour, baking powder, baking soda, cinnamon, nutmeg, cloves, allspice, and salt in a large bowl. Gradually add to the egg mixture, beating at low speed until blended. Fold in the shredded carrots, if using, and pour the batter into the prepared pan.

4. Bake until a toothpick inserted in the cake comes out clean and the cake springs back when touched, 45 to 50 minutes. Allow the cake to cool 10 minutes in the pan, then invert onto a wire rack and let cool completely, about 1 hour.

5. Once the cake is completely cooled, prepare the glaze: Whisk the confectioners' sugar with 1 to 2 tablespoons water until a pourable glaze consistency is achieved.

6. Drizzle the glaze over the cake. Top with the nuts or coconut. Store the cake on a cake platter with a lid or in a container with a tight-fitting lid.

DRESS IT DOWN
• Carrot Honey Loaf •

Rosh Hashanah honey cakes are commonly baked in loaf pans. Maybe there's a mysterious kabalistic reason for this old Jewish custom, or maybe they only had loaf pans back a thousand years ago when honey cakes were invented. Anyway, this recipe will yield two 9 x 5-inch loaf cakes.

Bake for 40 to 45 minutes. Keep one for yourself and pack up the other one to make nice with that cranky neighbor down the block.

QUICK TIP

Here are a few tips for measuring honey. If your recipe calls for oil or hot water, measure that first; then use the measuring spoons or cups for honey. Or you can spray the insides of your measuring utensils with cooking spray; the honey will slide out easily.

PAIR IT BALMA VENITIA MUSCAT BEAUMES DE VENISE

A sweet white from the Rhône valley.

Tart Green Apple Pie à la Mode

Kosher Status: Pareve • Prep: 45 minutes • Bake: 1 hour, 10 minutes •
Cool: 20 minutes • Total: 2 hours, 15 minutes • Yield: One 9-inch pie

Now this is so my thing. Sometimes I find your standard hot apple pie à la mode too sweet—so the contrasting tart green apples make this my perfect union of pie and non-dairy (pareve) ice cream. And we're talkin' about an exquisite, lasting food marriage, not like Hollywood marriages that don't even last till the tabloids go to press.

¼ cup all-purpose flour

½ cup granulated sugar

3 tablespoons packed light brown sugar

3 tablespoons cornstarch

½ teaspoon ground cinnamon

¼ teaspoon ground cardamom

¼ teaspoon kosher salt

Pinch of ground nutmeg

5 large Granny Smith apples, peeled,
    cored, and cut into ½-inch-thick slices

Grated zest and juice of 1 lemon

Two 9-inch frozen pie crusts, thawed

1 large egg, beaten with 1 teaspoon water

1 tablespoon turbinado sugar

1 pint vanilla or chocolate ice cream,
    for serving

1. Preheat the oven to 400°F.

2. Combine the flour, granulated sugar, brown sugar, cornstarch, cinnamon, cardamom, salt, and nutmeg in a large bowl. Add the apples and lemon zest and juice; toss to evenly coat the apples.

3. Place one crust in a 9-inch round pie plate and press lightly into place. Add the apple filling and top with the second crust. Press the edges together and decoratively crimp with a fork or make a design with your fingers. Brush the crust with the egg wash and sprinkle the turbinado sugar on top. Cut several 1-inch slits in the top of the crust to vent. Place the pie on a baking sheet and make a foil ring to cover the rim of the crust so it doesn't brown too quickly.

4. Bake 15 minutes, then reduce the oven temperature to 375°F. Bake until the top of the crust is golden brown and the fruit is tender when pierced with a knife (stick a thin knife into one of the vents), 45 to 55 minutes. If the crust is browning too quickly, cover it loosely with foil. Let cool 20 minutes before slicing. Serve each slice with a scoop of ice cream.

DRESS IT DOWN

• **Green Apple Crumble** •

Cut the apples in 1-inch chunks and toss with the flour, sugars, cornstarch, cinnamon, cardamom, salt, nutmeg, and lemon zest and juice in a large bowl. Transfer to a greased 8-inch square baking dish. Combine ¼ cup flour, ¼ cup rolled oats, ¼ cup packed brown sugar, and 3 tablespoons margarine in a medium bowl. Rub with your fingers until a coarse meal is formed; sprinkle over the apples.

Bake at 375°F until bubbly and golden brown, 45 to 50 minutes. Cool slightly and serve warm or at room temperature.

QUICK TIP

To keep your brown sugar from becoming hard as a rock, place a small piece or a heel of bread in the bag. Even stale bread will keep your sugar moist.

PAIR IT BARTENURA SPARKLING MOSCATO

Match the apple pie and ice cream with refreshing bubbles and texture. This wine's a real sweetie.

Caramel Apples with Crushed Nuts

Kosher Status: Pareve • Prep: 10 minutes • Cook: 20 minutes • Cool: 5 minutes •
Assemble: 10 minutes • Chill: 1 hour • Total: 1 hour, 45 minutes • Yield: 6 caramel apples

This was a horrific experiment beyond words. You'd never believe me if I told you the number of pots that needed to be soaked and scrubbed and soaked again; if I told you what it takes to make a pareve caramel that actually sticks to the apple without gluing your teeth together (I almost lost a tooth or two in this experiment); if I told you how I tried almond milk, coconut milk, nut-based creams, and things that should never be tried. But I don't want to mention it. If you knew, you would thank me profusely.

Not that I'm asking for gratitude. Heaven knows, I didn't do it to hear thanks. But I saved you all that time and cleaning and the waste of perfectly beautiful apples, not to mention the disappointment of a gang of kids eagerly waiting for a decent caramel apple. I saved you all that trouble and you haven't a clue. Except I'll tell you this: Hubby thinks I actually ruined our stovetop with this experiment. But it's over, done, behind me.

You're gonna love me for these. Never mind how I got there.

½ cup (8 tablespoons/1 stick) margarine

1 cup granulated sugar

1 cup vanilla soy milk

½ cup light corn syrup

¼ teaspoon kosher salt

Cooking spray

6 small Granny Smith apples, washed
and dried, stems removed

1 cup salted roasted peanuts, coarsely
chopped

1. Place the margarine, sugar, soy milk, and corn syrup in a large heavy-bottomed saucepan over medium-high heat. Bring to a boil, stirring continually, about 5 minutes. Cook, stirring often, until the mixture reaches 245°F on a candy thermometer, about 15 minutes. Remove from the heat and stir in the salt. Let cool for 5 minutes.

2. Line a sheet pan with wax paper and lightly spray with cooking spray.

3. Insert a popsicle stick or thick wooden candy stick into the center of each apple at the stem end. Spread the nuts on a plate. Holding an apple by the stick, dip in the caramel and swirl around to coat, letting the excess

drip off. While still holding the stick, let the caramel set for about 20 seconds, and then roll the apple in the nuts to coat evenly. Transfer to the prepared sheet pan, stick pointing up, and refrigerate until firm, about 1 hour. Repeat with the remaining apples.

4. Be sure to work quickly when coating the apples with caramel; it will begin to harden quickly. You may have to reheat the caramel slightly to finish coating the apples, but be careful because it will burn easily when there is less caramel in the pan.

DRESS IT UP

• **Caramel Fruit Bites** •

Sometimes, just a bite is all you need. I happen to love mini foods, little teasers that offer a variety of tastes and textures. Here's a great way to sample nature's bounty dipped in caramel or chocolate and garnished with your fave toppings, from coconut flakes to sprinkles to sea salt to slivered almonds. Just a bite, no need to indulge. Of course, you have to sample each one to make sure it's perfect; then try it with a different topping, sample, use another topping, sample . . .

Cut the apples into 1-inch chunks and skewer them with 1-inch pieces of banana and large green or red grapes. Dip some skewers in caramel and some in melted dark chocolate (see page 297), then roll them in or sprinkle on various toppings, such as sliced almonds, coconut flakes, crushed candy pieces, mini chocolate chips, or sea salt. Wrap a Styrofoam cube in festive paper and stick the skewers in the cube for a pretty presentation.

PAIR IT CARMEL SHA'AL LATE HARVEST GEWURZTRAMINER

Perfect for dessert, this complex late harvest wine is loaded with exotic fruit aromas and flavors.

Big Chewy Dark Chocolate Chunk Cookies

Kosher Status: Pareve • Prep: 10 minutes • Bake: 17 minutes • Total: 27 minutes • Yield: 12 cookies

My friend Aaron is famous for his killer dairy chocolate chip cookie recipe. But I wanted my cookies to be nondairy and better than Aaron's. Not that I'm competitive. I've perfected this wicked good bittersweet chocolate chunk cookie, with a soft chewy center and slightly crisped edges, just like those big gorgeous cookies from the bakery. And you can eat my yummy pareve cookies after any meal. Take that, Aaron!

2 cups all-purpose flour

½ teaspoon baking soda

½ teaspoon coarse flake sea salt

1 cup (16 tablespoons/2 sticks) margarine, at room temperature

⅔ cup packed light brown sugar

⅔ cup granulated sugar

½ teaspoon pure vanilla extract

2 large eggs, at room temperature

2 tablespoons honey

1½ cups 72% cacao bittersweet chocolate chunks or chocolate chips

1. Preheat the oven to 325°F. Line 2 baking sheets with parchment paper.

2. Whisk the flour, baking soda, and salt together in a large bowl.

3. Place the margarine in the bowl of an electric mixer and beat on high speed until smooth and creamy, 1 to 2 minutes. Add the sugars and vanilla and beat until combined. Beat in the eggs, one at a time, making sure to beat well after each addition. Mix in the honey, then the flour mixture. Add the chocolate chunks, stopping to scrape down the sides of the bowl as needed.

4. Drop the cookie dough, ¼ cup at a time, onto the prepared baking sheets and lightly press down in the center so the cookies will spread and bake evenly (keep 2 inches between each cookie). Bake until the edges are lightly browned, 15 to 17 minutes. Cool 2 minutes on the baking sheet, and then cool completely on a wire rack.

5. Once completely cooled, place the cookies in an airtight container or resealable plastic bag and keep them at room temperature, or freeze them in a resealable freezer bag and thaw them in the bag at room temperature before serving.

• Chocolate Chip Cookie and Cream Stacks •

Form cookie dough balls using a 1-tablespoon ice cream scooper or measuring spoon and your hands. Place the balls on the baking sheet, gently pressing down the centers. Bake until the edges are lightly browned, 9 to 11 minutes. Let cool completely on a wire rack. Stack 3 cookies with whipped cream in between. Add a final dollop of cream on top and garnish with chocolate curls.

Keep this dessert pareve by using nondairy whipped cream. To make your own homemade Nondairy Coconut Whipped Cream, see page 256.

PREP AHEAD

This cookie dough freezes perfectly. Form the dough into balls and freeze on a parchment paper–lined baking sheet. Place the frozen dough balls in a resealable plastic bag and freeze for up to 1 month. No need to thaw before baking, just bake as directed. You may need to increase the baking time by a few minutes.

QUICK TIP

To make chocolate chunks, use a knife to coarsely chop a bar of chocolate.

PAIR IT PSAGOT PRAT

Port and dark chocolate are made for each other. Let this port-style wine complement your cookies (or any other dark chocolate dessert)!

Salted Almond and Pistachio Bark

Kosher Status: Pareve • Prep: 15 minutes • Chill: 4 hours • Total: 4 hours, 15 minutes •
Yield: About 25 pieces of bark (each about 2 x 3 inches)

Bark is one of the easiest things to make. Just ask any tree.

Okay, the poet Joyce Kilmer may have written that only God can make a tree, but we mortals can make a pretty mean chocolate bark (I said that last part). All you need is a microwave and a fridge. And some chocolate.

So, like once a year I get my nails done—my fantasies about having a weekly stand-ing appointment are second only to my fantasies about living in a spa. Anyway, on the occasional days that I get there, they always have Food Network on. One day, I saw Ina Garten make a French chocolate bark, and I thought, How easy-peasy is that? I'm gonna try it. I think that show was at least four years ago, but I remembered it. I have a great memory for some things. My day to drive carpool, not so much; but a recipe idea I want to make stays with me forever.

1¾ pounds good-quality 60% cacao semisweet chocolate, chopped

1¼ cups roasted unsalted almonds, chopped

1¼ cups roasted shelled pistachios, chopped

½ teaspoon pure vanilla extract

1½ teaspoons coarse flake sea salt

1. Line a baking sheet with parchment paper.

2. Place the chocolate in a microwave-safe bowl and melt it in a microwave in 10-second intervals, stirring often, until smooth. Add ½ cup of the almonds, ½ cup of the pistachios, and the vanilla and stir well to coat the nuts. Use a rubber spatula to spread the mixture evenly on the prepared baking sheet. Sprinkle the salt and the remaining ¾ cup almonds and ¾ cup pistachios over the top. Cover and refrigerate until the chocolate is set, 2 to 4 hours.

3. Break the bark into pieces and store in an airtight container with parchment or wax paper between the pieces. The bark can be stored for about 1 week.

TIME-SAVER

Use 2½ cups trail mix in place of the almonds and pistachios.

VARIATION

Make **French Chocolate Bark** like Ina's, which is essentially a combo of dried fruits and nuts sprinkled on top of your bark (as opposed to mixed in). The fruits remind me of shiny jewels. (They know how to do it in France.) Dried apricots, cranberries, cherries, pineapple—anything you like works. Add cashews or peanuts or nuts of your choice. Just coarsely chop your topping; you will need about 2½ cups' worth.

• Kiddie Candy Bark •

Instead of making the bark with nuts and salt, try chopped-up candy bar pieces, crushed pretzels, or mini marshmallows. Experiment with interesting combinations.

PAIR IT CAPÇANES PERAJ PETITA

Not a sweet wine, but it's so fruity and versatile that it goes with most anything, even a salty/sweet dessert.

Sunday: 6:00 p.m.

Putting the mousse before the carte . . .

My mom went through a phase (a long phase) somewhere in my impressionable years when she would order her favorite dessert, chocolate mousse, first whenever we went to a restaurant. Yes, before the meal. That way, she didn't have to worry about saving room for dessert; it would always fit. This is a mother to love.

I inherited her infatuation with the wondrous chocolate mousse, and I always assumed that everyone delights in mousse as much as I do.

One Shabbos, Hubby and I had a newly engaged friend over for dinner. He brought his fiancée with him, so I wanted to celebrate the occasion with a super duper dessert. I made my Peanut Butter Chocolate Mousse and served it in martini glasses. I filled up each glass with this rich, decadent concoction (did they look gorgeous!), chilled them, and waited to make my grand entrance. I brought them out expecting applause, but there was only stunned silence. As I put them down, I realized that those glasses were way bigger than they had seemed when I filled them. Actually, kind of monstrous. I had just served a feast, and now I was planting a gallon of mousse in front of each person. People looked right and looked left, Hubby looked down, I looked heavenward—oh my God, what have I done? What if they don't share my obsession with chocolate and all things mousse, or what if they're just plain full?

Hubby felt so bad for me that he stuffed down his entire gallon. He loves this dessert, but after a crazy huge meal like that . . . I know him . . . I know his face . . . I saw he could barely eat any more, but he just kept shoveling it in so someone would eat my mousse.

I couldn't help thinking maybe I should have served the mousse first.

Well, the rest of the meal must have been great, 'cause that couple came back anyway. I've since learned to dish out much smaller servings—better to keep them wanting more, craving a second helping, and calling you for the recipe.

I now chill mousse in shot glasses of various sizes. That way, when I bring them to the table on a beautiful tray that I gingerly place in the center, people can grab whatever size suits them. And I almost always have a bowl of finger fruit on the side, for those rare birds who would pass up my mousse.

Olive Oil Dark Chocolate Mousse

Kosher Status: Pareve • Prep: 20 minutes • Chill: Overnight •
Total: 20 minutes plus overnight • Yield: 6 servings

I first learned about using fruity, high-quality olive oil in desserts—specifically in choco-late mousse—from executive chef Laura Frankel of Wolfgang Puck Kosher Catering. Just love the flavor and smooth, creamy texture it imparts.

Note that this mousse contains raw eggs. If you're concerned about the risks of eating raw eggs, you can use pasteurized eggs without affecting the results.

10 ounces high-quality 72% cacao bittersweet chocolate, finely chopped, or chocolate chips

8 large eggs, separated, at room temperature

¾ cup granulated sugar

½ cup extra virgin olive oil

1 teaspoon instant coffee granules dissolved in 2 tablespoons boiling water

Grated zest of 1 small orange (optional)

¼ teaspoon kosher salt

1. Place the chocolate in a microwave-safe bowl and melt in a microwave, stirring after each 10-second increment, until smooth, about 1½ minutes. Let cool slightly.

2. Place the egg yolks and ½ cup sugar in a medium bowl and whisk until pale yellow. Whisk in the olive oil, coffee, zest, if using, and salt until combined. Add the melted chocolate and whisk until smooth.

3. Beat the egg whites in the bowl of a stand mixer or with a hand mixer until soft peaks form. Gradually sprinkle in the remaining ¼ cup sugar and beat just until stiff peaks form. Add a generous spoonful of the egg white mixture to the chocolate mixture. Stir firmly until completely incorporated. Pour the chocolate mixture into the bowl of egg whites. Gently fold with a large spoon or rubber spatula until completely combined.

4. Divide the mousse into six 6-ounce ramekins and cover with plastic wrap. Refrigerate overnight.

• Olive Oil Dark Chocolate Mousse Shots •

Serve the mousse with various toppings in individual shot glasses on a vintage silver tray.

Try whipped cream, orange zest curls, coarse flake sea salt, fresh berries, or crushed nuts. For something really special, try my favorite, **Salted Nut Powder**. By hand or in a mini food processor or coffee grinder, combine 3 tablespoons shelled pistachios and 1 teaspoon coarse sea salt. Pulse until ground and slightly powdery but still with some rough chunks. Sprinkle on top of mousse before serving.

PREP AHEAD

The mousse can be made in advance and will last, tightly sealed, in the fridge for 1 week, or in the freezer for up to a month.

PAIR IT ELVI WINERY EL26 DULCE

The richness of this mousse deserves a rich, sweet red dessert wine.

Cherry Bourbon Hand Pies

Kosher Status: Pareve • Prep: 15 minutes • Chill: 30 minutes • Bake: 35 minutes •
Total: 1 hour, 20 minutes • Yield: 8 hand pies

Maybe I didn't quite spell it out for you, but you should know by now that I love pie, any pie. Pumpkin, apple, pecan, key lime, banana cream, lemon meringue, good ol' cherry—they all find a place in my heart and on my hips. I made this pie in a fit of nostalgia for my childhood when we used to eat apple hand pies in bulk from the local fast-food joint. I use frozen cherries because I simply cannot be bothered pitting fresh cherries, m'dear, not even with those cool contraptions they have these days.

This is so delish and divine. And it's all mine. When this came out of the oven, Hubby made the monstrous mistake of getting between a crazy cookbook author and her pie. He'll never do it again.

Flour, for rolling out the pastry

6 cups frozen pitted cherries, thawed and
    drained

1 cup granulated sugar

6 tablespoons Maker's Mark, or your
    favorite bourbon

¼ cup cornstarch

1 teaspoon pure vanilla extract

1 teaspoon kosher salt

One 1-pound package puff pastry
    (2 pastry sheets)

1 large egg, beaten with 1 teaspoon water

8 teaspoons turbinado sugar

1. Preheat the oven to 375°F. Line a baking sheet with parchment paper. Lightly flour your work surface.

2. Combine the cherries, sugar, bourbon, cornstarch, vanilla, and salt in a medium bowl. Working with one pastry sheet at a time, roll out to a 12 x 10-inch rectangle on the lightly floured surface. Using a pizza cutter, cut the pastry into four 6 x 5-inch rectangles. Working with one rectangle at a time, brush the edges lightly with the egg wash and place 3 to 4 tablespoons of the filling on one side. Fold the dough over so the short ends meet, forming a 5 x 3-inch packet. Seal the edges by crimping with a fork, cut 3 small horizontal slits down the middle to vent, and transfer to the prepared baking sheet. Repeat with the remaining pastry sheet and filling.

3. Refrigerate for 30 minutes. Brush the pies with the egg wash and sprinkle the turbinado sugar on top.

4. Bake the pies until golden brown, 30 to 35 minutes. Let cool completely.

DRESS IT DOWN

• **Warm Cherry Topping** •

Cook the cherry filling in a medium saucepan over medium heat until thickened and bubbling. Serve the cherry filling as a warm topping over a scoop of nondairy vanilla "ice cream" (omit the bourbon if you're serving it to children).

PAIR IT WEINSTOCK'S RED BY W

Just a hint of sweetness to pair well with sweet pies.

Sunday: 8:30 a.m.

There's something about a smile . . .

It touches the heart and soul of a person. I thought I knew how to smile, and then I met Mrs. E., who babysits for me. That woman has raised smiling to an art. And she has a repertoire—the warm, glad-to-meet-you smile; the sympathetic smile; the twinkling amused smiled. And it's not just her mouth that's upturned—it's her eyes, her cheeks; her whole face is radiant. After meeting Mrs. E. just once, Little Momma declared, "She's always smiling—she's my bestest friend."

Gooey Chocolate Cherry Cake

Kosher Status: Pareve • Prep: 15 minutes • Bake: 1 hour • Cool: 15 minutes •
Total: 1 hour, 30 minutes • Yield: 9 servings

For great moist chocolate cakes, the best of the best recipes call for buttermilk. If you go nondairy, you can use soy milk, but it just ain't the same. Yes, you can make a homemade version of buttermilk with soy milk and some lemon juice, but I also love using soy sour cream for that really moist texture. I think it's pretty ingenious.

The coffee really brings out the flavor of the chocolate, and the orange zest gives off little hints of fanciness. Oh, and the cherries—well, you gotta love cherries—and chocolate: I like how they sound together, and I loooove how they taste together. This is going to become your favorite easy-as-cake chocolate cake recipe.

Cooking spray

1¾ cups all-purpose flour

¾ cup unsweetened cocoa powder

2¼ cups granulated sugar

1 teaspoon baking powder

2 teaspoons baking soda

1 teaspoon kosher salt

2 large eggs, lightly beaten

½ cup canola oil

One 12-ounce container soy sour cream

1 tablespoon instant coffee granules, dissolved in 1 cup boiling water

Grated zest of 1 small orange

One 3½-ounce bar 72% cacao bittersweet chocolate, chopped

2 cups frozen pitted cherries, thawed and drained well

1. Preheat the oven to 350°F. Lightly spray one 9 x 13-inch baking pan or two 8-inch square baking pans with cooking spray.

2. Stir together the flour, cocoa powder, sugar, baking powder, baking soda, and salt in the bowl of a stand mixer fitted with the paddle attachment. With the mixer on medium speed, add the eggs, canola oil, and soy sour cream and mix until fully incorporated, about 2 minutes. Gently fold in the coffee and orange zest. Pour the batter into the prepared pan(s) and bake immediately.

3. After 20 minutes, remove the pans from the oven. Sprinkle the chocolate and arrange the cherries on top. Return to the oven and continue baking until a toothpick inserted in the center comes out clean, about 40 minutes more.

4. Cool the cake for 15 minutes in the pan. Serve warm or allow to cool completely on a wire rack.

VARIATION

For a classic moist, rich chocolate cake, omit the cherries.

DRESS IT UP

• **Red Wine Chocolate Cherry Cake** •

Replace the coffee with 1 cup dry red wine for a richer treat and stencil a bow, star, heart, or other shape or message of your choice on top of the cake with confectioners' sugar.

Draw and cut out the desired shape on thick cardstock paper. Remove the cooled cake from the pan and place the stencil on top. Dust with confectioners' sugar. Carefully remove the stencil and you'll be left with a beautiful decoration.

PAIR IT HERZOG LATE HARVEST ZINFANDEL

I love to pair chocolate with something that's really fun, like this late harvest zin. Actually, I love pairing chocolate with just about anything.

Cardamom-Scented Chanukah Cookies

Kosher Status: Dairy • Prep: 10 minutes • Chill: 30 minutes • Bake: 12 minutes • Cool: 10 minutes • Total: 1 hour, 2 minutes • Yield: About twenty-four 2-inch cookies

I feel like a good mom when I bake with my kids, especially for the holidays. Just a touch of cardamom transforms these bland little cookies into something super special.

1½ cups all-purpose flour, plus more for
  rolling

½ teaspoon baking powder

¼ teaspoon kosher salt

¼ teaspoon ground cardamom

¼ teaspoon ground ginger

8 tablespoons (1 stick) unsalted butter,
  at room temperature

¼ cup granulated sugar

¼ cup packed light brown sugar

1 large egg

1 tablespoon fresh orange juice

1 cup confectioners' sugar

Blue sugar or sprinkles, for decorating

1. Combine the flour, baking powder, salt, cardamom, and ginger in a small bowl. In a large bowl, beat together the butter and sugars with an electric mixer until light and fluffy. Add the egg and orange juice and beat until combined. Add the flour mixture and mix just until incorporated.

2. Wrap the dough in plastic wrap and chill in the refrigerator for 15 to 30 minutes.

3. Meanwhile, preheat the oven to 350°F. Line 2 baking sheets with parchment paper. Lightly flour your work surface.

4. Flour your rolling pin and cookie cutters. Roll out the dough to ¼ inch thick on the work surface. Cut into desired shapes and place them on the prepared baking sheets. Reroll the scraps as needed. Bake until the edges are just golden, 10 to 12 minutes. Cool 2 minutes on the baking sheet, then move to a wire rack.

5. Place the confectioners' sugar in a small bowl. Add water, 1 tablespoon at a time, and whisk until a smooth, thick, but pourable consistency is reached. Drizzle the frosting on the cookies and decorate them with blue sugar or sprinkles.

• Black and White Chocolate–Dipped Chanukah Cookies •

Our go-to Chanukah activity is cookie decorating. The kids love to pile on mountains of sprinkles, fluff, licorice, chocolate chips, mustard, and glue. (I threw those last two in to see if you're listening. If you're like Hubby, you'd be nodding and going, "Fine, fine.") And when our cousins Samara and Ilana come over to create their masterpieces, our humble cookies become candidates for the Kids' Cookie Hall of Fame. But we grown-ups deserve our day, too, so I recently added this slightly more refined chocolate ganache version to the mix. I mean, how many rainbow sprinkles can a person eat?

To make **Chocolate Ganache,** bring 1 cup heavy cream to a simmer in a small saucepan over medium heat. Place 4 ounces chopped milk chocolate in a small bowl and 4 ounces chopped white chocolate in another small bowl. Pour half of the warm cream into each bowl. Let sit for a few minutes, then stir with rubber spatulas to melt the chocolates. Let cool slightly before dipping your cookies. Divide the cookies into two equal batches. Dip the cookies in one batch in the milk chocolate, covering each cookie halfway; dip the cookies in the second batch in the white chocolate, dipping each cookie halfway. Sprinkle the frosted parts of the cookies with gold and silver decorating sugar.

MAKE IT PAREVE

These are so easy to make nondairy: just sub in margarine for butter. Because it's traditional to eat dairy delicacies on Chanukah, and I rarely have occasion to make dairy desserts, I seized the opportunity to use butter in this recipe. But it's a great quick cookie recipe and shouldn't be relegated to Chanukah—just use cookie cutters that are not holiday themed.

PAIR IT ALFASI LATE HARVEST SAUVIGNON BLANC

Some of the most complex wines are dessert wines, with a wide array of aromas. Sip this one alongside your cookies and enjoy the fruity, spicy sensation.

Chocolate Hazelnut Milk Shake Martinis

Kosher Status: Dairy • Prep: 5 minutes • Cook: 0 minutes • Total: 5 minutes •
Yield: Four 6-ounce milk shakes

When my sister and I were children, Monday afternoon meant special time with Daddy. He would pick us up from school and we'd head straight for Roosevelt Boulevard (the main drag in Northeast Philly), to a diner called Nifty Fifties. Really. Dad came to Pennsylvania from Transylvania in 1964, so he missed the American '50s scene. With its cool retro décor, neon signs, a jukebox, and costumed waitresses with teased-up hair, Nifty was his chance for a taste of that era. Best thing about the joint was the menu: kid heaven. We'd wallow in these "forbidden foods," 'cause Mom's idea of a great outing was the macrobiotic buffet at the health food store. I just loved bonding with Daddy over bubble gum milk shakes. Thick, creamy, pink, and perfect, they were the ideal after-school pick-me-up.

To my disappointment, I later discovered that there's nothing like a Nifty Fifties milk shake in Grown-up Land. This recipe is a mature—dare I say sophisticated?—take on a fondly remembered kid's classic.

1 cup milk

1½ cups vanilla ice cream

¼ cup chocolate hazelnut spread (such as Nutella)

½ to ¾ cup chocolate liqueur, such as Schmerling's or Godiva

½ cup seltzer, chilled

Combine the milk, ice cream, chocolate spread, and liqueur to taste in a blender; blend until smooth. Add the seltzer and stir to combine. Divide among four chilled martini glasses.

VARIATION

If you have nut allergies in your family, replace the chocolate hazelnut spread with plain chocolate spread or chocolate syrup.

PAIR IT WALDERS VODKA & VANILLA LIQUEUR

Forget about pairing. Just add a bit of this to your drink, sit back, and enjoy.

• **Chocolate Hazelnut Milk Shakes** •

Lose the liqueur and seltzer and up the ice cream to 1 quart.

Serve the kids their cool, creamy treat in tall milk shake glasses, each garnished with a maraschino cherry. Yields four 8-ounce milk shakes.

MAKE IT A MEAL

Ya think I would suggest serving dessert as a meal? Just look the other way while I whisper in your ear that this recipe is the perfect match for my Big Chewy Dark Chocolate Chunk Cookies (page 277). If you eat a few extra cookies (who's counting?), there may not be room for dinner—and then you don't have to cook. Well, okay, if you insist on healthful meals, serve these shakes alongside my Butternut Squash Mac 'n' Cheese (page 243), which is a lighter but still creamy version of that classic, and if made with whole wheat pasta, a healthful and proper balance to the milk shake guilt.

Friday: 1:10 p.m.

The "quick" Dobos torte that was never meant to be . . .

So I'm wondering what ever put it into my head to include a Dobos recipe in this book. It's pronounced "Dobosh," and this Hungarian doozy was a two-man (or one-woman) job in Ma and Uputzi's house. It was a masterpiece: sweet cake, bittersweet chocolate, rock-hard caramelized sugar top. Four days to make, and four minutes to eat—that's Hungarian baking for you. So I set out to come up with a riff that doesn't take the better part of a week. I mean, that's what I'm all about: quick results. To my mind, no recipe should schlep out for four days.

My adopted "grandmother," Miri, gave me her family cookbook, a beautiful hard-cover key to Hungarian baking secrets. I flipped it open to find a Dobos recipe—and there it was. But so complicated! It would be easier to play Liszt's Hungarian Rhapsody with oven mitts on both hands than to do this. So I surfed the net and found another authentic recipe that had no less than fifty-three steps. Fifty-three.

There's gotta be a quicker way.

So I got up bright and early one morning, determined to find the Northwest Passage to Dobosland. Hubby called it the First Annual Day of the Dobos. He knew this thing would take me no less than a whole day, if not a whole week. I stood there for hours, caramelizing, burning, and caramelizing some more, and then poured the glaze on top. And something really weird happened to my no-egg, no-cream, no-butter "buttercream." Maybe it didn't like my face, or maybe I had encountered the catastrophic Curse of the Angry Dobos, but it just wouldn't spread.

The kids came home from school and didn't even ask for a piece—and they always beg for a piece of anything that might be edible. They just glanced scornfully at the mess on the kitchen counter and went for the pretzels.

Around dusk, I tried a second time. And I'm proud to say that by 1:00 a.m., I presented my creation to a groggy but patient Hubby. We needed a hammer and chisel to slice it, and Hubby wondered aloud if this was some old Hungarian custom—a real sign of love when a man has to take a hammer and chisel to his lady's Dobos.

And that is why there is no Dobos recipe in this book. I dropped the idea rather than dishonor the memory of my grandparents, Miri, and every other Hungarian baker out there.

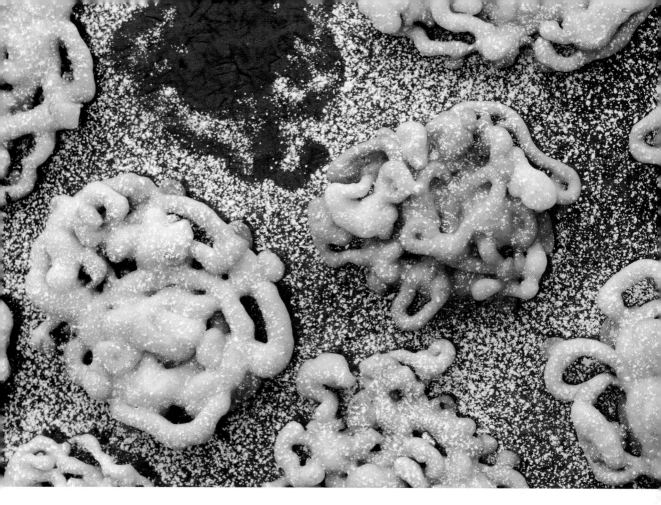

Funnel Cakes

Kosher Status: Dairy • Prep: 10 minutes • Cook: 6 minutes • Total: 16 minutes • Yield: 6 funnel cakes

Note: *If not serving immediately, keep the funnel cakes warm in a 200°F oven. Dust with confectioners' sugar just before serving.*

A few weeks ago, I went with my friend Tamar to a new restaurant, and I saw funnel cakes on the menu (served with basil ice cream, yet). OMG, I hadn't eaten these in years, not since I was a kid skipping through the Philadelphia Zoo. The guy there would make a fabulous funnel cake right before your eyes: It was like magic—hot, puffy, golden, fried magic—with confectioners' sugar on top.

And I got to thinking: How come I never shared the joy of funnel cake with my kids? So here it is, you guys—my most favorite dessert (after pie): funnel cake!

2 cups all-purpose flour

1 teaspoon baking powder

¼ teaspoon kosher salt

1 tablespoon granulated sugar

1⅓ cups whole milk

1 large egg, beaten

½ teaspoon pure vanilla extract

Juice of ½ lemon

Canola oil, for frying

Confectioners' sugar, for dusting

1. Sift together the flour and baking powder into a large bowl. Add the salt and sugar and stir. Whisk together the milk, egg, vanilla, and lemon juice in a medium bowl. Add the wet ingredients to the dry ingredients and whisk together.

2. Line a baking sheet with paper towels.

3. Pour the batter into a squeeze bottle or a pastry bag fitted with a large plain tip. Pour about ½ inch canola oil into a 9-inch sauté pan and heat over medium-high heat until the oil reaches 350°F. Squeeze ½ cup batter in a squiggly pattern all around the pan. Cook until set, about 30 seconds. Carefully flip with tongs and cook until golden brown on both sides, about 30 seconds more. Drain on the prepared baking sheet. Top with confectioners' sugar and serve immediately. Repeat with remaining batter.

DRESS IT UP

• Funnel Cakes with Basil Ice Cream •

Serve the funnel cakes topped with basil ice cream and a drizzle of hot fudge, if desired. (Don'tcha just love it when cookbooks say to add something irresistible "if desired," like it's an option? Once it's been suggested, how can you not desire it?)

Basil Ice Cream: Let a 1-pint container of vanilla ice cream soften at room temperature. Tear ⅓ cup packed basil leaves into small pieces. Put the leaves in a blender with a pinch of salt and ¼ teaspoon finely grated lemon zest. Blend for a second or two; scrape down the sides. Add ¼ cup ice cream to the blender and blend until the basil is pureed. Press the puree through a fine-mesh sieve; discard the solids. Mix the puree thoroughly into the rest of the ice cream. Freeze until solid, at least 4 hours.

PAIR IT BARTENURA BLUE BOTTLE MOSCATO

Pair this carnival treat with a classic bubbly sweet wine.

Orange-Scented Cheesecake

Kosher Status: Dairy • Prep: 20 minutes • Bake: 20 minutes plus 1½ hours • Cook: 15 minutes •
Cool: 1 hour • Chill: 4 hours • Total: 7 hours, 25 minutes • Yield: One 9-inch cheesecake

*Hands-down incredible, this cheesecake is one of the 101 ways to say "I love you." At least
to my neighbors. I am the only cheesecake lover in this house, so I had to walk this baby
over to Ilana and her six cheesecake-loving kids for a taste test. Well, they loved me back,
and it was one happy day on the block.*

2 cups graham cracker crumbs

⅓ cup plus ¼ cup granulated sugar

8 tablespoons (1 stick) unsalted butter,
  melted

1 cup fresh orange juice

½ cup packed light brown sugar

Four 8-ounce packages cream cheese,
  at room temperature

Grated zest of 2 oranges

1 cup sour cream

¼ cup all-purpose flour

½ teaspoon kosher salt

5 large eggs

1. Preheat the oven to 350°F.

2. Combine the graham cracker crumbs with ⅓ cup granulated sugar and the butter in a
   large bowl; stir until all the crumbs are moist. Press the crumb mixture evenly onto the
   bottom of a 9-inch springform pan. Bake until golden brown and set, 15 to 20 minutes.
   Cool completely. (Keep the oven on for the cheesecake.)

3. Meanwhile, combine the orange juice and brown sugar in a small saucepan; bring to a
   boil. Stir until the sugar dissolves. Simmer until the mixture thickens, 10 to 15 minutes.
   Set aside to cool.

4. In a stand mixer fitted with a paddle attachment, beat the cream cheese and the remaining ¼ cup sugar until smooth. Add the orange zest, sour cream, flour, and salt;
   beat for 2 minutes. Add the eggs one at a time, mixing well after each addition. Mix in
   the cooled orange juice and beat to combine.

5. Pour the cream cheese mixture on the crust and place the springform pan in a large roasting pan. Pour enough boiling water into the roasting pan to come halfway up the sides of the springform pan. Bake until just set in the center, about 1½ hours. If the top starts to brown too much, loosely cover with a piece of foil. Remove the cheesecake from the water bath. Cool 1 hour on a wire rack. Place in the refrigerator and chill at least 4 hours or overnight before removing the sides of the pan.

DRESS IT UP
• Candied-Orange Cheesecake •

Now this is what you serve when it's time to impress. Just a little more fuss for a whammo cheesecake.

Thinly slice 2 medium oranges and place in a medium saucepan. Add 1 cup sugar and 1 cup water; mix well. Simmer until the oranges are translucent and tender, about 30 minutes. Let cool slightly and arrange all over the top of the cooled cheesecake. To serve, drizzle a little of the syrup over slices of cheesecake.

PREP AHEAD

Prepare the orange slices and the cake and store them separately in the fridge. Top/decorate just before serving.

TIME-SAVER

You can use a store-bought graham cracker pie shell, but beware: This is a deep-dish cheesecake recipe, so you have enough filling for two store-bought pie shells; bake for 45 to 55 minutes. Also, when I'm feeling lazy, I don't always do the water bath, and the top doesn't crack. So if that aspect of the recipe scares you away, it's okay to bake the cheesecake without it.

PAIR IT HERZOG RESERVE LATE HARVEST CHENIN BLANC

A hearty dessert wine that will complement the rich orange cheesecake flavors.

Black and White Ice Cream Bombe

Kosher Status: Dairy • Prep: 12 minutes • Cook: 3 minutes • Freeze: 4 hours •
Total: 4 hours, 15 minutes • Yield: 8 to 10 servings

I should have been a doctor. Not because of my genius, or because I can stand seeing blood, but because of my handwriting. No one can read it, not even me.

Well, lately I've become a doctor of sorts. Call me Jamie Geller, D.D.—Doctor of Desserts. Just watch. I take a simple gallon of plain vanilla ice cream and doctor it up to make it a thing of beauty. This is one of those grab-your-camera-when-you-present-me desserts. It's delicious, too, and easier (way easier) than pie—the love of my life—after Hubby, the kids, and brisket.

One 1-gallon container vanilla ice cream

6 tablespoons heavy cream

6 ounces good-quality 60% cacao semisweet chocolate, chopped, plus more for garnish

3 ounces good-quality white chocolate, chopped

Whipped cream

1. Invert the container of ice cream onto a serving platter. Cut away the carton with a pair of scissors. Smooth the surface of the ice cream. Refreeze the ice cream until it hardens, about 2 hours.

2. Warm the heavy cream in a small saucepan over medium heat until just bubbling.

3. Melt 3 ounces of the semisweet chocolate in a double boiler over low heat or in a microwave-safe bowl in 10-second intervals in the microwave, stirring after each interval.

4. Slowly pour the warm cream into the melted chocolate, stirring continually, until incorporated and a smooth ganache forms. Let cool until slightly warm but still pourable.

5. Remove the ice cream from the freezer. Pour the ganache all over the ice cream, letting it drip down the sides. Freeze until the chocolate is set, about 2 hours.

6. Surround the ice cream with the white chocolate and the remaining 3 ounces dark chocolate. Serve topped with a dollop of whipped cream.

• **Black and White Sundae Bar** •

Serve the ice cream in scoops in beautiful individual bowls.

Surround them with bowls of chopped dark and white chocolate, crushed Oreo cookies, mini marshmallows, black licorice, slivered almonds, pitted black cherries, chopped brownie pieces, chocolate sprinkles, hot fudge, and sweetened whipped cream.

VARIATION

Choose three different flavors of ice cream to create colorful layers in a loaf pan. Line a loaf pan with plastic wrap, letting some of the wrap overhang the sides of the pan. Soften one flavor of ice cream enough to scoop and spread it in the bottom of the pan. Freeze until solid, about 1 hour. Repeat with the other two flavors, one at a time, making sure to freeze until solid, about 1 hour, after each layer. Unmold the ice cream by inverting the pan onto a serving platter and removing the pan and the plastic wrap. Smooth the ice cream, cover it with the ganache as instructed above, and freeze until the ganache is set, about 2 hours.

TIME-SAVER

Of course if you like vanilla, chocolate, and strawberry, you can just buy a tub of Neapolitan and call it a day.

QUICK TIP

Chocolate ganache is the mother of all chocolate sauces in the pastry world. It's supersimple to make this multipurpose sauce. All you have to remember is a 1:1 ratio of warm heavy cream to slightly cooled melted chocolate.

PAIR IT WALDERS VODKA & VANILLA LIQUEUR

After the kids go to bed, slice off a piece of the bombe and pour this right on top of the ice cream.

Cannoli Egg Rolls with Chocolate Sauce

Kosher Status: Dairy • Prep: 10 minutes • Cook: 6 minutes • Total: 16 minutes • Yield: 8 egg rolls

So I had a lot of frozen egg roll wrappers, which I usually use for, well, egg rolls—until one day I tried them for strudel and the next day for cannoli. Before you knew it, I was a wild egg roll wrapper woman—totally unstoppable.

2 cups ricotta cheese

6 tablespoons confectioners' sugar

Grated or finely chopped zest of 2 small lemons

½ cup coarsely chopped pistachios

2 teaspoons pure vanilla extract

8 egg roll wrappers, thawed

Canola oil, for frying

1 cup store-bought chocolate sauce, for serving

1. Make the filling: Combine the ricotta, sugar, lemon zest, pistachios, and vanilla in a medium bowl and stir well.

2. Lay out the egg roll wrappers on a large work surface. Working with one wrapper at a time, spoon about ¼ cup of the ricotta mixture across the middle of the wrapper, on the diagonal. Lightly brush all the edges with water. Turn the wrapper so that one corner is directly in front of you. Fold that corner up just enough to cover the filling. Fold each side over to meet in the middle and roll up from the bottom. Brush the final corner with water and press lightly to seal. Transfer to a baking sheet, seam side down. Repeat with remaining wrappers and filling.

3. Line a baking sheet with paper towels.

4. Heat about ¼ inch canola oil in a large skillet over medium-high heat. Fry the rolls, turning often, until golden brown on all sides, 5 to 6 minutes total. Remove the cannoli rolls with tongs and drain them on the prepared baking sheet. Serve warm or at room temperature with chocolate sauce on the side for dipping.

• Cannoli Cones •

Cones aren't just for kiddies. These grown-up cones overflowing with sweet ricotta make me feel young(er).

Dip the tops of 6 sugar cones in the chocolate sauce, letting the excess run down on the inside. Fill a pastry bag fitted with a wide tip, or a resealable plastic bag with a corner snipped off, with the ricotta filling. Pipe the filling into the cone and sprinkle with extra chopped pistachios for garnish. Variations: Finish some cannoli cones with a cherry on top. Also try filling sugar cones with fresh whipped cream and berries.

PAIR IT PORTO CORDOVERO PORT

Here's the place for that fab chocolate and port combo again. Nothing like the rich chocolate sauce in this dish to bring out the flavor in port.

Challah

1 Dough, 10 Sweet and Savory Recipes

Friday, 12:00 p.m.

It's not just bread.

Hubby never lets us call it bread. He always corrects us, "You mean . . . challah." He's right about that, of course.

In my almost eight years of marriage, I have made probably about 1,000 pounds of challah. Sounds crazy, right? Crazier still is that when I compare my wedding pictures to today's snapshots, it kinda sorta looks like I ate the entire 1,000 pounds all by myself. Either that or I had five kids in five minutes and lost the directions to the gym.

I knead my challah by hand. I don't own a bread machine. I know, I know, you'd think I'd be the first to run out and buy one. After all, I'm the queen of Quick & Kosher, and that's not just the way I cook. It's a metaphor for my entire life. (Did I tell you that Hubby and I dated for two weeks and married two months later?)

But when it comes to challah I don't own a bread machine, partly because it's pretty expensive, but mainly because I pray for my family as I knead the dough.

That's right. I pray. Okay, I shall now explain.

If you can stretch your notion of spirituality all the way into the kitchen, consider this. Challah is one of those foods that is a spiritual key, placing it front and center at the start of all our Shabbos and holiday meals. We eat challah every Shabbos as an allusion to the manna that God showered on the Israelites in the desert after they left Egypt. The manna would fall every day, but it was just enough for one day. The Israelites had to learn to trust in God for their daily sustenance and not worry about tomorrow. That's a pretty good lesson in itself. But the kicker is that every Friday a double amount would fall, so there would be enough to eat on Shabbos morning. We put two challahs on the Shabbos table, as a reminder of the Friday double portion of manna.

Every week, we enjoy our challah. At the same time, we deepen our faith in God, who loves us so much that He provides us with everything we need day after day, from paying the mortgage down to my daughters' Hello Kitty flip-flops. We reaffirm our allegiance to Shabbos, a day so special that we don't cook or bake; we just eat delicacies we prepared on Friday.

Sooooo, as I was saying, while I knead the dough of that holy bread, it's a nice, quiet interlude for prayers, both big (for world peace and ending global hunger) and small (please don't let this challah burn), for everyone that I know and love, for all those in need of healing, or who need to find a soul mate, or who need financial help.

You don't have to be in a house of worship, all squeaky clean, to pray. You can be up to your elbows in thick, sticky dough, with flour on your face. He'll hear you.

I'm sure you can pray when the mixer is going (and you can most certainly pray any other time of day or night), but I like to put my heart and soul—along with my fists and biceps—into my challah. It's true that I do everything else *chick chock* (an Israeli expression that means "in a jiffy"), but on this, I take my time.

That doesn't mean I won't give you time-savers in this chapter. There are plenty. And if you want to use a bread machine, please do. It's a lot easier on the knuckles.

WARNING: Check the capacity of your mixer. Most can't handle more than a few pounds at a time. Don't try going beyond that. You'll get smoke, splatter, and a scary-looking kitchen.

The Spiritual Significance
of Challah

There's another reason this unique bread pays spiritual dividends, but to understand it we have to visit ancient Israel for a minute. (Don't worry. I'll bring you back.) Back in the days of the Holy Temple in Jerusalem, people called *Kohanim* (a huge extended family, really) did not own farmland because their sole task was to serve in the Temple and teach the holy Torah to every Jew. The *mitzvah* (law) of giving them tithes and food gifts was mandated so they could devote themselves exclusively to this calling. One of those gifts was called "challah," which meant that whenever someone baked bread, he or she was to give a small portion of it to a friendly local Kohen. And the baker did not just drop a package on the doorstep and run. He would learn some Torah with the Kohen, maybe have a cup of tea and schmooze a while. This exchange not only fed the Kohanim and their families; it fortified the bond between average Israelites and their spiritual mentors. It was a great system.

Today there's no Holy Temple, but we still keep the mitzvah, called *hafrashas challah*, to elevate that simple act of baking bread to a spiritual activity. If you knead at least 2 pounds 10 ounces of dough, a small piece of raw dough is separated out (about the volume of an olive will do), wrapped completely in foil, and left in the oven till it's charred. After that, it's thrown away because today we are not permitted to practice specific Temple rituals in the absence of our Holy Temple in Jerusalem. This bit of challah is only a reminder of the ancient practice of giving challah to a Kohen. If more dough than that is kneaded, there's even a special blessing to say.

Challah Basics

The Bowl: So you are going to need a big momma plastic bowl (about 10 quarts) to make this challah dough recipe. It starts with 6 pounds of flour; and when you are done, you will have more than 10 pounds of dough.

The Flour: I always use flour that is high in gluten because gluten adds stickiness and sponginess to the dough. High-gluten flour will give you a nice chewy texture. Bread flour or bread machine flour are interchangeable with high-gluten flour. All-purpose flour can be subbed if necessary.

This recipe calls for a 6-pound bag of high-gluten (bread) flour. People are always e-mailing, texting, and calling me, asking, "Didn't you mean a 5-pound bag?" because they can't find the 6-pound bag in their stores. I lived in Queens and Monsey, two neighborhoods worlds and miles apart in New York; and in both necks of the woods, 6-pound bags are readily available. But fear not if you can't find them: 3¼ cups of high-gluten flour equals 1 pound, and 3¾ cups of all-purpose flour is equivalent to 1 pound.

The Yeast: Red Star is by far the best yeast on the market. If you plan to make challah and or use yeast regularly, buy it in bulk (Red Star comes in large 2-pound vacuum-sealed packages at Costco) so that you don't have to fiddle with lots of those little packets.

Blooming the Yeast: If the water is too warm it will kill your yeast. You're looking for the temperature of a baby's bath. Now, when I first started making challah I didn't have a baby, so I had no clue what that meant. Just to make sure we don't end up with dead yeast, water in the range of 90°F to 100°F is what we want here. Blooming, or proofing, the yeast is a way to make sure the yeast is indeed active. If the yeast doesn't become bubbly and frothy and about double in volume, your challah will not rise; discard the mixture and start over.

The Fridge/Freezer Effect: Because you may not want to eat all 10 pounds of dough at once (I did when testing for this chapter, and I'm telling you: all at once, not a good idea!), you can refrigerate or freeze your 2-pound pieces of dough. To freeze: Punch down the dough to release any air bubbles and form it into a round mass. Tightly wrap with plastic wrap and place in a 1-gallon resealable plastic freezer bag. Although it's not necessary, I like wrapping the dough in plastic wrap first, because it trains my dough to behave and not get a mind of its own and explode to alien proportions in my fridge.

The dough can be stored in the fridge for about 3 days. At 5 days it begins to ferment. While it will still be tasty, it may not rise—and who wants challah pita? The dough can be frozen for about 3 months. Just make sure to let it come to room temperature (in the bags, so it doesn't form a skin) before shaping.

Tips for Rolling: If your dough sticks to the work surface when you roll it out, resist the urge to add flour. Spray your work surface with cooking spray instead. If the dough is still really too sticky to work with, lightly oil the fingertips of one hand, rub your hands together to lightly coat both hands, and then work with the dough. If you have a large nonstick mat for rolling dough, that will work great, too.

The Pans: To make all the dressed-up variations on the following pages (and believe you me, you will want to try them all), you'll need the following equipment: baking sheets (at least two), 9-inch round baking pans, and 1-cup capacity jumbo muffin pans or individual 5-inch round challah roll pans. In addition, a bonus pan, although not required, is a 13-inch-long oval challah pan. Note that one recipe is dairy and requires a baking sheet and a 9-inch round baking pan.

How to Serve Challah: Challah is divine when served warm. If you're making it ahead and not serving it immediately, follow these instructions for storing and rewarming. For the first 24 hours, challahs can be stored, uncovered, in their baking pans. For convenience, once the challahs are completely cooled, or after 24 hours, place them in resealable plastic bags for up to 3 days. Before serving the challahs, remove them from the plastic bags and wrap them in aluminum foil. Heat them in a warm oven or warming drawer or on a hot plate until hot and soft. After 3 to 4 days, challahs really lose their freshness, but will still be beyond yum if sliced and toasted or turned into our Sunday morning staple, challah French toast!

Basic Pull-Apart Challah

Kosher Status: Pareve • Prep: 35 minutes • Rise: 2 hours, 15 minutes • Bake: 45 to 55 minutes •
Cool: 15 minutes • Total: About 4 hours • Yield: 10 pounds, 6 ounces dough, 5 challahs

It all starts here: your basic challah.

First things first: Master the dough. Traditional challahs are shaped by braiding six strands of dough into a beautiful braid, and I have a step-by-step video on how to do it on my website, www.JoyofKosher.com. But "pull-apart" challah skips the braiding and is way easier to make. It's pretty, too. Seven dough balls are positioned along the rim of an 8- or 9-inch round baking pan, and one dough ball sits in the center. This masterpiece looks like a beautiful flower. After you bake it up, all golden brown, each section can be easily pulled off. You don't even need a knife.

Traditionally, challah is sliced or torn, and the first bite is dipped in salt three times (it's a kabalistic thing) and then passed around to everyone. (We use kosher salt at our house because the large coarse flakes make it extra delicious.)

So this recipe is a riff on the challah dough recipe in my first book. I've been making it practically every week for the past seven years, so it's been tweaked and perfected to the point that Hubby and the kids purr with pleasure with every first bite. If I miss a week, there'll be whining and tears. (That's Hubby, but the children don't take it well, either.)

But weekly challah doesn't have to be boring. You can mix it up, changing the flavor in dozens of ways. That's what I like about this dough; it's very versatile. I'm not the type to sit there and patchka *with all different kinds of dough from scratch. So what I do is make at least six pounds of dough and divide it into five equal sections and store them in my freezer. (See instructions.) Then I use them one at a time to make the variations that follow. This way, it's like going shopping for prepared dough in my freezer instead of at the supermarket. Of course, you don't need to knead. Any of these recipes can be made with frozen dough (bread, challah, or pizza) from your supermarket freezer as well.*

It sort of amazes me that just by the strength of my hands and the love in my heart, plus a few basic ingredients, I can work this magic. You can, too.

2 ounces (¼ cup) active dry yeast

2 cups plus 3 tablespoons granulated
  sugar

6 cups warm water (90° to 100°F)

¼ cup kosher salt

6 pounds high-gluten (bread) or all-
  purpose flour (see page 320)

4 large eggs, separated

1¼ cups canola oil

Cooking spray

½ cup sesame seeds

½ cup poppy seeds

1. Bloom the yeast: Dissolve the yeast and 3 tablespoons sugar in 2 cups of the warm water in a medium bowl; set aside to bloom. If the yeast doesn't bloom after 5 minutes, discard the mixture and start over.

2. Place the salt, flour, and the remaining 2 cups sugar together in a very large bowl and stir together. Add the 4 egg yolks. Make a well in the middle and add the yeast mixture and the remaining 4 cups water. Start kneading together; add ½ cup canola oil. Knead for 10 minutes, adding another ½ cup canola oil, a small amount at a time, to create a workable dough. The dough will become a cohesive mass yet be a bit sticky. Rub a little of the remaining ¼ cup canola oil over the top and sides of the dough. Loosely cover the dough with a kitchen towel and place the bowl in a warm spot for 15 minutes.

3. After 15 minutes, the dough will have relaxed a bit and should be easier to work with. Lightly oil your hands and knead the dough again until smooth and satiny, 2 to 3 minutes. Rub a little oil over the top and sides of the dough. Cover with a kitchen towel and place the bowl in a medium garbage bag. Place the open end loosely underneath the bowl to trap air. Let the dough rise in a warm dark corner of your kitchen until doubled in size, about 1 hour.

4. Uncover the dough. With lightly oiled hands, punch the dough down to release air. Cover again with the bag, loosely tucked under, and let rise for 1 hour.

5. Divide the dough into five equal parts, about 2 pounds each. Preheat the oven to 375°F. Spray five 9-inch round baking pans with cooking spray.

6. Place one piece of dough on a smooth work surface. Squeeze out any air bubbles from the dough and roll it into a 12-inch rope. If the dough is sticking, lightly spray your work

surface with cooking spray. Cut the rope into eight equal pieces. Roll each piece into a ball. Place one ball in the center of the prepared pan and surround it with the remaining balls. Repeat with the remaining pieces of dough so you have five pans of challah. Loosely cover each pan with a kitchen towel or plastic wrap and let rise 15 minutes. (If you can't fit all the pans in your oven at once and you want your challahs to be as beautiful as possible, shape the remaining dough while the first round of challahs are in the oven so they don't rise for too much longer than 15 minutes before baking.)

7. Beat the egg whites with 1 teaspoon water in a small bowl and brush the challahs. Sprinkle each with sesame or poppy seeds or a combination of the two.

8. Bake for 10 minutes. Reduce the temperature to 350°F and bake until tops are dark golden brown, 35 to 45 minutes more. Let cool 15 minutes before serving warm, or cool completely on a wire rack.

DRESS IT UP

The Basic Pull-Apart Challah recipe will yield just over 10 pounds of dough, which you will separate into five equal pieces, about 2 pounds each.

You can make five Basic Pull-Apart Challahs as described above, or you can use each of the 2-pound pieces of dough to try one or more of the to-die-for dressed-up variations on the following pages. Each of the following dressed-up variations begins with 2 pounds of prepared Basic Pull-Apart Challah dough.

Shalom Bayis
*Pull-Apart
Challah,*
page 328

*Sun-Dried Tomato,
Garlic, and Herb
Braided Challah,*
page 331

Cran-Rosemary
Crown Challah,
page 330

Blueberry Apple
Challah Rolls,
page 333

Shalom Bayis Pull-Apart Challah

Kosher Status: Pareve • Prep: 15 minutes • Rise: 15 minutes • Bake: 45 to 55 minutes • Cool: 15 minutes • Total: About 2 hours • Yield: One 8-piece pull-apart loaf • photo on page 326

So what's a Shalom Bayis Challah?

Shalom Bayis *literally means "peace in the home."*

It really means peace in the family. Not just the absence of strife—true harmony.

I could give you all kinds of reasons to work toward this utopian goal. A transcendent reason is that God's presence can be found wherever there is unity and accord, especially in a happy home. But there's the plain, obvious fact that when a husband and wife are on the same page, going out of their way to please each other, they're both happy. They are better parents and the kids are happy. That's shalom bayis.

It's not always easy. Because people are people. Hubby and I have a great marriage ("tenks Gott!") but we don't see eye to eye on everything, especially food. We yin and yang our way through every restaurant menu. We wind up ordering ten different things—some for him, some for me, and some we'll share. We get away with it because we tell the waiter that I'm writing a cookbook and need to sample everything.

In a Jewish home, it's like there's this huge, invisible sign that reads SHALOM BAYIS! *over the doorway. Every member of the family tries to keep the peace. It means sometimes giving up something you want because someone else wants it more, or making it a point to remember each other's preferences.*

My sister, Shoshana, tells me that in her local Brooklyn bakery the biggest hit is a pull-apart Shalom Bayis Challah. Huh? It simply means that to accommodate differing tastes that are inevitable in a family, they make each ball out of a different kind of dough. So in one challah, you've got separate sections that are egg challah, water challah, whole wheat, and spelt, and so on. That way, everyone gets what he or she prefers and shalom bayis is preserved on an exquisite epicurean level.

That idea inspired me to this quick trick: challah toppings to suit every tastebud. I use cinnamon sugar for a sweet center, and then top each of the surrounding sections with sesame or poppy or sea salt or garlic powder or oats or caraway seeds or "everything." Make a topping for each member of the family (and your special guests!). There's nothing like knowing that this *piece of challah was made lovingly and especially for them.*

Cooking spray

2 pounds Basic Pull-Apart Challah dough
   (page 323)

1 large egg

¼ teaspoon cinnamon sugar

¼ teaspoon Everything Topping
   (page 336)

¼ teaspoon sesame seeds

¼ teaspoon freshly ground black pepper

¼ teaspoon poppy seeds

¼ teaspoon pretzel salt or coarse flake
   sea salt

¼ teaspoon old-fashioned rolled oats

¼ teaspoon caraway or flax seeds

1. Preheat the oven to 375°F. Spray a 9-inch round baking pan with cooking spray.

2. Place the dough on a smooth work surface. Squeeze out any air bubbles from the dough and roll it into a 12-inch rope. If the dough is sticking, lightly spray your work surface with cooking spray. Cut the rope into eight equal pieces. Roll each piece into a ball. Place one ball in the center of the prepared pan and surround it with the remaining balls. Cover loosely with a kitchen towel or plastic wrap and let rise 15 minutes.

3. Beat the egg with 1 teaspoon water in a small bowl. Brush the balls with the egg mixture. Sprinkle the middle ball with the cinnamon sugar and each of the other balls with one of the remaining seven toppings, taking care not to mix flavors.

4. Bake for 10 minutes. Reduce the temperature to 350°F and bake until the tops are dark golden brown, 35 to 45 minutes. Let cool 15 minutes in the pan and serve warm, or carefully transfer to a wire rack to cool completely.

VARIATION

Now is when you get to express your individuality or cater to your loved ones. Any topping you like will work. Here are some other suggestions: za'atar spice mix, pumpkin pie mix, minced onion or garlic (brush on some oil and add onion or garlic in the last 15 minutes of baking, to avoid burning). You need ¼ teaspoon of the topping of your choice for each ball.

Cran-Rosemary Crown Challah

Kosher Status: Pareve • Prep: 20 minutes • Rise: 30 minutes • Bake: 50 to 60 minutes •
Cool: 15 minutes • Total: About 2 hours • Yield: 1 large crown loaf • photo on page 327

*One of the central ideas of the Rosh Hashanah prayers is that we recognize God's total
control over everything—everything!—in the universe (and beyond). That's more than
most folks can envision. So we put it in human terms: We "crown" Him as our King.
Crown challahs are traditionally served on Rosh Hashanah, and throughout the entire
High Holiday season, to symbolize that concept.*

*Round challahs, in general, are traditional for this holiday, and lots of people just
coil one long, thick rope of dough into a spiral in the baking pan. (That's the easy way.)
But I like this dressed-up, more elegant way of making a round challah because it looks
more like a crown. I take the opportunity to discuss all these lofty ideas, in kid language,
with my children as we shape the dough together. It really helps to watch someone do
this. I have a video online at www.JoyofKosher.com that shows step-by-step instructions
for how to make crown challah.*

*You probably already know that cranberry and rosemary go wonderfully together. I
added a nice note of orange with some zest to keep it interesting. Dried cranberries with
fresh or dried rosemary work beautifully here. See how flexible I am?*

Cooking spray

½ cup coarsely chopped dried
  cranberries

1 tablespoon finely chopped fresh
  rosemary or 1 teaspoon dried

1 teaspoon grated orange zest

1 teaspoon extra virgin olive oil

2 pounds Basic Pull-Apart Challah dough
  (page 323)

1 large egg

1. Preheat the oven to 375°F. Spray a 9-inch round baking pan with cooking spray.

2. Combine the cranberries, rosemary, orange zest, and olive oil in a small bowl.

3. Place the dough on a smooth work surface. Cut the dough into three equal pieces. Roll
   each piece into a 24-inch rope. If the dough is sticking, lightly spray your work surface
   with cooking spray. Using a rolling pin, roll out each rope into a 3-inch-wide strip.
   Distribute the cranberry mixture among the strips, spooning it lengthwise down the

middle. Working quickly, bring the sides of the strips up and over the filling and pinch tightly to seal well.

4. Lay the filled ropes side by side, and pinch them together tightly at one end. Braid the ropes snugly, and pinch tightly to seal all three strands together at the other end. Hold the braid at each end; gently stretch and pull the braid to elongate. Tie the braid in a single loose knot, and tuck the loose ends under the bottom to secure. Place, bottom down, in the prepared baking pan. Lightly cover with a kitchen towel or plastic wrap and let rise 30 minutes.

5. Beat the egg with 1 teaspoon water in a small bowl. Brush the dough with the egg mixture and bake for 10 minutes. Reduce the temperature to 350°F. Bake until dark golden brown, 40 to 50 minutes. Let cool 15 minutes in the pan and serve warm, or carefully transfer to a wire rack to cool completely.

Sun-Dried Tomato, Garlic, and Herb Braided Challah

Kosher Status: Pareve • Prep: 20 minutes • Rise: 30 minutes • Bake: 55 minutes to 1 hour, 5 minutes • Cool: 15 minutes • Total: About 2 hours • Yield: 1 large loaf • photo on page 326

If you know how to braid hair, you can make a pretty three-strand braided challah. My special, dearest friend Monet loves to experiment in the kitchen and almost never follows a proper recipe. One Shabbos more than ten years ago, when she was entertaining (and experimenting on) thirty guests (including me), she improvised a special savory challah with an herb- and garlic-infused oil. What an experience!

Back then, I was into eating, not cooking, and couldn't care less how she did it. When I asked her about it recently, she gave me a blank stare. So this recipe is loosely inspired by that memory, since neither of us can be sure what was in the challah and what was in the oil. I may be imagining the sun-dried tomatoes in this distant recollection. So if this is not actually something Monet created, it's something special that she would serve at her table, even if she didn't. Come to think of it—this entire thing may be totally my own original recipe. Let's just say I'm channeling my inner Monet with this one.

Cooking spray

¾ cup sun-dried tomatoes in oil, drained
and coarsely chopped

1 tablespoon finely chopped fresh
oregano or 1 teaspoon dried

Kosher salt

1 teaspoon extra virgin olive oil

2 garlic cloves, finely chopped, or
1 tablespoon jarred chopped garlic

2 pounds Basic Pull-Apart Challah dough
(page 323)

1 large egg

Freshly ground black pepper

1. Preheat the oven to 375°F. Spray a baking sheet with cooking spray.

2. Combine the tomatoes, oregano, 1 teaspoon salt, the olive oil, and garlic in a small bowl.

3. Place the dough on a smooth work surface. Cut the dough into three equal pieces. Roll each piece into a 20-inch rope. If the dough is sticking, lightly spray your work surface with cooking spray. Using a rolling pin, roll out each rope into a 3-inch-wide strip. Distribute the tomato mixture among the strips, spooning it lengthwise down the middle. Working quickly, bring the sides of each strip up and over the filling and pinch tightly to seal well.

4. Lay the filled ropes side by side; pinch tightly together at one end. Braid the ropes snugly, and pinch to seal all three strands together at the other end. Tuck both ends under the braided challah to secure. Squish and push the challah a few times lengthwise and widthwise into a nice challah shape. Place the challah on the prepared baking sheet. Lightly cover with a kitchen towel or plastic wrap and let rise 30 minutes.

5. Beat the egg with 1 teaspoon water in a small bowl. Brush the dough with the egg mixture and sprinkle generously with the salt and pepper. Bake for 10 minutes. Reduce the temperature to 350°F and bake until dark golden brown, 45 to 55 minutes. Let cool 15 minutes in the pan and serve warm, or carefully transfer to a wire rack to cool completely.

QUICK TIP

You can use a baking sheet or a large (13-inch-long) oval challah pan to bake your three-braid challah.

Blueberry Apple Challah Rolls

Kosher Status: Pareve • Prep: 30 minutes • Bake: 30 to 35 minutes •
Cool: 15 minutes • Total: About 1½ hours • Yield: 10 rolls • photo on page 327

Apples and honey are the main symbolic foods of the Rosh Hashanah season. It's the start of the new Jewish calendar year, so they represent our hope that the coming year will be sweet. Folks love to get their own mini challah, and this recipe filled with apples, honey, and a shot of blueberries ensures that each and every one will be sweet and tasty. I added the blubes to the traditional apples and honey 'cause they're super healthy and 'cause I eat these babies like popcorn.

I once spent an entire summer eating two boxes of blueberries every day for lunch. Okay, so I'm really obsessive with food. I can get stuck on something for months until a new love comes along. As I write this, I'm into my third week of minestrone soup.

Oh, by the way, I always serve my challah warm. But be careful, 'cause the inside of this one retains a lot of heat. We want squeals of pleasure with that first bite, not burned tongues.

Cooking spray

2 large Granny Smith apples, peeled, cored, and diced

Juice of 1 lemon

½ cup granulated sugar

⅓ cup honey

1½ teaspoons ground cinnamon

Pinch of kosher salt

2 cups fresh blueberries or frozen, thawed and drained well

2 tablespoons all-purpose flour

2 pounds Basic Pull-Apart Challah dough (page 323)

1 large egg

¼ cup turbinado sugar

1. Preheat the oven to 375°F. Spray two jumbo (4-inch) muffin pans or 10 individual (4- to 5-inch) roll pans with cooking spray.

2. In a large sauté pan over medium heat, cook the apples, lemon juice, sugar, honey, cinnamon, and salt until the apples are tender and softened, 10 to 12 minutes. Remove from the heat and stir in the blueberries and flour. Set aside to cool.

3. Place the dough on a smooth work surface. Cut the dough into 10 equal pieces and roll them into balls. Using a rolling pin, roll out each ball into a 5-inch disk. If the dough is sticking, lightly spray your work surface with cooking spray. Evenly distribute the apple filling among the disks. Using your fingers, bring all the edges up around the filling and pinch tightly to seal. Place the rolls in the prepared muffin pans, seam side down.

4. Beat the egg with 1 teaspoon water in a small bowl. Brush the tops of the buns with the egg mixture and sprinkle with the turbinado sugar. Bake 10 minutes, then reduce the temperature to 350°F and bake until golden brown, 20 to 25 minutes more. Let cool 15 minutes in the pan and serve warm, or carefully transfer to a wire rack to cool completely.

TIME-SAVER

Combine apple pie filling with either blueberry or cherry pie filling for a quick fruity filling. You will need about 1¼ cups total.

Garlic Knots

Kosher Status: Pareve • Prep: 30 minutes • Bake: 20 to 25 minutes •
Cool: 5 to 10 minutes • Total: About 1 hour • Yield: 20 knots • photo on page 339

This was my first-ever challah dough experiment. Pizza shop–style garlic knots are fun, easy to tie, and perfect for a party, or just a special addition to your everyday meatball or ziti dinner. Just incredible how this one dough is so versatile! You'll never know you're eating the same base dough as in the cinn buns.

Cooking spray

12 garlic cloves, finely chopped, or 2
  tablespoons jarred chopped garlic

⅓ cup finely chopped fresh parsley or
  1½ tablespoons dried

¼ cup extra virgin olive oil

1 teaspoon kosher salt

2 pounds Basic Pull-Apart Challah dough
  (page 323)

1 large egg

1. Preheat the oven to 350°F. Spray two baking sheets with cooking spray.

2. Stir the garlic, parsley, olive oil, and salt together in a small bowl.

3. Place the dough on a smooth work surface. Cut the dough in half so that it is easier to handle. Loosely cover one piece of dough with a kitchen towel or plastic wrap while you are shaping the other. Squeeze out any air bubbles from the dough and roll it into a 15-inch rope. If the dough is sticking, lightly spray your work surface with cooking spray. Cut the rope into 10 equal pieces. Gently roll and stretch each piece into a 10-inch rope, and then tie it in a knot. Place the knots on a prepared baking sheet. Repeat with the other half of the dough. Beat the egg with 1 teaspoon water in a small bowl. Brush the knots with the egg mixture and bake for 12 minutes. Remove from the oven. Whisk the garlic mixture again and brush it on the knots with a pastry brush. Return to the oven for 8 minutes more for soft chewy knots or 13 minutes more for crunchy knots.

4. Let cool 5 to 10 minutes in the pan and serve warm, or carefully transfer to a wire rack to cool completely.

Everything Breadsticks

Kosher Status: Pareve • Prep: 20 minutes • Bake: 18 to 20 minutes •
Cool: 5 to 10 minutes • Total: About 1 hour • Yield: 10 sticks • photo on page 338

I really just want to try everything under the sun with this dough, and these breadsticks work to perfection, as if the dough was made with them in mind.

So when I was making these breadsticks, Hubby had a crazy brainstorm: wrap the dough around kielbasa, bake it, slice it on the diagonal, and serve with mustard—this kinda good should be illegal!

I found ready-made Everything Topping in a canister in the baking aisle of my supermarket. But when I suggested that online, I heard cries of "What?" and "Where can you find this ready-made Everything Topping?" So just in case you can't get it where you live, here's a homemade version; if you do track it down, sub 3 tablespoons for the garlic, sesame and poppy seeds, onion, and salt.

Cooking spray

2 teaspoons granulated garlic

2 teaspoons sesame seeds

2 teaspoons poppy seeds

2 teaspoons dried minced onion

1 teaspoon kosher salt

2 pounds Basic Pull-Apart Challah dough
   (page 323)

1 large egg

1. Preheat the oven to 350°F. Spray two baking sheets with the cooking spray.

2. Prepare the topping by mixing the garlic, sesame seeds, poppy seeds, dried onion, and salt in a small bowl.

3. Place the dough on a smooth work surface. Cut the dough in half so it is easier to handle. Loosely cover one piece of the dough with a kitchen towel or plastic wrap while shaping the other. Squeeze out any air bubbles from the dough and roll it into a 15-inch rope. If the dough is sticking, lightly spray your work surface with cooking spray. Cut the rope into 10 equal pieces. Roll each piece into a 10-inch rope. Place 2 ropes side by side and press them together tightly at one end. Twist the ropes six to eight times around each other and press the open end tightly to seal. Stretch the twisted dough to 10 inches long and transfer to one of the prepared baking sheets.

4. Repeat with remaining dough to form 5 more twists, for 10 twists total.

5. Beat the egg with 1 teaspoon water in a small bowl. Brush the sticks with the egg mixture, and sprinkle with the topping.

6. Bake until golden brown, 18 to 20 minutes. Let cool 5 to 10 minutes in the pan and serve warm, or carefully transfer to a wire rack to cool completely.

Everything Breadsticks, page 336

Garlic Knots, page 335

Sea-Salted Soft Challah Pretzel Rolls, page 340

Sea-Salted Soft Challah Pretzel Rolls

Kosher Status: Pareve • Prep: 30 minutes • Bake: 10 minutes •

Cool: 5 to 10 minutes • Total: About 50 minutes • Yield: 16 pretzels • photo on page 339

When I was a kid back in Philly, guys used to stand on the street corners every Sunday selling soft pretzels. We'd stop at a red light, wave a dollar bill out the window, and they'd run over and drop a bagful of them into our outstretched hands. The pretzels were shaped like figure eights and then purposely squished together so there were no holes. There would be four of them, attached to one another, stuffed into the bag. Imagine: four for a dollar—that was a long time ago.

Fast-forward to my Shabbos table as Hubby dips my challah into kosher salt and says, "This tastes like a soft pretzel." Lightbulb moment. I'm back at the street corner in Philly. Why not go all the way and shape my challah dough into pretzels? Even though this is not traditional pretzel dough, we're going to make the traditional pretzel shape, but hey, the dough swells up in the oven and there are no holes, just like Philly pretzels! Think of me when you make 'em.

I suggest serving these with mustard. I strongly suggest spicy mustard. I happen to love it. But that's up to you! You can also serve them dipped in melted butter if you're feeling really naughty (and dairy).

2 pounds Basic Pull-Apart Challah dough
  (page 323)
Cooking spray
¼ cup baking soda

2 cups hot water
1 large egg
2 tablespoons coarse flake sea salt
Mustard, for serving (optional)

1. Preheat the oven to 450°F. Line two baking sheets with parchment paper.

2. Place the dough on a smooth work surface. Cut the dough in half so it is easier to handle. Loosely cover one piece of the dough with a kitchen towel or plastic wrap while shaping the other. Squeeze out any air bubbles from the dough and roll it into a 15-inch rope. If the dough is sticking, lightly spray your work surface with cooking spray. Cut the rope into 8 equal pieces. Roll each piece into an 18- to 20-inch rope.

3. Make a U-shape with a rope on the work surface. Holding the ends, twist them together, and bring the ends down, pressing them onto the bottom of the U in order to form the shape of a pretzel. Place on a prepared baking sheet. Repeat with the remaining dough.

4. Combine the baking soda and hot water in a large bowl; whisk to dissolve. Using your hands or a large flat spatula, dunk the pretzels into the water, one at a time, completely immersing and soaking it for about 10 seconds. Remove the pretzel from the water and return it to the baking sheet.

5. Beat the egg with 1 teaspoon water in a small bowl. Brush the pretzels with the egg mixture, sprinkle with the salt, and bake until dark golden brown, about 10 minutes. Let cool 5 to 10 minutes in the pan and serve warm, or carefully transfer to a wire rack to cool completely. Serve with mustard.

Iced Cinnamon Buns

Kosher Status: Pareve • Prep: 20 minutes •
Bake: 25 to 35 minutes •
Cool: 10 minutes • Total: About 1 hour •
Yield: 8 buns

Last year, I was in Chicago to do a cooking demo and I was blown away by the huge, warm, happy crowd! My new favorite city after Jerusalem is Chicago. Really.

Anyway, while I was prepping, I chatted with some organizers of the event. You know. Just us girls. Dough talk. That's when Rebbetzin Ayelet (you don't have to go to school to become a rebbetzin—all you have to do is marry a rabbi) shared this fab idea for challah dough: Roll it out, sprinkle with sugar and cinnamon, roll it up like a jelly roll, cut it into 2-inch pieces, pack 'em tightly into a round baking pan, and bake till golden. She instantly became my bestest friend. I wanna go to her house for dinner.

And there's one more over-the-top topping on these buns: a simple sugar-water glaze. (Can't remember if that was my idea or hers. If you just love it, let's say it was hers; if not, I'll take the hit.)

These are scrumptious beyond words when served hot, hot, hot.

You might as well double the recipe—everyone will want another bun out of the oven. Once, when I was feeling unusually well behaved, I tried to ration one for my kids, cutting it into four pieces (then tried to snag a bite of each as tax). Nobody was happy, and boy, did they let me know it.

This recipe calls for making the buns in a 9-inch round pan. You can also make them in individual 1-cup jumbo muffin pans or 5-inch round individual challah pans. Cute. Personally, I love sticking my fingers into a large pan of buns and picking my fave. In a large pan, the buns will be a bit more doughy than the singles. But that's how I like them—not raw, kinda borderline, really doughy.

The margarine is optional. I came up with this idea when testing this recipe for the book. It certainly makes the buns super moist and sticky. On the other hand, I've been making the buns without the marg for the last year. In fact, when Miss Bouncy saw me adding the margarine, she cried, "No, Mommy, don't! You're going to mess it up." So cute—she didn't want to risk those buns! So it really is up to you, though I love my addition, if I do say so myself.

½ cup granulated sugar

½ cup packed light brown sugar

1½ tablespoons ground cinnamon

2 pounds Basic Pull-Apart Challah dough (page 323)

Cooking spray

6 tablespoons margarine, softened (optional)

1⅓ cups confectioners' sugar

1. Preheat the oven to 350°F.

2. Stir the granulated sugar, brown sugar, and cinnamon together in a small bowl.

3. Place the dough on a smooth work surface. Roll it out to form a 24 x 12-inch rectangle. If the dough is sticking, lightly spray your work surface with cooking spray. Spread 3 tablespoons softened margarine, if using, all over the dough. Sprinkle the sugar mixture over the margarine. Working with the longer side, roll the dough up tightly, like a jelly roll, ending with the seam underneath.

4. Melt the remaining 3 tablespoons margarine in the microwave and pour it into a 9-inch round baking pan. If you don't want to use the margarine, spray the pan with cooking spray. Cut the dough into 8 equal pieces. Place one piece, cut side up, in the center of the pan, and surround it with the remaining pieces, also cut sides up. It's okay if they do not touch; they will after they bake.

5. Bake until golden brown and bubbly, 25 to 35 minutes. Allow to cool in the pan about 10 minutes while you make the glaze: Whisk the confectioners' sugar with 3 tablespoons water in a medium bowl. Carefully transfer the buns to a serving platter. Drizzle the glaze over the buns and serve warm.

Gooey Pecan Sticky Buns

Kosher Status: Dairy • Prep: 30 minutes • Rise: 1 hour • Bake: 35 minutes •
Cool: 20 minutes • Total: About 2½ hours • Yield: 8 buns

Our dough is pareve, and that makes it our go-to for every kind of meal. But when I saw Bobby Flay make these buttery bits of heaven, I thought, Why stick to pareve buns when we can go authentically buttery, sticky, and nutty?

You'll be licking the platter, your fingers, your kids' platters, your kids' fingers—anything touched by these divine doughy buns.

The OJ gives the goo just a nice hint of tang. Make sure to use that baking sheet under the cake pan before these babies hit the oven, because it does bubble over a bit, and you don't want to be cleaning goo from the bottom of your oven—just the bottom of your plate. Don't crush your pecans too much; you still want large pieces or halves—but a little smaller is nice, too.

8 tablespoons (1 stick) unsalted butter

1¼ cups packed light brown sugar

½ cup heavy cream

¼ cup fresh orange juice or water

Pinch of kosher salt

¼ teaspoon ground cinnamon

¼ cup granulated sugar

2 pounds Basic Pull-Apart Challah dough
  (page 323)

Cooking spray

1 cup salted pecan halves, raw or roasted,
  lightly crushed

1. Melt the butter in a medium sauté pan over medium-low heat. Add 1 cup of the brown sugar and whisk to combine. Remove from the heat. Add the cream, orange juice, and salt; whisk until smooth. Set aside to cool slightly while shaping the buns.

2. Combine the cinnamon, granulated sugar, and the remaining ¼ cup brown sugar in a small bowl.

3. Place the dough on a smooth work surface. Roll out the dough into a 24 x 12-inch rectangle, about ¼ inch thick. If the dough is sticking, spray your work surface with cooking spray. Spread the cinnamon mixture evenly over the rectangle. Working with the longer side, roll the dough up tightly, like a jelly roll, into a log, ending with the seam underneath. Cut the log into 8 equal pieces.

4. Whisk the cooled butter mixture again and pour it into the bottom of a 9-inch round cake pan. Sprinkle the pecans all over. Place the buns in the pan, one in the center and seven around the edges, all cut side up. It's okay if they do not touch; they will after they rise and bake. Cover loosely with plastic wrap and let rise in a warm place for 1 hour.

5. Preheat the oven to 350°F.

6. Place the pan on a baking sheet, and bake until golden brown and bubbly, about 35 minutes. Let cool 20 minutes in the pan on a wire rack.

7. Serve warm on a plate that is slightly larger than the pan and that has edges to catch the goo. Place the plate on top of the pan and carefully invert the pan (using oven mitts if still warm) onto the plate, being sure to scrape out all the yummy goo onto the buns.

Holiday
Menus

Thursday: 5:15 p.m.

. . . .

So tonight I counted up how many holiday meals I cook in a year . . .

It can't be. It's crazy. One hundred thirty. Yup, read it again and let it sink in: 130. I'm including Shabbos, which translates into two banquets (plus a third meal) and the end of your diet *every week*.

With that much meal planning to do, I'm sure you'll want a suggestion or two. So I went through this book and put together menus for Shabbos and each of the holidays. By now, you're used to my confessions, so here goes: My great friend Tamar Genger, executive editor of JoyofKosher.com, helped me with these menus. Kinda like when your gal pal comes over and rummages through your closet and helps you realize that you really do have something to wear. Through her eyes, I see my recipes in a new light. I love Tamar for being who she is, and I'm grateful for her menu planning expertise.

Of course, with these menus, there's no reason you can't mix and match. Never mind that we racked our brains to make sure these menus are varied, satisfying, and nutritionally balanced (Tamar just happens to be a registered dietitian).

Shabbos

To the rest of the world, it's Saturday. But to us, it's Shabbos, and light years from our everyday life. At dusk on Friday, Hubby takes Angel Face with him to *shul* (synagogue) for services. And when they come home, the family gathers round the dining room table for a traditional, magnificent Shabbos meal. We eat together as a family, talk together, and sing together—yes, we sing. It's funny, but I've noticed that every family develops its own sound, its own harmony, even if they're not the most gifted voices in the world. The next morning, dressed in our Shabbos best (with sparkly headbands, lacy socks, and suits), we walk to *shul* together. Moments like these are when everything else stops, and all is right with the world.

Shabbos Dinner Menu

- Sun-Dried Tomato, Garlic, and Herb Braided Challah (page 331)
- Mock Crab Salad in Avocados (page 117)
- Crystal Clear Chicken Soup with Julienned Vegetables and Angel Hair (page 25)
- Moroccan Roasted Chicken (page 176)
- Colorful Mustard String Beans (page 107)
- Cranberry Couscous Eggplant Boats (page 101)
- Red Wine Chocolate Cherry Cake (page 294)

Shabbos Lunch Menu

- *Shalom Bayis* Pull-Apart Challah (page 328)
- Baked Carrot-Stuffed Gefilte Fish (page 59)
- Somewhat Sephardic Chulent (page 214)
- Daddy's Deep-Dish Potato Kigel/Kugel (page 91)
- Pastrami-Fry Salad with Creamy Chili Dressing (page 86)
- Toasted Marshmallow Nutty Caramel Brownies (page 258)

Kiddush

A Kiddush is a party buffet after Shabbos morning synagogue services are concluded. It can be held at the *shul* or in your home. People sponsor a Kiddush to celebrate any special event: a birth, a Bar/Bat Mitzvah, a great round of golf, an engagement. We customarily give a Kiddush for our newborn daughters. The Baby is now eight months old, but that's okay—any time up to a year is fine for the celebration. While it's not mandatory, having a Kiddush for a baby girl is said to guarantee that you'll marry her off to a fine upstanding young fellow—maybe even a doctor or a lawyer—when she and your bank account are ready. The Kiddush is your announcement to the immediate world, so you can invite the 'hood, and the 'hood will show up—with everyone including visiting Aunt Edna and Uncle Morris.

Small portions of fish and salads are tradish, and be prepared with lots of finger foods, pastries, and sweets, too. Add kugels and chulent only if you want to go the extra mile. A few impressive cakes decorating the table create a nice touch.

But be careful not to overdo. You don't want others to feel pressured to take out a second mortgage just to throw a lavish Kiddush. Better they should save it for the wedding, when their doctor son will marry your gorgeous daughter.

Below is a listing of great finger foods for a Kiddush (or any party). I've listed the dishes as meat, pareve, or dairy. Go ahead, mix 'em up—but not the milk with the meat!

MEAT

SAVORY

- Cocktail Meatballs with Sweet 'n' Sour Sauce (page 28)
- Ktzitzot (Israeli Mini Burgers) (page 33)
- Anita's Lachmagine (Miniature Ground Beef Pies) (page 38)
- Pastrami-Fry Salad with Creamy Chili Dressing/Pastrami-Fry Tomato Cups (pages 86 and 87)
- Triple Deli Pasta Salad with Creamy Italian Dressing (page 77)
- Pretzel-Crusted Chicken Skewers with Herbed Curry Mustard (page 161)
- Sesame Chicken "Sushi" with Hoisin Garlic Sauce (page 155)
- Mushroom Phyllo Cups (page 85)

DAIRY

SAVORY

- Cool Cucumber and Avocado Cream Shooters (page 69)
- Nacho Potato Bites (page 71)

- Purple, Orange, and White Chips (page 66)
- Waldorf Salad with Candied Walnuts and Blue Cheese (page 134)
- Fancy and Fresh Greek Pasta Salad (page 136)

SWEET

- Chocolate Hazelnut Milk Shake Martinis (page 298)
- Cannoli Cones (page 312)

PAREVE

SAVORY

- Eggplant Caviar Crostini (page 41)
- Lemon Lover's Hummus with Pita Crisps (pages 42 and 43)
- Falafel Poppers with Lemon Sesame Schug (page 46)
- Cilantro Corn Cakes with Avocado Aioli (page 50)
- Tropical Fruit Guacamole (page 51)
- Uputzi's Vegetarian Chopped "Liver" Pâté (page 53)
- Fancy Crudités with Garlic Ranch Dip (page 61)
- Baked Herbed Gefilte Fish (page 58)
- Mock Crab Salad in Avocados (page 117)
- Winter Citrus Salad (page 96)
- Rice Salad with Toasted Nuts, Apples, and Onion Dressing (page 102)
- Raw Root Vegetable Salad (page 108)
- Avocado Salad with Butter Lettuce and Lemon Dressing (page 116)

SWEET

- Nutty Caramel Brownies (page 257)
- Spiced Pumpkin Mousse (page 260)
- Big Chewy Dark Chocolate Chunk Cookies (page 277)
- Salted Almond and Pistachio Bark and Kiddie Candy Bark (pages 279 and 281)
- Olive Oil Dark Chocolate Mousse Shots (page 286)
- Cherry Bourbon Hand Pies (page 287)
- Holiday Carrot Honey Cake (page 267)
- Tart Green Apple Pie à la Mode with pareve/nondairy ice cream (page 270)
- Red Wine Chocolate Cherry Cake (page 294)
- Peaches and Jam Sweet Potato Cake (page 263)

Rosh Hashanah/High Holidays

The Jewish New Year brings hope for the future, but there's also a red flag. We're aware that our past activities are being judged and that our future blessings depend upon correcting wrongs and resolving to improve ourselves. Everyone wants the next year to be sweet! And that's why menus during our Rosh Hashanah and High Holiday season (which actually stretches for three weeks from Rosh Hashanah through Yom Kippur and Sukkos) emphasize the sweetest of sweet foods: honey. You can never have too much honey on Rosh Hashanah, but there's no telling where it will wind up!

Rosh Hashanah Menu

- Cran-Rosemary Crown Challah (page 330)
- Garlic Honey Brisket (page 198)
- Sweet and Sticky Stuffed Cornish Hens (page 166)
- Apple Challah Kugel Towers (page 95)
- Raw Root Vegetable Salad (page 108)
- Holiday Carrot Honey Cake (page 267)

Erev (Eve of) Yom Kippur Menu

Yom Kippur is a 25-hour fast day, so you want a hearty, filling meal that goes easy on salt and other spices that could make you thirsty.

- Basic Pull-Apart Challah (page 323)
- Our Family Fricassee (page 171)
- Red Hasselback Potatoes (page 98)
- Zucchini and Red Bell Pepper Sauté (page 121)
- Big Chewy Dark Chocolate Chunk Cookies (page 277)

Sukkos

Sukkos is when we camp out in our own backyards for a week—eating, sometimes sleeping—in a flimsy hut called a *sukkah*. Not built to last. That's the idea, 'cause we're re-creating the temporary dwellings of our ancient Israelite ancestors after their exodus from Egypt. But I'll bet theirs weren't as pretty as ours. They didn't have Little Momma, Miss Bouncy, and Angel Face as interior decorators!

During *Chol Hamoed*—the middle days of Sukkos week, when excursions are permitted—it's become our family custom to go apple picking and use the fruit for all kinds of holiday desserts. It seems that other families have the same idea, as there are usually lots of daddies lifting toddlers up to the branches "one more time," older kids filling up their baskets, and mommies wondering how on earth they'll use up 30 pounds of apples when they get home.

Sukkos Menu

- Blueberry Apple Challah Rolls (page 333)
- Sour Mash Whiskey-Glazed Whole Roasted Turkey (page 168)
- Stuffed Baked Onions (page 81)
- Marshmallow-Topped Sweet Potato Casserole (page 111)
- Easy Scallion Cornbread (page 112)
- Roasted Brussels Sprouts with Herb "Butter" (page 122)
- Tart Green Apple Pie à la Mode (page 270)

Shemini Atzeres/Simchas Torah

After eight days of Sukkos, just when you think it's all over, two more days of festivities begin. Bring on the food! (Like is anybody still hungry? When does the diet start?)

Shemini Atzeres/Simchas Torah Menu

- *Shalom-Bayis* Pull-Apart Challah (page 328)
- Deconstructed Meatball Bruschetta (page 29)
- Stuffed Veal Rolls with Smoky Tomato Sauce (page 181)
- Wilted Spinach with Crispy Garlic Chips (page 124)
- Purple, Orange, and White Chips (omit the sour cream) (page 66)
- French Chocolate Bark (page 280)

Chanukah

The most precious Chanukah gift I ever got was Bruiser. For his Chanukah B-day, we don't do candles—they're in the menorah. We do Funnel Cakes with powdered sugar, Birthday Pancake Towers, and Chanukah Cookies. Even without a birthday, Chanukah is another excuse to party. This time, we're celebrating the defeat of one of the earliest attempts to destroy Jewish culture and religion. That kind of challenge has hit us over and over in our history. And, hey, we're still here. So let's eat.

Chanukah Menu (Dairy)

- Everything Breadsticks (page 336)
- Winter Citrus Salad (page 96)
- Latkes with Caviar and Cream (page 127)
- Country Spinach, Tomato, and White Bean Soup (page 248)
- Creamy Tomato Penne (page 128)
- Cardamom-Scented Chanukah Cookies (page 295)

Purim

The Jewish Halloween? No way. The Purim story is replete with hidden identities and mysterious behind-the-scenes Divine manipulation. Simplicity on the surface masks deep meaning. So you will find normally serious, responsible adults parading around in costume, a little giddy, on this day of over-the-top festivity. A really neat custom is to bring food gifts (called *mishloach manos*) to friends and neighbors. Like many families, we usually try for a theme, matching our costumes and the foods we give and those we eat at our late afternoon Purim banquet. This year my favorite place—Israel—inspired me.

Purim Menu

- Sea-Salted Soft Challah Pretzel Rolls (page 340)
- Lemon Lover's Hummus with Pita Crisps (pages 42 and 43)
- Eggplant Caviar Crostini (page 41)
- Ktzitzot (Israeli Mini Burgers, page 33)
- Falafel Poppers with Lemon Sesame Schug (page 46)
- Mediterranean Lamb Skewers (page 223)
- Yerushalmi Kugel (page 118)
- Caramel Apples with Crushed Nuts (page 273)

Mishloach Manos

- Tricolor Hummus Trifles with Pita Crisps (page 43)
- Pretty Cornbread (page 113)
- Caramel Fruit Bites (page 274)
- Big Chewy Dark Chocolate Chunk Cookies (page 277)
- Salted Almond and Pistachio Bark (page 279)
- French Chocolate Bark (page 280)
- Kiddie Candy Bark (page 281)
- Blueberry Apple Challah Rolls (page 333)
- Garlic Knots (page 335)
- Everything Breadsticks (page 336)
- Sea-Salted Soft Challah Pretzel Rolls (page 340)
- Iced Cinnamon Buns (page 342)
- Gooey Pecan Sticky Buns (page 344)

Passover (Pesach)

Family Seders: four questions, four cups of wine, kids up late, lotsa matzoh—followed by a week of holiday meals, morning and night. Extended family, guests, neighbors, all come by to eat, and my mom and mom-in-law both wonder aloud, "Do you really have to cook this much?"

The answer is yes.

The trick is to stock up on everything you need from the get-go, so I generally start off with 20 pounds of potatoes, 6 dozen eggs, and a bag of onions bigger than Bruiser!

Kosher for Passover Recipes

Assuming you've got ingredients labeled "Kosher for Passover," many of the recipes in this book can be adapted for the holiday. Nope, not the challah recipes, nor any recipe *not* on the list below. When I refer to a recipe as adaptable, I mean strictly that recipe, not necessarily the other recipes under that heading.

Keep in mind that *every* ingredient must be kosher for Passover, including items such as mustard, mayo, teriyaki sauce, and soy sauce. These are, of course, imitations of the year-round products that exclude the ingredients that are not permitted on Passover.

In addition, lots of things may seem as though they would be naturally K for P, but processed items can have all sorts of additives or hidden ingredients that render them *not* kosher for Passover use. So look carefully at those labels.

Some of my recipes are inherently fine for Passover; others require adjustments noted in the following chart. To keep my criteria simple, I followed generally accepted Ashkenazic customs with regard to permitted ingredients. Sometimes I suggest serving "rolls" or other items that are *gebrokts* (foods that are made with matzoh meal), which is common, but not a universal custom. If you've never heard of "Passover rolls," you probably don't eat gebrokts.

But whether or not you use matzoh meal, Passover should not pose great limitations on your holiday cuisine if you look at cooking creatively. So if you've ever wondered, "What in the world can I serve during Passover?"—my answer is "plenty!"

Recipe	Page	Passover Adjustment
Crystal Clear Chicken Soup with Julienned Vegetables and Angel Hair (Meat)	25	Substitute Passover "noodles" for angel hair pasta.
Chicken Noodle Alphabet Soup (Meat)	27	Substitute Passover "noodles" for alphabet noodles.
Cocktail Meatballs with Sweet 'n' Sour Sauce (Meat)	28	Substitute matzoh meal for bread crumbs. Substitute Passover mustard and honey for honey mustard. Substitute olive or vegetable oil for canola oil. Substitute Passover soy sauce for Worcestershire sauce.
Ktzitzot (Israeli Mini Burgers) (Meat)	33	Substitute matzoh meal for bread crumbs. Omit cumin. Substitute olive or vegetable oil for canola oil.
Ktzitzot Pita Sandwiches (Meat)	34	Substitute Passover mayonnaise for tahini and hummus. Substitute Passover "rolls" for pita.
Eggplant Caviar (Pareve)	40	Substitute matzoh for pita chips.
Eggplant Caviar Crostini (Pareve)	41	Substitute matzoh for crostini.
Lemon Sesame Schug (Pareve)	46	Omit tahini. Serve with matzoh.
Tropical Fruit Guacamole (Pareve)	51	Substitute Passover potato chips for tortilla chips.
Uputzi's Vegetarian Chopped "Liver" Pâté (Pareve)	53	Substitute matzoh for crackers.
Baked Herbed Gefilte Fish (Pareve)	58	Kosher for Passover
Fancy Crudités with Garlic Ranch Dip (Pareve)	61	Substitute almond milk or whole, low-fat, or skim milk for soy milk. Note: When using cow's milk, recipe will take on dairy status. Substitute olive or vegetable oil for canola oil.
Chilled Coconut Berry Soup (Pareve)	63	Substitute almond milk or whole, low-fat, or skim milk for coconut milk. Note: When using cow's milk, recipe will take on dairy status.
Baked Sweet Potato Chips (Pareve)	66	Substitute Passover mustard and honey for honey mustard.
Cool Cucumber and Avocado Cream Soup (Dairy)	68	Substitute matzoh for sourdough bread. Substitute yogurt for Greek yogurt

Recipe	Page	Passover Adjustment
Smashed Red Potato Nachos (Dairy)	70	Kosher for Passover
Poppy's Sour Cream Potato Soup (Dairy)	72	Omit pasta
Triple Deli Pasta Salad with Creamy Italian Dressing (Meat)	77	Omit the pasta, add more lettuce and vegetables and toss with dressing to taste.
Cranberry Chestnut Challah Stuffing (Meat)	79	Substitute regular or whole wheat matzoh farfel for cubed challah.
Hearty Mushrooms with Herbs and Wine (Meat)	84	Substitute Passover mustard for Dijon mustard.
Pastrami-Fry Salad with Creamy Chili Dressing (Meat)	86	Substitute white vinegar for rice vinegar. Omit cumin.
Daddy's Deep-Dish Potato Kigel/Kugel (Pareve)	91	Substitute olive or vegetable oil for canola oil.
Pastrami Potato Kugel (Meat)	92	Substitute olive or vegetable oil for canola oil. Substitute Passover mustard for mustard.
Spiced Apple Challah Kugel (Pareve)	94	Substitute matzoh farfel for cubed challah. Substitute almond milk or whole, low-fat, or skim milk for soy milk. Note: When using cow's milk, recipe will take on dairy status.
Winter Citrus Salad (Pareve)	96	Kosher for Passover
Winter Citrus Brûlée (Pareve)	97	Substitute regular sugar for turbinado sugar.
Red Hasselback Potatoes (Pareve)	98	Kosher for Passover
Raw Root Vegetable Salad (Pareve)	108	Substitute olive oil for toasted sesame oil. Substitute Passover soy sauce for soy sauce.
Sweet Potato Casserole	110	Kosher for Passover
Avocado Salad with Butter Lettuce and Lemon Dressing (Pareve)	116	Substitute Passover mustard for Dijon mustard.
Yerushalmi Kugel (Pareve)	118	Substitute cooked Passover egg "noodles" for angel hair.
Latkes with Caviar and Cream (Dairy)	127	Substitute matzoh meal for cornmeal. Substitute olive or vegetable oil for canola oil.
Waldorf Salad (Dairy)	132	Kosher for Passover

Recipe	Page	Passover Adjustment
Greek Pasta Salad with Creamy Feta Dressing (Dairy)	135	Omit pasta. Add more vegetables and toss with dressing to taste.
Chicken Sausage and Sweet Potato Hash with Baked Eggs (Poultry)	145	Omit cumin.
Coq au Vin with Veal Sausage, Thyme, and Merlot (Poultry)	148	Kosher for Passover
Slow Cooker Turkey Spinach Meatloaf (Poultry)	157	Substitute matzoh meal for bread crumbs.
Sweet and Sticky Citrus Drumsticks (Poultry)	165	Substitute Passover mustard for Dijon mustard.
Our Family Fricassee (Poultry)	171	Substitute matzoh meal for bread crumbs. Omit rice.
Moroccan Roasted Chicken (Poultry)	176	Omit cumin.
Slow Cooker Moroccan-Style Chicken (Poultry)	177	Omit cumin and couscous.
Crispy Salt and Pepper Chicken with Caramelized Fennel and Shallots (Poultry)	179	Substitute potato starch for flour.
Stuffed Veal Rolls with Smoky Tomato Sauce (Meat)	181	Substitute matzoh meal for bread crumbs.
BBQ Short Rib Sandwiches with Avocado (Meat)	183	Omit dry mustard. Substitute olive or vegetable oil for canola oil. Substitute Passover soy sauce for Worcestershire sauce. Substitute Passover "rolls" for baguettes.
Short Rib Sliders with Flavored Mayo on Garlic Toast (Meat)	185	Omit wasabi mayonnaise. Substitute Passover "rolls" for slider rolls.
Crispy Fried Red Onions (Pareve)	185	Substitute potato starch for flour.
Skirt Steak with Salsa Verde (Meat)	191	Omit cumin, tortilla chips, and rice.
Garlic Honey Brisket (Meat)	198	Substitute Passover mustard for Dijon mustard. Substitute potato starch for flour.
Argentinean Brisket with Chimichurri (Meat)	200	Omit cumin. Substitute olive or vegetable oil for canola oil.
Loaded Burgers with Special Sauce (Meat)	205	Substitute Passover "rolls" for sesame buns. Substitute finely diced pickles sweetened with sugar for sweet pickle relish. Substitute French fries for onion rings.

Recipe	Page	Passover Adjustment
Balsamic London Broil (Meat)	208	Kosher for Passover
"Buttery" Crusted Beef Pot Pie (Meat)	220	Omit peas. Substitute Passover "rolls" for baguette.
Mashed Potato Beef Cottage Pie (Meat)	221	Omit peas.
Teriyaki and Scallion Rainbow Trout (Pareve)	227	Substitute potato starch for flour. Substitute Passover teriyaki sauce or Passover soy sauce combined with sugar for teriyaki sauce.
Blackened Tilapia Tacos with Cumin Avocado Sauce (Dairy)	230	Omit cumin. Substitute matzoh for tortillas.
Salmon with Lemon Velvet Cream Sauce (Dairy)	234	Substitute potato starch for flour.
Poppy and Grandma's Layered Rakott Crumpli	239	Substitute matzoh meal for bread crumbs.
Roasted Summer Squash Lasagna (Dairy)	241	Substitute matzoh for lasagna noodles.
Blue Cheese, Pear, and Arugula Pizza (Dairy)	245	Substitute matzoh for pizza dough.
Sorbet Cups with Strawberry Kiwi Salsa (Pareve)	255	Kosher for Passover
Birthday Pancake Towers (Pareve)	265	Use a Passover yellow cake mix. Substitute almond milk or whole, low-fat, or skim milk for soy milk. Note: When using cow's milk, recipe will take on dairy status.
Salted Almond and Pistachio Bark (Pareve)	279	Kosher for Passover
Kiddie Candy Bark (Pareve)	281	Use only Kosher for Passover mix-ins.
Olive Oil Dark Chocolate Mousse (Pareve)	285	Kosher for Passover
Chocolate Hazelnut Milk Shake Martinis (Dairy)	298	Substitute chocolate spread for chocolate hazelnut spread.
Orange-Scented Cheesecake (Dairy)	305	Substitute Passover cookies for graham crackers.
Black and White Ice Cream Bombe (Dairy)	308	Kosher for Passover
Black and White Sundae Bar	310	Use only Kosher for Passover toppings.

Shavuos

There's thunder and lightning at Mt. Sinai, God is giving the Ten Commandments to Moses, and the world will never be the same. And every year, we reaffirm our commitment to God's User Handbook for the World—the Torah. Sacred texts tell us that on the morning the Jews received the Torah, the stony, barren terrain of Mt. Sinai became miraculously lush with greenery. And to commemorate that event, we fill our homes with flowers and plants for the holiday!

That's it, in a nutshell . . .

In any case, unlike the other festivals that are usually celebrated with lavish meat meals, the custom on Shavuos is to eat dairy for at least one of the meals. Just love the chance to dress up some of my everyday fave foods in their holiday duds.

Shavuos Menu

- Garlic Knots (page 335)
- Smashed Red Potato Nachos (page 70)
- Roasted Vegetable Summer Lasagna (page 242)
- Wilted Spinach with Crispy Garlic Chips (page 124)
- Waldorf Salad with Candied Walnuts and Blue Cheese (page 134)
- Candied-Orange Cheesecake (page 307)

Food Glossary

baba ghanoush (Arabic) A Middle Eastern dish made of eggplant, olive oil, and seasonings. Considered very chic in some circles, it's same ol' same ol' to those who grew up with it.

boureka (Hebrew) A puff pastry you can stuff with anything! Since you ask, I'll tell you that this sort of dish is found in cultures all around the world. Started in Asia (maybe) as *burga*. Made their way to Asia Minor and renamed *börek*. When Sephardic Jews reached Turkey, it reminded them of their own dish, empanada (see below). Well, it's a quick slip of the tongue to go from börek-empanada to boureka. Anyway, that's the legend. They became phenomenally popular in Israel, and after a soggy swim in the Atlantic emerged on American shores.

chrein (Yiddish) Horseradish, that hot stuff Jews love to pile on their gefilte fish (see below). It has remarkable health benefits, but we were hooked on it long before those discoveries. Newcomers often need time to adjust their palates and their psyches to the "extra strong" varieties. Just remember, "the pain of *chrein* is mainly in the brain."

empanada (Spanish origin) Dough folded around a stuffing, popular in Western Europe, Latin America, and Southeast Asia. Those sixteenth-century Spanish explorers really got around. You'll find reminders of their fave foods everywhere.

gefilte fish (Yiddish) Literally "stuffed fish" because originally fish skin was wrapped around the minced fish. Today, the skin is rarely used and the fish is boiled or baked as balls or loaves. Carp, whitefish, and/or pike (individually or in combination) are often used. GF is so ingrained in the Jewish psyche that it's almost a sin to leave it off a Shabbos menu.

hummus (Turkish, Arabic) A dip that dates back to thirteenth-century Egypt, it's made from mashed chickpeas, tahini, olive oil, lemon juice, garlic, and salt. People in the know pronounce it with that throat-grating sound: chummus. Thanks to a huge ad campaign by Sabra Dipping Co., you'll find it right alongside the guacamole and salsa at Super Bowl parties.

meza (Turkish, Persian) Middle Eastern appetizers. In most places, you need to serve at least a half dozen different kinds to be considered hospitable. In some places, meza can be a whole meal.

pita (Greek) The Middle Eastern pocket flatbread you use to cheat on diets.

schug (Hebrew) Middle Eastern hot sauce made from hot peppers, seasoned with coriander, garlic, and other spices. In Yemen, it was believed to have serious medicinal properties; if you could stomach it, you felt great afterward.

tabouleh (Arabic) Originally from Syria/Lebanon, this is a salad made with bulgur, tomatoes, olive oil, lemon juice, and finely chopped parsley and mint.

za'atar (Arabic) A blend of herbs, sesame seeds, and spices including oregano, hyssop, rosemary, and basil.

Hebrew/Yiddish/Yinglish Glossary

Hebrew is the original language of the Bible, spoken by Jews throughout the centuries and today by Jews in Israel and the world over.

Yiddish is a language that evolved throughout the Jewish sojourn in the European diaspora. It is based largely on German, but contains numerous words in Hebrew and other languages.

"Yinglish" is a modern combination of Yiddish and English. It is not a language. Except to some people.

a bissel (Yiddish) A little; not much. As in "I'll just take *a bissel* more of that incredible dessert, thanks. Okay, maybe *a bissel* more . . . *noch* (another) *a bissel* . . ."

a shaynem dank (Yiddish) Literally "thank you very much," but often with a touch of irony, as when your mother-in-law insists on showing you how to fix her son's favorite meal because "you'll never be able to do this yourself," or when said hubby presents you with a beautiful new sweater in a huge size "to make sure it will fit."

Ashkenazim (Hebrew) Jews whose ancestry goes back to Central or Eastern Europe. They are so tightly associated with borscht, bagels, and babka that many people believe that Ashkenazic Jews invented them. Never believe folk legends! Those foods are classic Ukrainian, Polish, and Czech, respectively.

Bar Mitzvah (Hebrew) A festive occasion for which the mother of the Bar Mitzvah boy typically loses fifteen pounds so she can squeeze into a fabulous dress. Oh, and the thirteen-year-old Bar Mitzvah himself (the term refers to both the boy and the celebration) is now counted as a Jewish man. There's no adolescence in Judaism. Either you're a child or an adult. Girls become Bas Mitzvah (aka Bat Mitzvah), an official Jewish woman, when they're only twelve, 'cause girls are better than boys.

chessed (Hebrew) A kindness, Jewish-style, i.e., typically over-the-top. Such as when your neighbor asks you to take in her mail while she's on vacation, so while you're at her place, you also water the lawn, weed the flower bed, and, on the last day, leave supper at the door because you know she'll be hungry when she gets home.

chick chock (Hebrew) An Israeli expression meaning superquick, because Israelis like to do everything—from checking out at the supermarket to flying a plane—with as little interference as possible.

"Ess, ess, mein kindt." (Yiddish) "Eat, eat, my child." What we grew up hearing day in and day out. It's in our bones and on our hips. See *Mangia! Mangia!* below.

fancy schmancy (Yinglish) Really fancy, with a touch of sarcasm, as in "now that you bought that fancy schmancy grill, do you know how to cook on it?" See *hotsy-totsy*.

farklempt (Yiddish) Overcome with emotion, choked up. "I'm so *farklempt,* I can't talk right now; just give me a minute." Totally opposite of stiff upper-lipped, Jews are easily, often, and visibly *farklempt* on any occasion involving gifts or grandchildren, or any time "Sunrise, Sunset" is played.

farmished   (Yiddish) Confused, distracted. "I was so *farmished*, I put in salt instead of sugar."

far-fetched   Not a Yiddish word, but it should be.

hotsy-totsy   (Yinglish) Like *fancy schmancy*, but usually referring to a person, not a thing. "Since her promotion, she's such a hotsy-totsy executive, even her kids need an appointment to talk to her."

Kohen (pl. Kohanim)   (Hebrew) In ancient Israel, a "priest" in the Holy Temple of Jerusalem. Today, one who is descended from Kohanim.

Mangia! Mangia!   Italian for *Ess, ess, mein kindt.* Ever since ancient Rome met ancient Jerusalem, there's been heated debate over which mothers stuff their kids more.

maven   (Yiddish) An expert; a judge of quality. You can be a *maven* of anything: cooking, shoes, jewelry, gardening, music, nail polish.

mensch   (Yiddish) Literally "a man" but so much more! Someone who is courteous, thoughtful, understanding, and who always says and does the right thing. Every Jewish mother wants her kid to "be a *mensch*." If a person is dubbed *nisht kan mensch* (not a mensch), he's an uncouth louse.

mitzvah   (Hebrew) A commandment stipulated in Jewish law, but it has come to mean any kind act because kind, thoughtful behavior is inherent in the body and spirit of the law. "You're actually giving me your great-grandmother's secret recipe? What a *mitzvah*!"

nebach   (Yiddish) Poor thing! (You've just got to pity that person.)

nosh   (Yiddish) Snack. Both a noun and a verb, as in English. "I need to *nosh*; don't tell me the only *nosh* you have around is carob chips!"

nu   (Yiddish) "So what do you think of this? Isn't it amazing? Never seen anything like it in all my born days, and I do mean never." Second meaning: (with tapping foot) "We're late again. We're always late. What can possibly be taking you so long? How many hours does it take to put on lipstick anyway?" *Nu*, is it any wonder why we use just the one word to convey all that? This is why I love Yiddish.

pareve   (Hebrew) Not dairy, not meat. A food that's permissible to eat with either one, or can go it alone. Example: eggs, fruit, vegetables. While fish is considered pareve, too, it may not be combined directly with meat.

patchka   (Yiddish) Fuss. Both a noun and a verb. "I never thought I'd bake bread because it's such a *patchka*. I have no time to *patchka* in the kitchen."

pupik, pipik   (Yiddish) A chicken's tummy. Really. A delicacy outside of my house. Whether you pronounce it with a *u* or an *i* depends on whether your people came from Russia or southern Poland.

schlep, schlepping   (Yiddish) To lug; lugging. A noun/verb combination not found in English. It can also refer to lugging oneself someplace. "We *schlepped* all the way out to Long Island only to discover that Aunt Myra and Uncle Sol weren't home. I told you we didn't need to *schlep* all that food."

schmaltz   (Yiddish) Literally, fat, often chicken fat that was used in cooking before we ever heard the word cholesterol. Today *schmaltz* also means excessively sentimental. "I can't stand a movie that has too much *schmaltz*."

schmooze   (Yiddish) Another great verb/noun combination. It means to talk, discuss, chatter. "It's okay, honey, we can leave now; I was just *schmoozing* with some friends." As a noun, it takes on a more serious tone: "The rabbi gave him a *schmooze* he'll never forget."

Sephardim, Sephardic   (Hebrew) Referring to Jews who lived in Spain, Portugal, North Africa, or Middle Eastern countries (or are descended from them). A Jew from Caucasus, Arab countries, or North Africa can be referred to as Mizrachi (literally, eastern), though they are generally grouped with Sephardim in Israeli parlance. Though based on the same Torah laws, Sephardic culture and customs differ from those of European Jews (see Ashkenazim on page 365), who regard them as exotic. No word on what the Sephardim think of Ashkenazim.

Shabbos   (Hebrew) A weekly oasis of peace, calm, and communing with our Creator. It comes every Friday night–Saturday along with bountiful meals, family time, and friendly camaraderie.

shalom bayis (Hebrew) Family harmony. Sometimes it's easy, sometimes not. Definitely worth the effort.

shmear (Yiddish) A smear, a dab. Yup, another noun/verb. "I'll take just a *shmear* of cream cheese on that bagel."

shoin (Yiddish) Done! There! "We had just arrived, and *shoin*—he knew all our names!"

shtetl (Yiddish) A small Jewish town in Eastern Europe prior to World War II. Most people who have nostalgia for the *shtetl* of old have never been in one.

shtick (Yiddish) Almost untranslatable, I guess you could say that *shtick* could be a sly trick, or attitude ("Don't give me that *shtick*!"); or it could mean a person's way of doing things ("Nobody can copy his *shtick*"); or a relationship ("We had a real teacher/student *shtick* going"); or paraphernalia you bring to a wedding to entertain the bride and groom ("She has the most creative wedding *shtick* I've ever seen."). I told you it was untranslatable.

"tenks Gott" (Yinglish) Thank God. As in, "tenks Gott we finally finished this glossary."

Many Thanks

Nachum, Bracha Miriam, Rochel Naami, Yaakov Yosef, Avraham Yitzchak "AY," and **Noa Rivka,** you are my entire life. All has meaning because of you. **Mommy and Daddy,** I've thanked you publicly and privately online and offline, in numerous books, blog posts, and face-to-face. Yet I will never be able to adequately express my gratitude for the support you give me day in and day out, every day of my life. **Karen "Grandma,"** I love you like a mother. Thank you for treating me like a daughter and picking me up and putting me back together again and again (and again). **Cassie Jones,** I worried about working with a new editor, meeting new standards—would my message be tweaked beyond recognition? Would my voice be edited so that it was no longer my own? Our work together has been incredible and enriching. I thank you for your encouragement, for letting me be me, and for enhancing my book in all the right places. Simply, I love working with you and being your friend. The **William Morrow/HarperCollins team: Kara Zauberman, Liate Stehlik, Lynn Grady, Shelby Meizlik, Heidi Richter, Tavia Kowalchuk, Megan Traynor,** and **Andrea Rosen**. You have a great crew with great energy. I knew from the moment I met you that I had met my publishing dream team. Thank you for making this book a real success. Thanks to the William Morrow production and design team for making such a beautiful book: **Emin Mancheril, Mary Schuck, Paula Szafranski, Joyce Wong, Ann Cahn, and Karen Lumley. Judy Linden,** your deep interest and caring for your authors turns them from clients into true friends. Thank you for making my dreams come true. **Stonesong Team: Alison Fargis, Ellen Scordato, Emmanuelle Morgen,** and **Sarah Passick,** an honor and pleasure to be represented by you. **Charlotte Friedland,** we've shared so much together since my first pitch and our first meeting—books, blessings, and baby celebrations. We share a brain and a voice. I thank you for always working with me, writing with me, and improving me, and for helping me present the spiritual pillars of the world—the principles of Torah and Judaism—in a way that everyone can understand and appreciate. **Sheilah Kaufman** and **Paula Jacobson, "S+P,"** my recipe testers, editors, and dear friends. **Terry H. Tretter,** a new and exacting member of the recipe testing team, it was a pleasure to work with you. **Andrew** and **Carrie Purcell,** your food photography and styling bring beauty to these pages. I have yet to meet a more giving, talented, exceptional team. **Paige Hicks,** you've got great style and a great personal-

ity. It was an absolute pleasure to be with you on set. Photography assistant **Elizabeth Drago,** food styling assistants **Dana Bonagura,** and **Micah Morton,** and prop styling assistant **Kira Corbin,** assistants extraordinaire, the shoot ran smoothly and beautifully thanks to your professionalism. **Zoe Berkovic,** you brought my writing to life by pouring your creative heart and soul into the lifestyle photo shoot. I thank you for a rewarding and fulfilling experience. **Jessica Leiser,** thank you for bringing beauty and style to our personal story. Photography assistant **Chris Dinerman,** makeup artist **Olga Postolachi,** makeup assistant **Jane Cebotari,** wardrobe stylist **Naila Ruechel,** and wardrobe styling assistant **Nakima Benjamin,** thank you for enhancing the shoot with your talents, your originality, and, above all, your calm, pleasant attitudes. **Breindy Noscow,** thank you for sharing your beautiful home and grounds. **Ahuva Staum** and **Chana Tziporah Smith,** thank you for your Passover research. Thank you, **Melissa Kaye Apter** from **Lil' Miss Cakes** for the beautiful desserts on pages 252, 302, and 349. You lent a sweet hand at the very last minute and I will be forever grateful. Thanks to your hubby, Lil' Mr. Cakes, for hand delivering the goods all the way to Monsey in the early a.m. Thank you to my beloved profes-

sional family, the **Kosher Media Network Team: Henry Kauftheil, Charlie Harary, Menachem Rubin, Tamar Genger** (my friend, my right hand, my always-there-for-you-never-let-you-down most awesome partner in kosher crime, JoyofKosher.com is a success because of you), **Shifra** and **Shloimy Klein "SSK"** (the magazine would be absolutely nothing without you), **Melinda Strauss** (event planner extraordinaire), **Milt Weinstock, Yehuda Yovitz, Mrs. Pearl, Rochel Shechter, Jodi Samuels, Allen Ganz,** and **Grant Silverstein**. A super-duper thank-you to **Stacey Bender,** my friend and principal at BHGPR, who always thinks big and delivers bigger—humongous hugs to you!

Incredible thanks to **Royal Wine Corp** and **Mordy Herzog,** specifically, for always believing in me and supporting me, and to **Gary Landsman** equally for his support and for the fantastic wine pairings in this book. A super-special thank-you to my **Manischewitz** family, **Paul Bensabat, Alain Bankier,** and **David Rossi;** I treasure our relationship. Special thanks to **AllinKosher.com** for supplying all the fresh and wonderful food for the recipe development and testing stages of this book.

For comments, questions, and to subscribe to my magazine—or just to say hi—visit me at **JoyofKosher.com.**

Index

Note: Page references in *italics* indicate photographs.